3718 2242

GLOBAL WARMING
and AGRICULTURE

Impact Estimates by Country

GLOBAL WARMING and AGRICULTURE

Impact Estimates by Country

William R. Cline

CENTER FOR GLOBAL DEVELOPMENT
PETERSON INSTITUTE FOR INTERNATIONAL ECONOMICS
Washington, DC
July 2007

William R. Cline is a senior fellow jointly at the Center for Global Development (since 2002) and the Peterson Institute for International Economics (since 1981). During 1996–2001, he was deputy managing director and chief economist at the Institute of International Finance. He was a senior fellow at the Brookings Institution (1973–81); deputy director of development and trade research, office of the assistant secretary for international affairs, US Treasury Department (1971–73); Ford Foundation visiting professor in Brazil (1970–71); and lecturer and assistant professor of economics at Princeton University (1967–70). He is the author of 22 books, including *The United States as a Debtor Nation* (2005), *Trade Policy and Global Poverty* (2004), *Trade and Income Distribution* (1997), *International Debt Reexamined* (1995), and *The Economics of Global Warming* (1992), which was selected by *Choice* for its 1993 "Outstanding Academic Books" list and was the winner of the "Harold and Margaret Sprout Prize" for best book of 1992 on International Environmental Affairs, awarded by the International Studies Association.

CENTER FOR GLOBAL DEVELOPMENT
1776 Massachusetts Avenue, NW, Third floor
Washington, DC 20036
(202) 416-0700   FAX: (202) 416-0750
www.cgdev.org

Nancy Birdsall, *President*

**PETER G. PETERSON INSTITUTE
FOR INTERNATIONAL ECONOMICS**
1750 Massachusetts Avenue, NW
Washington, DC 20036
(202) 328-9000   Fax: (202) 659-3225
www.petersoninstitute.org

C. Fred Bergsten, *Director*
Edward Tureen, *Director of Publications,
  Marketing, and Web Development*

Typesetting by BMWW
Printing by Kirby Lithographic Company, Inc.
Cover by Naylor Design, Inc.

Printed in the United States of America
09 08 07   5 4 3 2 1

Library of Congress Cataloging-in-Publication Data

Cline, William R.
  Global warming and agriculture :
    impact estimates by country /
    William R. Cline.
      p. cm.
  Includes bibliographical references and index.
    ISBN-13: 978-0-88132-403-7 (alk. paper)
    1. Global warming—Environmental aspects.   2. Plants—Effect of global warming on.   3. Crops and climate.   I. Title.

  S600.7.G56C58 2007
  338.1'4—dc22   2007018892

The views expressed in this publication are those of the author. This publication is part of the overall programs of the Center and the Institute, as endorsed by their Boards of Directors, but does not necessarily reflect the views of individual members of the Boards or the Advisory Committees.

Contents

Figures

Box

Preface

Public policy on global warming has reached a critical new phase. Calls for action are escalating, reflecting such developments as heightened public awareness after Hurricane Katrina, the influential documentary film by former US Vice President Al Gore, and the high-profile "Stern Review" by Sir Nicholas Stern for the UK Treasury. In the United States, several states are adopting measures to discourage carbon dioxide emissions, and the Supreme Court has ruled that CO_2 is a pollutant to be regulated by the Environmental Protection Agency. Internationally, the European Union has established a functioning system of trading in carbon emission permits. Under the United Nations Framework Convention on Climate Change, negotiations could begin later this year on the post-Kyoto regime after 2012.

Relatively little attention has gone, however, to the likely impact of global warming at the country level, especially in the developing world, and the social and economic implications in China, India, Brazil, and the poor countries of the tropical belt in Africa and Latin America. This book, on the stakes for world agriculture, by William R. Cline of the Center for Global Development and the Peterson Institute for International Economics, makes a major contribution on this score. Cline's analysis has sobering implications for all concerned about global poverty and long-term economic development. This study starkly confirms the asymmetry between potentially severe agricultural damages in many poor countries and milder effects in rich countries.

Cline provided an early broad analysis of climate change 15 years ago in the pioneering Institute book, *The Economics of Global Warming*. In this new study, he uses agricultural impact models of two separate types, "Ricardian" statistical economic models and process-based agronomic crop models, combined with leading climate model projections, to develop comprehensive estimates for agricultural effects in over 100 countries. He develops a "consensus" set of geographically detailed estimates for changes in temperature and precipitation by the 2080s and applies these climatic changes to the agricultural impact models.

His findings confirm the view that aggregate world agricultural impacts will be negative, if moderate, by late this century, rather than the alternative view that world agriculture would actually benefit in the aggregate from business as usual global warming over that horizon. His findings also confirm in greater detail and on a more systematic basis than previously available the prognosis that damages will be disproportionately concentrated in developing countries.

The findings of this study strongly suggest that policymakers in both industrial and developing countries should have a keen interest in helping ensure that international action begins in earnest to curb global warming from its business as usual path. Otherwise losses in agricultural output potential could be severe in Africa, South Asia, and Latin America in particular. Policymakers concerned about the future of global poverty thus also need to be concerned about the future of global warming.

<table>
<tr><td>NANCY BIRDSALL</td><td>C. FRED BERGSTEN</td></tr>
<tr><td>President</td><td>Director</td></tr>
<tr><td>Center for Global Development</td><td>Peterson Institute for</td></tr>
<tr><td>June 2007</td><td>International Economics</td></tr>
<tr><td></td><td>June 2007</td></tr>
</table>

■ ■ ■

The Peter G. Peterson Institute for International Economics is a private, nonprofit institution for the study and discussion of international economic policy. Its purpose is to analyze important issues in that area and to develop and communicate practical new approaches for dealing with them. The Institute is completely nonpartisan.

The Institute is funded by a highly diversified group of philanthropic foundations, private corporations, and interested individuals. About 30 percent of the Institute's resources in our latest fiscal year were provided by contributors outside the United States, including about 12 percent from Japan.

The Institute's Board of Directors bears overall responsibilities for the Institute and gives general guidance and approval to its research program, including the identification of topics that are likely to become important over the medium run (one to three years) and that should be addressed by the Institute. The director, working closely with the staff and outside Advisory Committee, is responsible for the development of particular projects and makes the final decision to publish an individual study.

The Institute hopes that its studies and other activities will contribute to building a stronger foundation for international economic policy around the world. We invite readers of these publications to let us know how they think we can best accomplish this objective.

Acknowledgments

I thank Rachel Block for massive and skillful research assistance. In particular, she developed the grid conversion and mapping methods set forth in appendices A and B. I also thank Arvind Nair for excellent research assistance in the second phase of this study. I thank, without implicating, Robert Mendelsohn and Richard Morgenstern for comments on an earlier draft. I am also indebted to participants in a study group that reviewed an initial draft of this study at a meeting in Washington on December 5, 2006. Special thanks go to Ariel Dinar for calling my attention, and facilitating access, to new results in the World Bank studies on Africa and Latin America.

1

Introduction and Overview

In the long list of potential damages from global warming, the risk to world agriculture stands out as among the most important.[1] In the development of international policy on curbing climate change, it is important for policymakers to have a sense of not only the aggregate world effects at stake but also the distribution of likely impacts across countries, for reasons of equity.

This study seeks to sharpen understanding of the prospective impact of unarrested global warming on world agriculture for two reasons. First, there has been some tendency in the literature in the past decade toward the view that agricultural damages over the next century will be minimal and indeed that a few degrees Celsius of global warming would be beneficial for world agriculture. This study seeks to provide a rigorous and comprehensive evaluation of whether the aggregate global agricultural impact should be expected to be negative or positive by late in this century and of how large the aggregate impact is likely to be.

Second, there is relatively wide recognition that developing countries in general stand to lose more from the effects of global warming on agriculture than the industrial countries. Temperatures in developing countries, which are predominantly located in lower latitudes, are already close to or beyond thresholds at which further warming will reduce rather than increase agricultural potential, and these countries tend to have less capacity to adapt. Moreover, agriculture constitutes a much larger fraction of GDP in developing countries than in industrial countries, so a given percentage loss in agricultural potential would impose a larger propor-

---

1. Others include sea level rise, species loss, loss of water supply, tropospheric ozone air pollution, hurricane damage, impact on human health and loss of life, forest loss, and increased electricity requirements. For an early quantitative analysis, see Cline (1992).

tionate income loss in a developing than in an industrial country. This study seeks to provide more detailed and systematic estimates than previously available for the differential effects across countries, and in particular between industrial and developing countries.

To assess the impact of climate change on agriculture, it is essential to take account of the effects through at least the latter part of this century. A small amount of warming through, say, the next two or three decades might provide aggregate global benefits for agriculture (albeit with inequitable distributional effects among countries). But policy inaction premised on this benign possibility could leave world agriculture on an inexorable trajectory toward a subsequent reversal into serious damage. The delay of some three decades for ocean thermal lag before today's emissions generate additional warming is a sufficient reason not to stop the clock at, say, 2050 in an analysis of the stakes of climate change policy for world agriculture over the coming decades.[2] For this reason, this study chooses the final three decades of this century (the "2080s" for short) as the relevant period for analysis. Climate projections for several climate general circulation models (GCMs) are available for this period within the program of standardized analysis compiled by the Intergovernmental Panel on Climate Change (IPCC).

This study reaches two fundamental conclusions. The first is that by late in this century unabated global warming would have at least a modest negative impact on global agriculture in the aggregate, and the impact could be severe if carbon fertilization benefits (enhancement of yields in a carbon-rich environment) do not materialize, especially if water scarcity limits irrigation. This finding contradicts optimistic estimates such as those by Richard Tol (2002) and Mendelsohn et al. (2000), who find that baseline warming by late in this century would have a positive effect on global agriculture in the aggregate (discussed later). Moreover, in the business as usual baseline, warming would not halt in the 2080s but would continue on a path toward still higher global temperatures in the 22nd century, when agricultural damages could be expected to become more severe. The second broad conclusion is that the composition of agricultural effects is likely to be seriously unfavorable to developing countries, with the most severe losses occurring in Africa, Latin America, and India. Although past studies have tended to recognize that losses will tend to be concentrated in developing countries, this study provides more comprehensive and detailed estimates on such losses than previously available.

---

2. Warming at the ocean's surface is initially partially dissipated through heat exchange to the cooler lower layers of the ocean. Only after the lower levels warm sufficiently to reestablish the equilibrium differential from the surface temperature does the "committed" amount of warming from a given rise in carbon concentration become fully "realized."

Main Features of the Book

The principal features of this study that distinguish it from previous analyses include the following: First, this study provides unusual geographical detail. The estimates are obtained in a systematic methodology for more than 100 countries, regions, and regional subzones of the largest countries. In contrast, previous studies have tended either to provide global estimates with breakdowns only by a few large regions (often continental) or to focus on one or more specific countries without developing comparable estimates for other countries and regions.

Second, there is a direct link from the GCM estimates to highly detailed country climate change estimates. In contrast, other studies have often tended to prepare country models for agricultural impact functions but then apply broad hypothesized changes in temperature and precipitation to illustrate but not formally quantify the corresponding climate change impacts on agriculture.

Third, this study uses a central or "consensus" climate projection approach. Many studies instead show a wide range of climate outcomes. Although for some purposes it is desirable to consider such ranges, they tend to leave the diagnosis so ill-defined that they risk policy paralysis. The experience of the past two decades shows that a wide spectrum of estimates tends to be invoked as evidence that there is too much uncertainty to warrant action, even though in principle greater uncertainty could justify greater action if policymakers are risk averse.

Fourth, this study seeks a preferred synthesis of the two main families of quantitative estimates: summary statistical "Ricardian" models and detailed crop process models. This approach permits a more balanced set of estimates than applying models from one family to the exclusion of the other.

It should be noted at the outset that the estimates developed in this study would not have been possible without the benefit of the previous contributions of researchers who developed the agricultural impact models applied. In particular, they include Robert Mendelsohn in the Ricardian school and Cynthia Rosenzweig in the crop model school.

Plan of the Book

Chapter 2 briefly surveys the findings of several leading existing studies on the agricultural impact of climate change. Chapter 3 discusses three fundamental issue areas: carbon fertilization, irrigation, and induced effects from international trade. Gauging the influence of higher atmospheric concentrations of carbon dioxide on crop yields ("carbon fertilization") is crucial to arriving at meaningful estimates of agricultural impact.

Impact estimates may be unduly optimistic if they fail to adequately account for additional irrigation requirements, or if they rely on statistical models that conflate benefits from warmer climates with the greater incidence of irrigation in such climates. Studies that incorporate induced effects of world trade may give an unduly benign view of the impact of global warming by reducing estimated output losses without calculating the additional costs or considering the ability of poor countries to pay for additional food imports.

Chapter 4 develops the baseline projections of temperature and precipitation used in this study. These are business as usual projections premised on the absence of serious international programs of emissions taxes or restraints. They therefore provide a benchmark for judging the possible damages from inaction and hence benefits of abatement. As set forth later, both the baseline emissions scenario chosen and the set of GCMs for which projections are available should be seen as intermediate rather than extreme at either the high or low end.

It is well known that there is less agreement among the GCMs about climate change prospects at the regional level than at the global level. This study seeks to overcome this problem by taking the average across six GCMs of detailed geographical results on future climate change. The principle for policymaking should not be to ignore the country-specific profile of climate effects because there is uncertainty but to take the best central estimate available, which in the absence of quality weightings by GCM will simply be the average.

This approach nonetheless requires overcoming two important obstacles. First, each GCM has a different "grid resolution," or size of geographical unit with specific results (measured in degrees of latitude height and longitude width of the grid cells). Second, even for a single model, results typically are not mapped to countries. This study converts individual GCM results to estimates at a standardized global grid resolution (90 latitude cells of 2° height by 120 longitude cells of 3° width), as discussed in appendix A, and maps these standardized cells into corresponding national territories, as discussed in appendix B.

Chapter 5 then turns to the application of the projected climate changes to two frameworks of models of agricultural impact to estimate the corresponding prospective effects for agricultural capacity by country, regional grouping of smaller countries, or subnational zones of the largest countries. The first is a family of "Ricardian" or cross-section models relating agricultural capacity statistically to temperature and precipitation on the basis of statistical estimates from farm survey or county-level data across varying climatic zones. The classical economist David Ricardo developed the theory that the value of land depends on the difference between its fertility and that of the least fertile land just brought into cultivation at the margin. The seminal Ricardian agricultural impact model (Mendelsohn, Nordhaus, and Shaw 1994) argued that statistical regressions relating land values to climate differences could capture the impact of climate on agricultural productivity and thus be used to calculate prospective effects of global warming.

Model estimates in this family are available for the United States (Mendelsohn and Schlesinger 1999), Canada (Reinsborough 2003), many countries in Africa (from the World Bank farm surveys reported in Kurukulasuriya et al. 2006), major countries in Latin America (also from World Bank farm surveys; see appendix G), and India (Mendelsohn, Dinar, and Sanghi 2001). These country-specific models in the first framework are applied to countries accounting for 35 percent of global agricultural output and about half of the number of countries. Where country-specific studies are not available, the estimates apply the Mendelsohn-Schlesinger Ricardian model for the United States to the climate estimates for the country in question. However, in these cases the weighting given to the Ricardian estimates in arriving at the final preferred estimates is reduced and the weighting of crop models is increased, because of the considerably lesser reliability of US model parameters when applied to other countries.[3] The Mendelsohn-Schlesinger Ricardian results are also used in chapter 5 to investigate the sensitivity of results to variability among the six climate models used.

Chapter 5 then turns to the second framework for the impact estimates, which consists of region-specific calculations synthesized from estimates by agricultural scientists in 18 countries as applied to alternative GCM projections of climate scenarios (Rosenzweig and Iglesias 2006, Rosenzweig et al. 1993). This framework is based on crop models and may thus be seen more as a set of input-output process calculations, in contrast to the approach of indirect inference of climatic effects using the Ricardian land value approach. For the United States, Mendelsohn and Schlesinger (1999) also provide a reduced form impact equation summarizing crop model results. Regional estimates within the United States are obtained by applying this model to the corresponding climate estimates. The overall crop model estimates for the United States are then obtained as the simple average of the Rosenzweig-Iglesias and Mendelsohn-Schlesinger estimates. For all other countries the crop model estimates are from Rosenzweig and Iglesias (2006).

A synthesis of these two sets of estimates then provides the basis for the preferred estimates of this study. Together the Ricardian and crop model frameworks should provide a relatively comprehensive basis for evaluating the impact of global warming on agriculture. This study does not use the third approach that has sometimes been applied. This approach categorizes existing land area by land "types" with related productive potential and investigates the change in the distribution of these categories

---

3. See, for example, the discussion of Ricardian estimates for the United States versus Canada later.

as a consequence of global warming. As discussed later, Darwin et al. (1995) apply this approach. However, both the specific results of that study and more fundamentally the underlying concept (which in the case of the Darwin et al. study uses length of growing season as the key determinant for categorization) seem considerably less reliable than the Ricardian and crop model approaches used in this study. Chapter 5 concludes with a comparison of the estimates in this study with impact estimates from some of the underlying model studies themselves.

Chapter 6 turns to dynamic considerations, in particular the question of whether technological change can be expected to be so rapid and profound that policymakers should not worry about possible adverse effects of global warming on agriculture because such effects will simply be swamped by gains from improved varieties and other technological changes. Chapter 7 presents this study's principal findings and policy conclusions.

The appendices first discuss the climate projections: the method for converting different climate model results to a standardized grid (appendix A), the method for translating the standardized results into country-level estimates (appendix B), and the method of calculating grid land area at different latitudes (appendix C). They next present detail on the definition of the regions and subzones in this study (appendix D) and on the development of the database on agricultural land and output (appendix E). Country results are then presented in detail for the Mendelsohn-Schlesinger models as applied in the present study (appendix F), and further detail is provided on the parameters of the India, Africa, and Latin America models (appendix G). Appendix H reports the present and future temperature and precipitation estimates by country in monthly detail, and appendix I reports the analysis of the degree of dispersion across GCMs in future climate projections.

2

Brief Survey of Existing Literature

The voluminous literature on the impact of global warming on agriculture broadly contains three types of quantitative estimates: those from application of agronomic crop models (e.g., Adams et al. 1990, Rosenzweig et al. 1993, Reilly et al. 2001), Ricardian models (e.g., Mendelsohn, Nordhaus, and Shaw 1994), and land zone studies premised on the shift of geographical areas from one agronomic class to another due to climate change (e.g., Darwin et al. 1995). In general, there has been some trend from pessimism toward optimism over time, especially for the United States.[1] But as discussed later, there are grounds to doubt the extent of this swing toward optimism. At the same time, there has been a relatively persistent diagnosis that developing countries stand to lose disproportionately from the agricultural effects of global warming, in large part because these countries are predominantly located in the lower latitudes, where temperatures are already near or above optimal levels for agriculture. This chapter briefly reviews some of the main studies in the existing literature.[2]

Environmental Protection Agency (1989). The US Environmental Protection Agency (EPA 1989) provided important early estimates of the impact on US agriculture by 2060 of a doubling of atmospheric concentration of carbon dioxide (CO_2) above preindustrial levels, or benchmark $2 \times CO_2$

---

1. Thus, my estimates in Cline (1992, 131) based on the studies then available placed US agricultural losses from benchmark $2 \times CO_2$ warming at 0.3 percent of GDP; Nordhaus and Boyer (2000, 76) placed them at 0.07 percent based on Darwin et al. (1995); and Mendelsohn and Neumann (1999, 320) estimated *gains* amounting to 0.2 percent of GDP.

2. For helpful surveys, see NAST (2001) and Kurukulasuriya and Rosenthal (2003).

warming, based primarily on crop model analysis subsequently published in Adams et al. (1990). The study identified net losses of about $6 billion to $34 billion at 1982 prices if carbon fertilization effects were excluded and a range of about ±$10 billion if carbon fertilization effects were included assuming a boost from 330 parts per million (ppm) to 660 ppm atmospheric concentration of CO_2. In Cline (1992), I argued that attributing this much carbon fertilization was inappropriate because carbon-equivalent doubling would include noncarbon gases with less than carbon doubling and because equilibrium long-term warming from 660 ppm carbon concentration would be considerably higher than realized warming by 2060 because of ocean thermal lag. On this basis I gave two-thirds weight to non–carbon fertilization estimates and one-third weight to with–carbon fertilization estimates and, after converting to 1990 dollars, arrived at a central estimate of $17.5 billion losses, or 0.3 percent of 1990 US GDP (Cline 1992, 92–94).

Rosenberg and Crosson (1991) Study on Missouri, Iowa, Nebraska, and Kansas. A study prepared for the US Department of Energy (Rosenberg and Crosson 1991) at about the same time studied four states in depth: Missouri, Iowa, Nebraska, and Kansas (MINK). The study used actual climate conditions in the 1930s as an analogy for the climate by the 2030s. It concluded that warming by the 2030s would reduce agricultural production in the MINK area by 17.1 percent without considering carbon fertilization, by 8.4 percent after allowing for carbon fertilization from a rise in carbon concentration from 350 to 450 ppm, and by only 3.3 percent after further taking farmer adaptation into account (Rosenberg and Crosson 1991, 11–12). The study's result, that losses might be relatively modest, was for much less warming than the usual benchmark $2 \times CO_2$ warming.

Environmental Protection Agency (1994). Rosenzweig and Iglesias (1994) extended the EPA analysis to the global level. As set forth in Rosenzweig et al. (1993), the new set of estimates used the crop model approach to analyze the impact of benchmark $2 \times CO_2$ global warming on yields for wheat, rice, maize, and soybeans in 18 countries. The study included a world food trade model that translated the yield impact estimates into corresponding impact on food production, food prices, and the number of people globally at risk of hunger. The query-based system in Rosenzweig and Iglesias (2006) that reports yield estimates from the country models developed in Rosenzweig et al. (1993), using various climate models and scenarios, serves as one of the two broad sets of models used in the present study and is discussed in chapter 5. For purposes of this chapter, the following discussion refers to Rosenzweig et al. (1993).

The crop models in Rosenzweig et al. (1993) relied on the following agronomic influences of global warming:

> Higher temperatures during the growing season speed annual crops through their development (especially grain-filling stage), allowing less grain to be produced.

This occurred at all sites except those with the coolest growing-season temperatures in Canada and the former USSR. . . . At low latitudes . . . crops are currently . . . nearer the limits of temperature tolerances for heat and water stress. Warming at low latitudes thus results in . . . greater yield decreases than at higher latitudes. . . . . [Other causes of falling yields are a] [d]ecrease in water availability . . . due to a combination of increase in evapotranspiration in the warmer climate, enhanced losses of soil moisture and, in some cases, a projected decrease in precipitation in the climate change scenarios; [and] poor vernalization . . . [i.e.,] the requirement of some temperate cereal crops, e.g. winter wheat, for a period of low winter temperatures to initiate or accelerate the flowering process (p. 14).

The study used three climate models (GISS, GFDL, and UKMO) that, for benchmark $2 \times CO_2$ warming by 2060, generated estimated global mean warming of about 4°C (GISS and GFDL models) to 5.2°C (UKMO model).[3] The study reported that it used the following yield enhancements for carbon fertilization at 550 ppm: 21 percent for soybeans, 17 percent for wheat, and 6 percent for rice. As discussed in chapter 3, these enhancements may have been somewhat overstated in light of more recent open-field experimental results.

For wheat, the yield impacts identified in the study showed large negative effects globally without carbon fertilization, mixed results with carbon fertilization, and negative results even with carbon fertilization for the developing countries reported (excluding China). Thus, under level 1 adaptation and without carbon fertilization, global wheat yields fell in the range of 16 to 33 percent for all three climate models.[4] With carbon fertilization, however, global yields fell in only one model (UKMO by 13 percent) while rising in the other two (GISS by 11 percent and GFDL by 4 percent). In contrast, for five developing countries (Brazil, Egypt, India, Pakistan, and Uruguay), the simple average impact on yields ranged from –36 to –57 percent without carbon fertilization and from –10 to –42 percent with carbon fertilization. The chief exception among developing countries was China, for which yields fell by a range of 5 to 17 percent without carbon fertilization but rose by 0 to 16 percent with carbon fertilization. The United States experienced yield declines of 21 to 33 percent without carbon fertilization but declines of only 2 to 14 percent with carbon fertilization.

At the global level the impacts were most severe for maize, which showed reductions of 20 to 31 percent without carbon fertilization and reductions of 15 to 24 percent with carbon fertilization. Rice also showed negative global results, at a range of –2 to –5 percent with carbon fertilization and –25 percent without. Soybeans in contrast showed a pattern across models that resembled that for wheat: uniform losses without carbon fertilization (by 19 to 57 percent) but mixed results with carbon fer-

3. GISS, GFDL, and UKMO stand for Goddard Institute for Space Studies, Geophysical Fluid Dynamics Laboratory, and United Kingdom Meteorological Office, respectively.

4. As discussed in chapter 5, the study included three levels of adaptation: none, moderate (level 1), and intensive (level 2).

tilization; gains in two models (GISS and GFDL, 5 to 16 percent) but losses in the third (UKMO, –33 percent). The overall results of the study were negative, showing an increase in world cereal prices by 10 to 100 percent even with level 1 adaptation and a corresponding rise in the number of people globally at risk from hunger from a baseline of 641 million to a range of 681 million to 941 million.

Intergovernmental Panel on Climate Change (1996). In the Second Assessment Report of the Intergovernmental Panel on Climate Change (IPCC 1996), the authors of the chapter on agriculture concluded that

> global agricultural production can be maintained relative to baseline production in the face of climate changes likely to occur over the next century (i.e., in the range of 1 to 4.5°C) but . . . regional effects will vary widely . . . [and] it is not possible to distinguish reliably and precisely those areas that will benefit and those that will lose. . . . [L]ower-latitude and lower-income countries have been shown to be more negatively affected. . . . Low-income populations depending on isolated agricultural systems, particularly dryland systems in semi-arid and arid regions, are particularly vulnerable to hunger and severe hardship. Many of these at-risk populations are found in Sub-Saharan Africa . . . (IPCC 1996, 429–30).

The survey reported temperature thresholds from underlying crop physiology as follows: for wheat, optimum range of 17°C to 23°C with minimum of 0°C and maximum of 35°C; potatoes similarly at 15°C to 20°C optimum, 5°C minimum, and 25°C maximum; and rice and maize located at higher optima (25°C to 30°C), minima (7°C to 8°C), and maxima (37°C to 38°C) (IPCC 1996, 432). The authors noted that "higher temperatures would . . . increase crop water demand. Global studies have found a tendency for increased evaporative demand to exceed precipitation increase in tropical areas" (p. 433–34). Regional tables reported results of various studies, typically for benchmark $2 \times CO_2$ warming, with wheat, maize, soybeans, and rice the most frequently studied crops but including others as well. The study summaries typically showed large ranges of either losses or gains for most regions. However, there were nearly uniformly negative and large impacts on yields in two regions: Africa–Middle East and Latin America. Losses tended to dominate but in smaller magnitudes in South and Southeast Asia, East Asia, the United States, and Canada; moderate gains tended to dominate in Australia–New Zealand, the former Soviet Union, and Western Europe.[5] As discussed later, these patterns broadly resemble those found in the present study (except for Australia, where significant losses are identified).

---

5. As summary indicators, the number of negative and positive entries, respectively, in the yield impact tables and the median entry were as follows: Africa–Middle East, 9 negative, 1 positive, and –29 percent median; Latin America, 16, 3, and –17; South and Southeast Asia, 27, 17, –6; East Asia, 18, 11, –6; Australia–New Zealand, 4, 6, +11; former Soviet Union, 5, 5, +4; Western Europe, 3, 5, +10; United States, 9, 7, –6; and Canada, 5, 3, –16.

The IPCC authors cited the findings of Reilly, Hohmann, and Kane (1994), who incorporated the Rosenzweig et al. (1993) estimates of losses for benchmark $2 \times CO_2$ warming into a different trade model to calculate economic effects (change in producer and consumer surplus) against the present global agricultural base. They estimated that without carbon fertilization or adaptation, benchmark warming would impose global damage ranging from $116 billion (at 1989 prices) to $248 billion across three climate models but that after incorporating carbon fertilization and level 1 adaptation, the range of impacts would shrink to +$7 billion for GISS, –$6 billion for GFDL, and –$38 billion for UKMO (IPCC 1996, 452). They found that some agricultural exporting countries could gain even though they experienced yield reductions because of higher world prices and similarly that food-importing countries could lose despite yield increases domestically, for the same reason.

Importantly, this Second Assessment Report reported relatively high carbon fertilization impacts, which the authors set at +30 percent for C3 crops (most crops except maize, millet, sugarcane, and sorghum [IPCC 1996, 429]). As discussed later, the estimates from more recent open-field research are considerably lower. The report may thus have been overly optimistic about agriculture. Moreover, its central conclusion that "global agricultural production can be maintained" disguised two key issues: at what cost and with what differential impacts especially on developing countries?

US Department of Agriculture (1995). In 1995 researchers at the Economic Research Service of the US Department of Agriculture (USDA) prepared estimates of the world agricultural impact of global warming using a completely different framework from the crop model estimates previously dominant: land zone change (Darwin et al. 1995). They classified global agricultural land into six categories based on length of growing season. These were LC1, < 100 days and cold (e.g., Alaska); LC2, < 100 days and dry (e.g., Mojave Desert); LC3, 101 to 165 days (e.g., Nebraska); LC4, 166 to 250 days (e.g., Northern European Union); LC5, 251 to 300 days (e.g., Tennessee and Thailand); and LC6, >300 days (e.g., Florida and Indonesia). They judged LC1 and LC2 as mainly usable for rough grazing, LC3 for short-season grains, LC4 for maize, LC5 for cotton and rice, and LC6 for sugarcane and rubber. They placed the current global distribution of land across the six classes (from LC1 to LC6) at 17.3, 32, 13, 10, 7.7, and 19.7 percent, respectively, with global land area at a total of 13.1 billion hectares (Darwin et al. 1995, 9).[6] Considering that LC1 and LC2 are marginal for agricultural production, it is sobering that about half of world land area is currently in these two categories. The authors divided the

---

6. Note that this compares with my estimate of 3 billion hectares in farmland; see table E.1 in appendix E.

world into eight regions.[7] They identified production profiles characteristic of each land class in each region for four agricultural sectors (wheat, other grains, nongrain crops, and livestock) and nine other economic sectors.[8] They placed the value of crops at 2.5 percent of world output and livestock at 1.4 percent.

The authors applied their future agricultural resources model (FARM) to simulate the impact of climate change on world agriculture "by altering water supplies and the distribution of land across the land classes within each region" (Darwin et al. 1995, 16). For this purpose, they use equilibrium $2 \times CO_2$ results from four climate models: GISS, GFDL, UKMO, and OSU (Oregon State University). The resulting averages across the four models show the following percent changes in global land class coverage: LC1, –45.6 percent; LC2, –9.8 percent; LC3, +28.2 percent; LC4, +47.5 percent; LC5, +11.3 percent; LC6, –23.0 percent (Darwin et al. 1995, 20). Weighting by current rents, they find that "the total value of existing agricultural land declines . . . [so] climate change will likely impair the existing agricultural system" (p. 20). In one aggregation, they identify changes in "agriculturally important land" in three groupings. The average across the four climate models shows an increase in such land by 34.2 percent in the high latitudes, a decrease by 32.7 percent in the tropics, and a small increase (1 percent) in other areas. So once again the stylized fact of gains in the high latitudes and losses in the low latitudes tends to be supported, this time by a land zone rather than crop model approach.

For the United States, the authors find that cold LC1 declines (by an average of 54 percent), whereas land suitable for agriculture rises. However, "most of this impact will occur in Alaska" (Darwin et al. 1995, 22). As will be shown in table 4.2, even with global warming by late this century, average temperatures in Alaska would remain close to zero (rising from –5.1°C to 1.1°C), which casts serious doubt on how meaningful the rise in agricultural land would be. As for existing farmland as opposed to newly suitable land, climate change would shift about 7 percent of agricultural land to shorter growing seasons, weighting by existing rents (four-model average). Moreover, there would be a decline of about 25 percent in land in category LC4, "suggesting potential negative effects in the U.S. Corn Belt;" and an average 1 percent decline in LC6 and a 2 percent rise in LC2, which "implies that soil moisture losses may reduce agricultural possibilities" (p. 22).

The study then goes on to calculate changes in output and prices in the world regions and sectors, but it does not present any equations revealing

---

7. The eight regions are the United States, Canada, European Community, Japan, other East Asia (China, Hong Kong, Taiwan, and South Korea), Southeast Asia (Thailand, Indonesia, Philippines, and Malaysia), Australia–New Zealand, and rest of world.

8. The sectors are forestry; coal, oil, and gas; other minerals; fish, meat, and milk; other processed foods; textiles, clothing, and footwear; other nonmetallic manufactures; other manufactures; and services.

the basis for the calculations. It first reports the change in "supply," defined as changes in the amounts firms would be willing to sell at unchanged prices. These changes must inherently be broadly the change in expected yields, although the authors do not explicitly say so. The four-model average places this change for cereals and with no adaptation at –23.6 percent for the world and –33.5 percent for the United States, and the authors state that these results are extremely close to those estimated by Rosenzweig et al. (1993) for the three overlapping climate models. Including farm-level adaptation shrinks the supply impact to an average decline of 4.3 percent globally and 17.8 percent for the United States. The next step in the analysis shrinks the effects much further, however. The authors emphasize the change in production, defined as changes in what firms are willing to sell and consumers are willing to buy *at new market prices*. These changes shift to a four-model average *increase* of 0.6 percent globally and a decrease for the United States of only 3.8 percent (p. 28).

So the Darwin et al. (1995) study arrives at minimal changes in production globally in large part because it expects the adverse impact on yields to push up prices and clear the market at little change in actual output. Surely, however, this approach ignores the major loss in consumer surplus that would be associated with this outcome. It would thus seem that the "production" results of the study are much less relevant than the "supply" results as a guide to welfare impact. Indeed, Cline (1992, annex 3A) shows that the welfare loss should be expected to be at least as large (in percentage terms) as the decline in yields. Implicitly the Darwin et al. (1995) study assumes resources are drawn away from other sectors of the economy to help keep up agricultural production, but it does not explicitly address the opportunity cost of this increased call on resources from the rest of the economy.

Even the supply effects may be unduly sanguine because they seem likely to exaggerate easy gains from adaptation. The authors argue that the simple adaptation measure of "allowing farmers to select the most profitable mix of inputs and crops on existing cropland" would eliminate 78 to 90 percent of the initial climate-induced reductions in world cereal supply (p. 28). No reported equations spell out the components of this shift, and this effect far exceeds that in Rosenzweig et al. (1993, table 6). Those authors find, for example, that for wheat in Argentina, the United States, and Eastern Europe and the former Soviet Union, the inclusion of level 1 adaptation (which would clearly encompass changing the crop pattern and input mix) reduces the impact of benchmark warming on yields from –21 to –12 percent (UKMO model). Their shrinkage of loss through adaptation amounts to only about 40 percent (i.e., 9/21), less than half the Darwin et al. (1995) estimate.

Finally, the study obtains a small but positive net world output effect only after including newly suitable land. But as noted, it is mostly in Alaska for the United States and Siberia for Russia and so should be taken with a grain of salt. The study does omit carbon fertilization and under-states gains from that standpoint. Broadly, however, its approach seems less satisfactory than the crop model approach because of its ascription of production characteristics by extremely aggregated land classes and regions and especially because of its focus on output rather than yields and corresponding inattention to losses in consumer surplus.

Reilly et al. (2001). For the United States, an even more optimistic set of estimates was subsequently prepared by the Agriculture Sector Assessment Team of the US National Assessment of the Potential Consequences of Climate Variability and Change within the US Global Change Research Program (Reilly et al. 2001). Primarily supported by the USDA, the study cautiously summarized that "climate changes . . . will not imperil crop production in the US during the 21st century" (p. xi). Its actual estimates were much more dramatic. Under the transient climate predicted for 2090, averaging the two climate models employed, the authors showed US dry-land yields with farm-level adaptation rising by an average of 89 percent for cotton, 80 percent for soybeans, 29 percent for corn, 24 percent for wheat, and 11 percent for rice, with the only decline to be found in pota-toes (by 11 percent) (p. 39). The corresponding changes in irrigated yields with adaptation were estimated at 110 percent for cotton, 36 percent for soybeans, 11 percent for rice, 4 percent for corn, 4 percent for wheat, and –14 percent for potatoes (p. 41).

The source of these extremely favorable estimates is an enigma.[9] Reilly et al. (2001) states that the 1989 EPA study had been "in many ways the most comprehensive assessment to date" (p. 17). Yet as noted earlier, the EPA study showed US losses of 2 to 14 percent for wheat yields even after taking account of carbon fertilization, a sharp divergence from the 24 per-cent gain identified in Reilly et al. (2001). Even though the latter study is once again a crop model approach (based on estimates at 45 sites), the au-thors do not explain why their results are so much more favorable than earlier crop model estimates. Nor does the report state the amount of yield enhancement assumed from carbon fertilization, although it indi-cates that this effect accounts for one-third to one-half of the yield in-creases simulated and their estimates of it "should be regarded as upper limits to actual responses in the field" (p. xi).

The report indicates that the temperature increases indicated in the climate models used are 5.8°C by 2095 for the Canadian model and 3.3°C by then for the Hadley model, and the corresponding precipitation changes

---

9. Nor does a further examination of the underlying studies seem to shed much light. Con-sider the results for wheat in Tubiello et al. (2002), an underlying study. It reports losses of 4 to 30 percent by 2090 for winter wheat and of 16 to 24 percent for spring wheat, using the Canadian climate model (pp. 265–66). In contrast, the National Assessment Synthesis Team (NAST) summary study reports all wheat results for the Canadian model as positive, in a range of 4 to 14 percent (Reilly et al. 2001, 39).

are 17 and 23 percent (Reilly et al. 2001, 30). These precipitation increases seem unduly large. Thus, in table 4.2 based on six climate models, US precipitation by the 2080s under "business as usual" global warming would be expected to rise by 49 percent in Alaska (where there is almost negligible agricultural land) but by 11.5 percent in the Southern Pacific Coast, 5.6 percent in the Pacific Northwest, 5.1 percent in the Rockies-Plains, and only 3.5 percent in the Lakes-Northeast region. Precipitation would decline by 2.3 percent in the Southeast and by 11 percent in the Southwest and Plains (see appendix table D.1 for definitions of regions). Reilly et al. (2001) do acknowledge "the 'wet' nature of the scenarios employed" (p. xi). For temperature increases, for the six US regions in table 4.2 excluding Alaska, the unweighted average would be an increase of 5.1°C, comparable to the Canadian model result but much higher than the Hadley model used in Reilly et al. (2001).

Taken together, the climate model scenarios used would seem to exaggerate increased precipitation seriously and understate temperature increases. The authors are cautionary about their carbon fertilization effects and avoid summary language that would be much more consistent with the dramatic gains they report ("massively beneficial" would be more apt than their "will not imperil"). There seems to be no reason to disagree with their caution, so the estimates in the study would seem to provide little more than a qualitative result that previous crop model estimates may have understated potential US gains.

Fischer et al. (2002). An important recent study in the land zone school is that by Fischer et al. (2002). They develop an agroecological zone model that identifies suitability of land for agricultural production and simulates the change in the availability of suitable agricultural land that can be expected from climate change. For the present climate, they use the same detailed dataset at the 0.5° latitude by 0.5° longitude grid level[10] used in the present study. They apply the FAO/UNESCO Soil Map of the World for information on soils, elevation, and slope. Their database incorporates information on land use and population distribution. A key concept in their model is the length of growing period, defined as the number of days per year when both water availability and temperature permit crop growth. They identify four groupings of major food products: two adapted to higher temperatures (C3: soybeans, rice, and cassava; C4: millet, sorghum, maize, and sugarcane) and two adapted to lower temperatures (C3: wheat and potatoes; C4: sorghum and maize). They develop five "thermal climate" categories: tropics, subtropics, temperate, boreal, and arctic. Thresholds for these classifications are the number of months with average temperatures above 18°C, below 5°C, and between 10°C and 18°C. They then

---

10. From the IPCC Data Distribution Center Web site, http://ipcc-ddc.cru.uea.ac.uk maintained for the IPCC by Climate Research Unit, University of East Anglia, United Kingdom.

identify 154 "land utilization types" that match crops to climate zones.[11] Potential yields correspondingly vary by land utilization type.

The authors then apply three of the same general circulation models (GCMs) used in the present study to simulate the impact of climate change by the 2080s on agricultural production.[12] They find that for rain-fed cereal production based on one crop per year, land currently under cultivation would experience a decrease in production potential by 3.5 percent globally. However, they also find that if multiple cropping is allowed (more than one crop per year) where the length of growing period is sufficient, there would instead be a gain of 4 percent. If irrigation is further considered, under the assumption that "(i) water resources of good quality are available, and (ii) irrigation infrastructure is in place" (Fischer et al. 2002, 35), the global gain reaches 9 percent. They also find, however, that developing countries would experience worse results than industrial countries. Among 117 developing countries, the average impacts across the three GCMs indicate that 39 with a population of 2.5 billion (in 2080) would gain 5 percent or more in agricultural potential; 29 with 1.1 billion people would experience no change; and 49 with a population of 4.2 billion would experience losses of 5 percent or more, causing aggregate net losses of about 89 million metric tons of cereal capacity for the developing countries as a group (or about 5 percent).[13]

The meaning of the multiple-cropping and irrigation results would seem ambiguous, because there is no clear analysis of whether the corresponding potential of both has already been exploited and hence whether the increment from future global warming could be expected to occur because of the relaxation of current constraints. Nor is there an analysis of the prospective availability of irrigation water, a key issue as discussed in chapter 3. Perhaps more importantly, however, results of the agroecological zone model appear to be buoyed crucially by the expectation of large gains in the high latitudes, where today's temperatures are the coldest. Thus, output potential is calculated to rise by 20 to 50 percent for both Canada and Russia. In contrast, the crop models (Rosenzweig and Iglesias 2006) used in the present study indicate that Canada and Russia would experience losses without carbon fertilization and negligible to modest gains even including carbon fertilization (see table 5.8 in chapter 5). Similarly, Ricardian model estimates for Canada show virtually no change in

---

11. For example, there is one land utilization type for sugarcane: tropics and subtropics. In contrast, for wheat there are 4 for hibernating (boreal, temperate, and subtropics) and 12 for nonhibernating (boreal, temperate, subtropics, and tropics).

12. The models are ECHAM4/OPYC3, HadCM2, and CGCM1. The latter two are earlier versions of the corresponding models applied in the present study (see table 4.1 in chapter 4).

13. The 5 percent interpretation here is based roughly on global cereal production shown in table 6.1 after allowing for 30 percent expansion in future production by developing countries.

productive potential from global warming (Reinsborough 2003). It would thus seem that the land zone transformation school may tend to overstate global gains from climate change by attributing excessive benefit to the warming of cold high-latitude regions, in contrast to prospective effects identified by more detailed biophysical treatment in the crop models on the one hand and revealed by economic behavior models in the Ricardian school on the other hand.

Recent Secondary Studies. In their influential study of economically optimal response to climate change, Nordhaus and Boyer (2000) rely heavily on the estimates of Darwin et al. (1995) in calibrating regional impacts on agriculture. As a result, their impact estimates for warming associated with a doubling of CO_2 are highly optimistic. They show agricultural *gains* of about 0.5 percent of GDP for China and Japan and about 1 percent of GDP for Canada, Australia, New Zealand, and Russia. They identify only a slight loss for the United States (0.07 percent of GDP). In contrast, they estimate sizable agricultural losses for OECD Europe and Eastern Europe (0.6 percent of GDP). The largest agricultural losses they apply are from two sources other than Darwin et al. (1995): Sanghi, Mendelsohn, and Dinar (1998) for India, discussed later, and a study attributed to Sanghi but not bibliographically referenced for Brazil. These two studies form the basis for their agricultural losses of about 1.5 percent of GDP for India and for middle-income countries.

Tol (2002) draws upon several underlying studies to identify agricultural impact of benchmark warming for nine regions. His table of the "original" estimates for five studies (including some of those examined above) shows significant and dominant negative results for 2.5°C warming. Of a total of ten variants of the studies and hence 90 regional outcomes, all but 22 are negative. For Africa, 9 out of the 10 variants are negative, with a median outcome of –0.68 percent of agricultural GDP impact (and an average of –1.2 percent). After he makes his own adjustments to the estimates by adding the influence of carbon fertilization to those results omitting it, and adding an estimate of the contribution of adaptation based on Darwin et al. (1995) when otherwise not present, he arrives at the remarkable conclusion that the effect of benchmark warming would be positive in all regions, with gains ranging from a low of 0.47 percent of agricultural GDP in Africa to 2.65 percent in Central Europe and the former Soviet Union and 3.1 percent in centrally planned Asia. On average his inclusion of adaptation contributes a positive impact equivalent to 1.24 percent of agricultural GDP. As argued above, however, the Darwin et al. (1995) results appear seriously to overstate the impact of adaptation. In addition, Tol's heavy reliance on Darwin et al. (1995) is vulnerable to its misleading focus on output rather than yields without considering corresponding opportunity costs of resources required from the rest of the economy and losses in consumer surplus. Moreover, it seems likely from the vintage of the studies considered by Tol that several of them include what would now be seen as an over-statement of the carbon fertilization effect.

Even within the generally overoptimistic estimates prepared by Tol, the usual latitudinal pattern of regional differences emerges. Latin America, the Middle East, and Africa have the lowest gains (and hence largest losses if the whole set of estimates is too optimistic), whereas Russia and Eastern Europe have among the largest gains. (His highest gains for centrally planned Asia are somewhat of an anomaly, considering that China is not usually included as among the biggest winners.)

Jorgenson et al. (2004, 9) draw on the estimates of Reilly et al. (2001), on the optimistic side, and Adams et al. (1990), on the pessimistic side, to estimate that in a central climate scenario with 2.4°C global mean warming and 3.1°C US warming by 2100, the average impact on agriculture over the present century would range from a decline of 26 percent to an increase of 20 percent. They note, "Under the pessimistic view, the unit costs for crop agriculture . . . rise continuously with rising temperatures . . . However, under the optimistic view [there are initial benefits that begin to reverse] when the rise in U.S. mean temperature reaches a threshold of just under 3.3°C . . ." (Jorgenson et al. 2004, 10).

In a recent survey prepared for the OECD, Hitz and Smith (2004) find that agricultural impacts of global warming are uncertain below about a 3°C temperature increase but that at larger temperature increases the literature broadly indicates reductions in yield. Grain yields decline above temperature thresholds, CO_2 fertilization effects eventually saturate, and "eventually . . . geographical shifting cannot compensate for higher temperatures" (p. 44). They note that Parry et al. (1999) find adverse effects even at 1°C increase in global mean temperature and that Rosenzweig, Parry, and Fischer (1995) find sharply increasing adverse effects above 4°C, even with adaptation, in contrast to benefits at 2.3°C global mean temperature increase. Hitz and Smith (2004) argue that the potential reductions are small relative to baseline increases in agricultural output. They judge that

the existing disparities in crop production between developed and developing countries were estimated to increase. These results are a reflection of longer and warmer growing seasons [as a consequence of global warming] at high latitudes, where many developed countries are located, and shorter and drier growing seasons in the tropics, where most developing countries lie. Results in mid-latitude regions are mixed (Hitz and Smith 2004, 43).

Stern Report for the UK Government. At the time this study was being completed, a particularly important study prepared for the UK government was released. The Stern Review (2006) provides an overall evaluation of the prospective damages of global warming and costs of limiting climate change through abatement of emissions of CO_2 and other greenhouse gases. It is notable for providing substantially higher estimates of damage than most past studies, in a range of 5 to 20 percent of GDP by

2200 (as well as "now and forever" when the indefinite future is converted to once-for-all equivalence), and for estimating significantly lower abatement costs than in most previous studies, at only 1 percent of GDP to keep atmospheric concentration of greenhouse gases from rising above 550 ppm equivalent of CO_2.

For purposes of this study the report provides a useful metastudy on agricultural impacts of global warming. Key evaluations in the study include the following: First, there is a parabolic "hill function" for agricultural impact, and location on the hill depends on geographic location and other factors. For 1°C warming there would be "modest increases in cereal yields in temperate regions." With 2°C already there would be "sharp declines in crop yield in tropical regions (5–10% in Africa)." At 3°C warming there would be 150 million to 550 million additional people at risk of hunger if carbon fertilization is weak, and agricultural yields in higher latitudes would be likely to peak. At 4°C warming agricultural yields would decline by 15 to 35 percent in Africa, and entire regions would move out of production (e.g., parts of Australia) (Stern Review 2006, 57).

Water stress is one reason for adverse agricultural effects. The review judges that already dry areas such as the Mediterranean basin and parts of southern Africa and South America would experience a 30 percent decline in water runoff for 2°C warming and 40 to 50 percent reductions for 4°C, although there would be increased water availability in South Asia and parts of Northern Europe and Russia. The review cites recent Hadley Centre results indicating that the proportion of land area experiencing extreme droughts would increase from 3 to 30 percent and that in Southern Europe 100-year severity droughts would increase to 10-year frequency with 3°C warming (Stern Review 2006, 62).

The review summarizes agricultural effects as follows:

> In tropical regions, even small amounts of warming will lead to declines in yield. In higher latitudes, crop yields may increase initially for moderate increases in temperature but then fall. Higher temperatures will lead to substantial declines in cereal production around the world, particularly if the carbon fertilization effect is smaller than previously thought, as some recent studies suggest (p. 67).

The review notes that whereas work based on the original predictions for carbon fertilization suggested rising yields for such crops as wheat and rice (but not maize) for 2°C to 3°C of global warming but declines once temperatures reach 3°C or 4°C, the "latest analysis from crops grown in more realistic field conditions suggests that the effect is likely to be no more than half that typically included in crop models." The review estimates that with weak carbon fertilization, worldwide cereal production declines by 5 percent for 2°C warming and by 10 percent for 4°C warming (with some entire regions potentially too hot and dry to grow crops in the latter case). At higher temperatures such as 5°C to 6°C warming, "Agricultural collapse across large areas of the world is possible . . . but clear empirical evidence is still limited." The review argues that previous crop studies using a quadratic functional form, as in Mendelsohn, Nordhaus, and Shaw (1994), which give a symmetrical reduction in yields for either temperature increases or decreases from the optimal level, tend to understate damage from warming. Recent studies suggest that instead the relationship is highly asymmetrical, with temperature increases above the optimal level "much more harmful than comparable deviations below it" (Stern Review 2006, 67).

The review considers that agricultural impacts will be strongest across Africa and Western Asia (including the Middle East), with crop yields falling 25 to 35 percent with weak carbon fertilization (and 15 to 20 percent even with strong carbon fertilization) once warming reaches 3°C to 4°C. It notes that because maize does not benefit much from carbon fertilization, maize-based agriculture in parts of Africa and Central America would likely suffer declines in yields.

The review takes note of studies that are optimistic about adaptation and incorporation of newly suitable land at high latitudes but points out that transition costs are often ignored and that population movements needed to realize such opportunities could be very disruptive. It adds that many existing estimates do not include the impacts of short-term weather events such as floods, droughts, and heat waves.

In its most specific summary agricultural estimate, the review cites the Parry, Rosenzweig, and Livermore (2005) analysis using Rosenzweig and Parry (1994) data to estimate that benchmark global warming of about 3°C would boost cereal production by 3 to 13 percent in developed countries, reduce it by 10 to 13 percent in developing countries, and cut global production by 0 to 5 percent in simulations of three climate models (GISS, GFDL, and UKMO). The review thus appears to judge the multicountry crop model results of the suite of studies reviewed above (Rosenzweig et al. 1993; Rosenzweig and Iglesias 1994, 2006) as still the most reliable despite numerous successive studies. The review does not mention the optimistic studies of Darwin et al. (1995) and Reilly et al. (2001) discussed above. Nor does it mention the country-specific estimates of Mendelsohn et al. (2000), whose results are reviewed in chapter 5 in comparison to the results of the present study.

Intergovernmental Panel on Climate Change (2007). Finally, as this study went to press, the IPCC released the policymakers' summary of its Working Group II contribution to the Fourth Assessment Report (IPCC 2007b), with release of the full report scheduled for later in the year. For agriculture, the report endorses the prognosis of modest initial gains followed by subsequent losses in the middle and higher latitudes but early losses in the lower latitudes. It states:

> Crop productivity is projected to increase slightly at mid to high latitudes for local mean temperature increases of 1–3°C depending on the crop, and then decrease beyond that in some regions. At lower latitudes, especially seasonally dry and tropi-

cal regions, crop productivity is projected to decrease for even small local temperature increases (1–2°C), which would increase risk of hunger. Globally the potential for food production is projected to increase with increases in local average temperature over a range of 1–3°C, but above this it is projected to decrease. Adaptations such as altered cultivars and planting times allow low and mid- to high latitude cereal yields to be maintained at or above baseline yields for modest warming. Increases in the frequency of droughts and floods are projected to affect local production negatively, especially in subsistence sectors at low latitudes (p. 6).

In terms of vulnerable regions, the report notes that already "in the Sahelian region of Africa, warmer and drier conditions have led to a reduced length of growing season with detrimental effects on crops" (p. 4). It notes that as early as 2020, between 75 million and 250 million people in Africa are projected to be exposed to increased water stress from climate change.

Agricultural production, including access to food, in many African countries and regions is projected to be severely compromised by climate variability and change. The area suitable for agriculture, the length of growing seasons and yield potential, particularly along the margins of semi-arid and arid areas, are expected to decrease. This would further adversely affect food security and exacerbate malnutrition in the continent. In some countries, yields from rain-fed agriculture could be reduced by up to 50% by 2020 (p. 10).

For other regions,

crop yields could increase up to 20% in East and Southeast Asia while it [sic] could decrease up to 30% in Central and South Asia by the mid-21st century. . . . As a result of reduced precipitation and increased evaporation, water security problems are projected to intensify by 2030 in southern and eastern Australia. . . . Production from agriculture and forestry by 2030 is projected to decline over much of southern and eastern Australia. . . . In Southern Europe, climate change is projected to worsen conditions (high temperatures and drought) in a region already vulnerable to climate variability, and to reduce water availability. . . . In Central and Eastern Europe, summer precipitation is projected to decrease, causing higher water stress. . . . In Northern Europe, climate change is initially projected to bring mixed effects, including some benefits such as . . . increased crop yields. . . . However, as climate change continues, its negative impacts . . . are likely to outweigh its benefits." In North America, "Moderate climate change in the early decades of the century is projected to increase aggregate yields of rain-fed agriculture by 5–20%, but with important variability among regions. Major challenges are projected for crops that are near the warm end of their suitable range or depend on highly utilized water resources (pp. 11–12).

Unfortunately, the policymakers' summary is silent on the crucial question of recent scientific estimates of prospective carbon fertilization. It also tends to focus on the next few decades rather than the latter part of this century. Broadly, however, the report is consistent with the findings of this study.

3

Key Issues: Carbon Fertilization, Irrigation, and Trade

Before proceeding to the main estimates of this study, it is important to highlight three major issues. The first is carbon fertilization. The estimates developed in this study depend crucially on the yield enhancement assumed for this effect. As set forth in this chapter, recent scientific studies using open-field rather than laboratory conditions find a considerably lower enhancement than often used in past studies. Accordingly, this chapter considers these recent estimates to develop an independent central carbon fertilization effect for use in the estimates of this study. This carbon fertilization effect is then imposed on the without–carbon fertilization results from the agricultural impact models applied to obtain the estimates including carbon fertilization.

The second issue is irrigation. This chapter reviews the controversy on whether model estimates have adequately taken irrigation into account. There is still considerable room for doubt that they have done so. The estimates in this study, however, do not attempt to quantify any corresponding correction.

The third issue is whether to incorporate feedback from international trade when examining the impact of global warming on agriculture. This chapter sets forth the reasons why such effects are not incorporated in the country-specific impact estimates of this study.

Carbon Fertilization

The extent to which carbon fertilization could alleviate any adverse effects of global warming on agriculture has been a central issue in analysis of the severity of these effects. Carbon dioxide is an input in photosynthesis, which uses solar energy to combine water and carbon dioxide to produce carbohydrates, with oxygen as a waste product.[1] In addition, higher atmospheric concentrations of carbon dioxide reduce plants' stomatal (pore) openings and hence the loss of water to respiration. So-called C3 crops, which include rice, wheat, soybeans, fine grains, legumes, and most trees, benefit substantially from additional atmospheric carbon dioxide. Benefits for C4 crops, which include maize, millet, sorghum, and sugarcane, are much more limited.[2]

Recent research based on experiments with the free air concentration enrichment (FACE) method suggests that past estimates of the carbon fertilization effect have been substantially overstated as a consequence of relying on "studies made within chambers at small scales" rather than "field crops under fully-open-air conditions at an agronomic scale." Thus, Long et al. (2005, 1, 5) find that with carbon dioxide elevated to 550 to 575 parts per million (ppm), the FACE experiments show "the yield increase is 11% for C3 crops and 7% for all five major food crops, which is one-third to one-quarter of the direct effect of CO_2 modelled in the recent assessment for Europe and the USA by Darwin & Kennedy (2000)."

In a more recent study, Long et al. (2006) report that FACE studies indicate that at 550 ppm carbon dioxide concentration, yield increases amount to 13 percent for wheat in contrast to 31 percent in laboratory studies, 14 percent instead of 32 percent for soybeans, and 0 percent instead of 18 percent for C4 crops. Among the major crops, C3 species account for roughly three-fourths and C4 for one-fourth of total value.[3] If the central C3 increment is set at 12 percent, considering the two Long et al. studies, and a

---

1. This process occurs in two stages. In the first, a light-dependent reaction, the pigment chlorophyll absorbs light and loses an electron, which becomes stored in the high-energy molecules NADPH and ATP. In the second, a light-independent reaction, these high-energy molecules are used along with the enzyme RuBisCO to capture carbon dioxide from the atmosphere in what is called the Calvin cycle.

2. In C3 crops RuBisCO is located in mesophyll cells, which are in contact with the atmosphere through stomatal pores in the epidermis. In these cells, "RuBisCO is not CO_2 saturated in today's atmosphere. . . . In contrast, in C4 crops . . . RuBisCO is localized to bundle sheath cells in which CO_2 is concentrated to three to six times atmospheric [levels. This is] sufficient to saturate RuBisCO and in theory would prevent any increase in CO_2 uptake with rising $[CO_2]$" (Long et al. 2006, 1918). However, these crops may also benefit indirectly from increased efficiency in water use as a consequence of reduced stomatal conductance with rising carbon dioxide.

3. Global production value circa 2004 stood at the following estimated levels: wheat, $94 billion; rice, $120 billion; soybeans, $49 billion; cotton, $23 billion, or a total of $286 billion for the four major C3 crops; and at $68 billion for maize, $25 billion for sugarcane, and $6 billion for sorghum, or a total of $99 billion for the three major C4 crops. These estimates are compiled from USDA (2005, 2006), IMF (2006), UN FAOSTAT database, and Federal Register (2006). It is assumed that the sugar output yield of sugarcane is 0.063, the ratio for Brazil, and the Philippines price for sugar is applied.

modest allowance of 3 percent yield increase for C4 crops is made, then the weighted average increment in yield from carbon fertilization would be 9 percent at 550 ppm.

This study examines the period 2070–99. At the midpoint of 2085, the central scenario used in this study—scenario A2 of the Special Report on Emissions Scenarios (SRES) from the Intergovernmental Panel on Climate Change (IPCC)—places atmospheric carbon dioxide concentration at 735 ppm (IPCC 2001a, 807). The carbon fertilization effect rises less than linearly with atmospheric carbon concentrations (Long et al. 2006, Mendelsohn and Schlesinger 1999). If Mendelsohn and Schlesinger (1999) is followed and the relationship is specified as logarithmic, then at 735 ppm the effect should be about two-thirds larger than at 550 ppm.[4] On this basis, the central estimate of the carbon fertilization effect by the 2080s is set in this study at a 15 percent increase in yield. This impact is considerably smaller than that assumed in some past studies.[5]

Two past studies in particular are of relevance to this study: Mendelsohn and Schlesinger (1999), or MS; and Mendelsohn, Morrison, Schlesinger, and Andronova (2000), or MMSA. Using an atmospheric concentration of 735 ppm of carbon dioxide by the 2080s, and applying the future world average temperature and precipitation for land weighted by farmland area—16.2°C and 2.44 mm per day (see table 4.3 in chapter 4)—the MS "reduced form" equation for output per hectare gives an estimate of $333.2 without carbon fertilization and $376.6 with carbon fertilization, an increase of 13 percent.[6] Applying the MS Ricardian function gives corresponding estimates of land rental equivalent of $34 per hectare without carbon fertilization and $45.9 with carbon fertilization, an increase of 32.1 percent.[7] As discussed in chapter 5, for the Ricardian estimates it is necessary to translate the percent change in land rental equivalent into corre-

---

4. With the present concentration at 350 ppm, the typical 550 ppm concentrations are a ratio of 1.57 to today's concentration, and a future concentration of 735 ppm would be 2.1 times today's concentration. The ratio of the logarithm of the latter to that of the former is 1.64 to 1.

5. Note that Tubiello et al. (2007) have argued that Long et al. (2006) overstate the difference between FACE and non-FACE experimental results and contend that in any event the principal crop models have applied much more conservative carbon fertilization than those cited by Long et al. For the purposes of the present study, the most important point in this debate is that the central estimate used here, 15 percent yield enhancement at 735 ppm against a 350 ppm base, is fully consistent with the preferred crop model cited in Tubiello et al. (2007). Namely, the agroecological zone model cited in table 2 of Tubiello et al. (2007) indicates that a rise from 350 to 735 ppm would boost yields by 16 percent for wheat and rice, 21 percent for soybeans, and 7 percent for maize. Applying the corresponding world output value shares, the weighted increase would be 14.8 percent.

6. See equation (5.1) in chapter 5.

7. See equation (5.2) in chapter 5.

sponding potential output changes, which are about half as large.[8] When this translation is done, the 32 percent MS Ricardian carbon fertilization for land rental equivalent represents an output impact on the order of 16 percent. For both the MS "reduced form" and Ricardian functions, then, the carbon fertilization effect is relatively similar to the 15 percent used in this study (for 735 ppm).

In contrast, in the subsequent MMSA study, the version of the MS model used to arrive at global (rather than just US) estimates, the exercise just outlined generates a Ricardian model increase of land rental equivalent from $34 per hectare to $49.6 per hectare, an increase of 45.9 percent. Again applying a global ratio of about half, carbon fertilization as estimated in MMSA would boost output potential by about 23 percent, which is considerably larger than the 15 percent used in this study. The MMSA function explicitly increased the carbon fertilization parameter used in the MS equation, but it would appear that this increase resulted in a significant overstatement of carbon fertilization.[9]

The Irrigation Question

A persistent question about the Ricardian statistical estimates of how agriculture responds to changing climate has been whether they have adequately taken account of irrigation. One issue is whether benefits attributed to warmer climates are overstated because in fact these benefits reflect high values of land and output per hectare attributable instead to irrigation combined with the fact that there is a higher incidence of irrigation in warmer regions. Another issue is whether climate impact projections using these models address the availability of water for irrigation.

Evapotranspiration (the combined loss of moisture from soil through evaporation and plants through stomatal transpiration) increases with temperature. The need for irrigation rises as conditions become drier. It rises as a function of the difference between evapotranspiration and precipitation. Because global warming will increase both temperature and precipitation, the implications for soil moisture and the need for irrigation depend on the outcome of the race between rising temperature and rising precipitation.

An extremely simple test for the United States shows the incidence of irrigation is positively related to temperature and negatively related to

---

8. The ratios of net revenue per hectare to output per hectare used in chapter 5 range from a low of about 40 percent in the United States to a high of 78 percent in Africa. This ratio is applied to the percent change in land rental equivalent to obtain the corresponding percent change to be expected in output potential.

9. The MMSA Ricardian function is similar to equation (5.2) in chapter 5 (the MS function) but changes the coefficient on the logarithm of the ratio of carbon concentration to today's 350 ppm from 480 to 687 (Mendelsohn et al. 2000, 559).

precipitation. Using state data for agriculture and state capital data for temperature and precipitation, figure 3.1a shows the relationship across US states between the ratio of irrigated crop area to harvested crop area (percent) and annual average daily temperature (°C). Figure 3.1b shows the same incidence of irrigation as related to average annual precipitation (mm per year).[10]

Broadly the scatter diagrams show higher incidence of irrigation for higher temperatures and lower incidence of irrigation with higher precipitation. There are three states that are outliers to the temperature trendline: Nevada (irrigation incidence at 136 percent of harvested cropland), Utah (114 percent), and Wyoming (119 percent).[11] All three have extremely high irrigation incidence but relatively low temperatures. The anomaly is explained by the low precipitation in all three, as they become the upper-left observations in figure 3.1b.[12] Many of the states have low irrigation incidence, but some have extremely high incidence, as indicated by the difference between median (8.2 percent) and average irrigation (29.5 percent).

A simple statistical regression for these data shows the following, with *t*-statistics in parentheses:

$$Z = 24.1 + 3.73\ T - 0.0455\ P;\ \text{adj. } R^2 = 0.21$$
$$(1.57)\quad(3.22)\quad(3.29)$$

Although the degree of explanation is moderate at only about 20 percent, the coefficients on temperature (T) and precipitation (P) are highly significant.

To anticipate the following climate analysis, for the United States the estimates in this study indicate that baseline global warming by the 2080s would cause the farmland-weighted averages for annual temperatures to rise by 5.4°C and the corresponding averages for precipitation to fall by 4.3 mm per year.[13] If these changes are applied to the simple regression equation, the incidence of irrigation would need to rise by 20.3 percentage points as a consequence of climate change. The increase would be almost entirely from higher temperature; the slight decline in precipitation would have little effect, except in the sense that the failure of precipitation to rise would mean that the race between temperature and precipitation would be won hands down by temperature.

---

10. Temperature and precipitation are from NOAA (2007). Irrigated and harvested crop land are from USDA (2004).

11. Greater than 100 percent incidence implies that some irrigated land is used for pasture rather than crops and/or that some irrigated land is left fallow.

12. Note also that Carson City at 4,687 feet elevation and average annual temperature of 10.7°C may not be as representative of statewide conditions as is the case for most capitals. Thus, also in Nevada, Las Vegas at 2,028 feet has average annual temperature of 20.1°C.

13. Calculated from table 4.2 and appendix table E.1.

Figure 3.1a   Irrigation and temperature for US states

irrigated crop area as percent
of harvested crop area

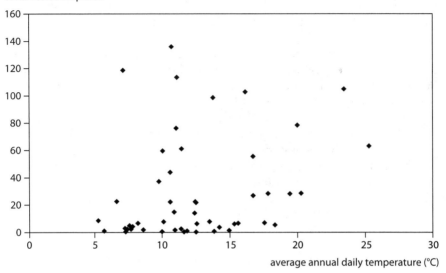

average annual daily temperature (°C)

Figure 3.1b   Irrigation and precipitation for US states

irrigated crop area as percent
of harvested crop area

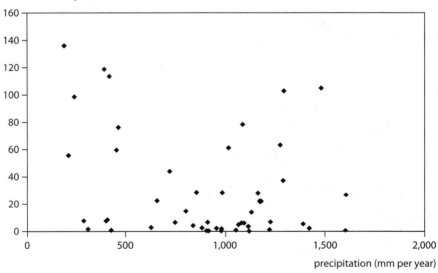

precipitation (mm per year)

Viewed in this way, the irrigation issue raises two questions for most model estimates. First, have they included the costs of additional irrigation, which requires large capital outlays? Second, have they carefully considered the availability of water for additional irrigation? The broad answer to both questions would seem to be in the negative, suggesting that the Ricardian models may well tend toward an optimistic bias regarding treatment of irrigation.

The seminal empirical Ricardian function for the United States is that estimated in Mendelsohn, Nordhaus, and Shaw (1994). In an early comment (Cline 1996), I argued that the application of their results to global warming scenarios faced the problem that such an exercise implicitly assumed that water was infinitely available for irrigation at the present price, whereas there were strong grounds for concern about water scarcity and increased incidence of droughts as a consequence of global warming. In a subsequent comment, Darwin (1999) suggested that the Mendelsohn-Nordhaus-Shaw function itself could contain a statistical bias by failing to remove the influence of irrigation on the measured relationship of productivity to temperature and precipitation (along the lines just suggested). Quiggin and Horowitz (1999) further criticized the Mendelsohn-Nordhaus-Shaw function by pointing out that its quadratic term for October temperature had the wrong sign (positive), indicating that there was no limiting optimal temperature for that term. The two authors also usefully sharpened the argument on the Ricardian approach by pointing out that whereas some crop models lacking attention to adaptation might be subject to the "dumb farmer" critique, the Ricardian approach instead "implicitly assumes zero adjustment costs and therefore yields a lower-bound estimate of the costs of climate change" (Quiggin and Horowitz 1999, 1044).

In response to the critique of Darwin (1999) about possible irrigation bias, Mendelsohn and Nordhaus (1999) reestimated their model as follows. First they estimated an equation for irrigation as a function of the climate and control variables. Then they included predicted irrigation from this equation as an independent variable in an expanded climate impact Ricardian function. They argued that it would be incorrect to include irrigation directly (rather than predicted irrigation) because of the endogeneity of irrigation to climate. Then when they conducted their climate change impact exercise using the revised Ricardian function, they found that the effects were somewhat more rather than less favorable after removing the influence of irrigation.[14] They concluded that concerns about irrigation bias were not warranted.

---

14. The authors found that in the function without irrigation, a temperature increase of 2°C and precipitation increase of 8 percent would boost net revenue by 3.3 percent, whereas in their revised function removing the influence of irrigation, crop net revenue would rise by 10.4 percent.

Their equation for incidence of irrigation has key information in itself, however, that could instead suggest concern about a possible substantial rise in the need for irrigation in a hotter, drier climate. If their equation is applied to their suggested climate scenario (+2°C temperature, +8 percent precipitation), the result is an estimated 19 percentage point increase in the incidence of irrigation.[15] If the temperature increase were considerably larger and precipitation change negligible or slightly negative, as suggested above for the 2080s baseline examined here, by implication the expected increase in irrigation would be much larger, using the Mendelsohn-Nordhaus equation. So once again there are two key questions for their analysis: Who would pay for the extra irrigation, and would it be feasible given possible water constraints?

Moreover, their conclusion of benign results turns crucially on the precipitation variable. Their two-stage results boost the marginal effect of an extra 1 inch per month in precipitation from $123 per hectare to $218 per hectare. Their interpretation is that once the influence of irrigation is removed, precipitation is relatively more important to agricultural performance. But then their large boost to precipitation in their climate change scenario becomes the key to the favorable impact, and as noted the set of climate model estimates presented below shows a much less favorable precipitation change in the baseline by the 2080s.[16]

More fundamentally, however, the Mendelsohn-Nordhaus reestimation failed to escape the problem of the wrong sign for a key quadratic term on temperature. Indeed, a closer inspection of their equation shows that it has entirely implausible estimates for high warming as a result. In particular, in their formulation the underlying variables are temperature in degrees Fahrenheit minus the average temperature, with both linear and quadratic terms on this "demeaned" temperature variable. This yields the following structure:

---

15. Calculated from their seasonal temperature and precipitation linear and squared coefficients applied to demeaned variables from the base US climate from table 4.2, for the base, and their specified changes in temperature and precipitation.

16. Note further that the change in the temperature coefficient in their two-stage results is problematic. The marginal impact of 1°F swings from –$17 per hectare originally to +$4 per hectare. If one accepts the notion that US agriculture on average is below optimal temperature, then this marginal effect might not be implausible. But then the real question becomes whether their coefficients on the squared terms for temperature are reliable, because it is the nonlinear adverse effect of going well beyond optimal temperature that is the concern. By the construction of their variables, which are "demeaned" (subtract mean temperature from temperature and mean precipitation from precipitation), their model unfortunately forces the nonlinear effects to be symmetrical for both a decline and an increase in temperature. As noted above, recent studies suggest instead an adverse asymmetry for temperature increases. Moreover, the mixture of positive and negative coefficients for the squared temperature terms across different seasons means that their function is not strictly hill-shaped but questionably gives nonlinear positive gains to October temperatures, as noted by Darwin (1999).

$$y = \alpha + \sum_i \beta_i \Delta T_i + \sum_i \gamma_i (\Delta T_i)^2$$

where y is crop revenue per acre per year, α is a constant term, i is the seasonal month (January, April, July, or October), and ΔT_i is the increase in temperature (in degrees Fahrenheit) above the base period averages. The level of base temperature itself does not appear because in the base period the temperature term disappears: Temperature *is* average temperature for the month, and the base demeaned variable is zero.

For a climate scenario with an increase in temperature specified as ΔT uniformly across the four seasons,[17] the change in revenue per hectare is then simply:

$$\Delta y = \Delta T \sum_i \beta_i + (\Delta T)^2 \sum_i \gamma_i$$

In the reestimated Ricardian function in Mendelsohn and Nordhaus (1999), the sum of the linear coefficients on demeaned temperature is $4.10 per acre, and the sum of the quadratic coefficients is $1.52.[18] So there is an unlimited rise in net revenue per hectare with higher temperatures. An extra 2°F boosts the net revenue output measure by about $14 per hectare. As the temperature increase doubles successively to 4°F, 8°F, 16°F, and 32°F, the boost to output per hectare becomes respectively $41, $130, $455, $1,688, and so forth. The climate function states literally that if temperature rose to that on the sun (11,000°F), net revenue would rise by $121 million per hectare. In short, it violates both common sense and the underlying hill-shaped Ricardian function postulated by the authors.

What one seems to be left with in the reestimated Mendelsohn-Nordhaus analysis of irrigation is one reliable result and one failed result. The reliable result is that irrigation does indeed rise for hotter and drier counties. The failed result is a Ricardian function for the impact of climate on agriculture. The empirical estimate should be rejected just as an empirical estimate of an upward-sloping demand curve (higher price offered, larger volume purchased by consumers) should generally be rejected, regardless of the *t*-statistics. On this basis, the irrigation issue stands as follows: First, there should indeed be concern that additional irrigation will be required under global warming. Second, there simply remains ambiguity as to whether the Ricardian functions successfully elim-

---

17. As indicated in appendix tables H.1 and H.2, the change in average temperature by 2070–99 for the US Lakes-Northeast region, for example, is almost identical at 6.3°C for January, April, and July and almost the same at 5.3°C for October.

18. The seasonal detail is as follows, for January, April, July, and October, respectively: linear, –133, +91.1, –128, and +174; quadratic, –1.88, –4.66, 0.17, and 7.89 (Mendelsohn and Nordhaus 1999, 1054).

inate any bias in estimate from irrigation, because in the specific test designed for this purpose Mendelsohn and Nordhaus instead estimate a function that must be rejected on first principles.[19]

Trade as Moderator?

Finally, a crucial conceptual issue is whether to examine the impact of global warming on agriculture with or without incorporating induced effects operating through international trade. The estimates of this study do not incorporate trade feedbacks for the following reasons.[20]

First and foremost, there is a "let them eat cake" flavor to the notion that trade will greatly reduce losses from global warming. Poorer nations are most likely to experience greater agricultural losses. A focus on trade implicitly argues that these countries can limit their losses from global warming by shifting to agricultural imports rather than producing those products at home. The problem is that they may face difficulties increasing export earnings from other goods in order to pay for their new food import needs. Incorporation of world trade moderation of global warming damage to agriculture should at the minimum include corresponding estimates of the terms-of-trade losses of the poorer countries as they find it necessary to export additional volumes of (likely) labor-intensive manufactures in order to import more food.

Second, Cline (1992, appendix 3A) shows that in a closed system, which is the case for the world as a whole, the welfare losses from a negative shock to agricultural yields are at least as large in percentage terms as the percent decline in yields. Basically consumer surplus losses exceed pro-

---

19. Nor does the further work by Mendelsohn and Dinar (2003) appear to lay this issue to rest, because it asks a different question: "whether farmers that have access to irrigation water have higher farm values" (p. 331). Not surprisingly, it finds that they do. But the study does not attempt to simulate the costs of additional irrigation, or investigate the availability of water for the additional irrigation, that could be necessitated by a hotter and drier (or hotter and only marginally wetter) climate.

20. Note that although the regions for which average yield impacts are reported in the crop model source used in this study (Rosenzweig and Iglesias 2006) are defined for consistency with one such trade model (the basic linked system [BLS]), the yield impact estimates themselves are for the direct effect of climate change without considering such induced effects (see table 5.7 in chapter 5). In general incorporation of induced effects, whether domestic or from international trade, would be unlikely to change the direct yield estimates by much. For example, an area experiencing a negative yield shock from climate change would be likely to encounter a positive second-round yield offset from the standpoint of greater applications of fertilizer and other nonland inputs but a negative second-round aggravation from the incorporation of more marginal land. Trade would tend to moderate both effects, because less of the new shortfall of output would be resolved by higher prices and induced domestic output response; but this trade moderation would be of the second-round yield effects, not of the first-round direct climate impact.

ducer surplus gains.[21] Reduction in global average yields from climate change cannot be offset by recourse to trade at the global level.

Third, studies that focus on world agricultural output change, rather than direct yield impact or ex ante impact on agricultural potential, tend to generate impact estimates that are misleadingly small because they tend to report output change but not losses in net welfare after accounting for loss of consumer surplus. Demand for food is price inelastic. As an illustration, suppose demand were completely price inelastic but yields fell 50 percent. Output would have to rise back to the original level at what could be enormous costs of additional inputs; yet a study reporting the "output" effect would find that there was no impact whatsoever.

Fourth, trade feedbacks are omitted in the present study in part because to include them would add an additional layer of hypothetical and circumstantial analysis to an already difficult analysis focused on biophysical effects. It is not even clear that there are particularly meaningful medium-term agricultural supply functions available on a multicountry basis in today's international economy, yet it would be necessary not only to identify them but also to project them for the distant future. It is useful to recall that in 1973 the United States imposed an embargo on soybean exports in order to avoid inflationary effects of rising prices; it is also the case that many nations are inclined to impose agricultural import barriers in the name of food self-sufficiency. Incorporating probabilities of such distortions would further complicate adding trade feedbacks to the analysis.

In sum, for several reasons incorporating induced effects based on a trade model could easily obscure rather than clarify the central diagnosis of prospective effects of unmitigated global warming on world agriculture.

---

21. Consumer surplus is the amount of saving by consumers represented by the difference between what they actually have to pay for the good and the amount they would be willing to pay if necessary. Producer surplus is the corresponding difference between what producers receive and what they would be willing to accept if necessary. The sum of the two is the area between the downward-sloping demand curve and the upward-sloping supply curve. Because a reduction in agricultural yield shifts the supply curve upward without a corresponding upward shift in the demand curve, it unambiguously reduces the sum of consumer and producer surplus. The percent reduction in the sum of producer and consumer surplus is likely to be at least as large as the percent reduction in yield.

4

Country-Level Climate Projections

The agricultural impact estimates of this study combine two sets of existing models to arrive at consistent geographically detailed estimates. The first set of models is from climate science; the second set is from agronomy and economics. This chapter sets forth what may be viewed as consensus general circulation model (GCM) climate projections for business as usual warming by the 2080s. These estimates are then used in the following chapter in applying the agronomic-economic impact models.

The Climate Models

The new agricultural impact estimates of this study use the base climate and model scenario results available on the Intergovernmental Panel on Climate Change (IPCC) Data Distribution Centre Web site maintained for the IPCC by the Climate Research Unit, University of East Anglia, United Kingdom.[1] For the base climate of 1961–90, climate data are available at the $0.5° \times 0.5°$ grid resolution level ($360 \times 720 = 259{,}200$ cells). The analysis here selects two climate variables: temperature and daily precipitation. These data are available as monthly averages. The estimates here first obtain the annual average of these monthly averages, for each cell in the base grid. The base climate data are consolidated to averages for the stan-

---

1. See http://ipcc-ddc.cru.uea.ac.uk. The other institutions participating in maintaining the Data Distribution Centre are the Deutsches Klimarechenzentrum (DKRZ/MPI) in Hamburg, Germany and the Center for International Earth Science Information Network (CIESIN) at Columbia University, New York.

Table 4.1 General circulation models used for scenarios

Name	Organization/model	Author	Grid resolution	Climate sensitivity parameter (°C)
ECHAM4/ OPYC3	German Climate Research Centre, European Centre/ Hamburg Model #4	Roeckner et al. (1996); Zhang et al. (1998)	2.8° × 2.8°	2.6
HadCM3	UK Hadley Centre for Climate Prediction and Research Coupled Model #3	Gordon et al. (2000)	2.5° × 3.75°	3.0
CSIRO-Mk2	Australian Commonwealth Scientific and Industrial Research Organisation Model #2b	Gordon and O'Farrell (1997)	3.2° × 5.6°	3.7
CGCM2	Canadian Centre for Climate Modeling and Analysis GCM #2	Flato and Boer (2001)	3.7° × 3.7°	3.6
GFDL-R30	US Geophysical Fluid Dynamics Laboratory R-30 Resolution Model	Knutson et al. (1999)	2.25° × 3.75°	3.4
CCSR/NIES	Japanese Centre for Climate System Research	Emori et al. (1999)	5.6° × 5.6°	3.5

Source: IPCC (1999; 2001a, 478, 538).

dard grid G used in this study, latitude height of 2°, and longitude width of 3° (90 × 120 = 10,800 cells) using the method set forth in appendix A.

The changes in climate variables from the present to a future target date as calculated by six GCMs are then similarly converted to standard grid G and added to the corresponding base period average climate variables to obtain temperature and precipitation at the future period, 2070–99. Table 4.1 reports the models, their grid resolution, and their climate sensitivity parameter S. This parameter indicates global mean surface warming to be expected from a doubling of carbon dioxide–equivalent atmospheric greenhouse gas concentration above preindustrial levels.

The scenario used for all six models is SRES A2 in the IPCC's Special Report on Emissions Scenarios (Nakićenović and Swart 2000). It is one of the six scenarios used in the IPCC's Third Assessment Report and the only scenario for which all six climate models providing data to the IPCC Data Distribution Center include projections.

Among the six scenarios considered by the Third and Fourth Assessment Reports of the IPCC, scenario A2 was the next to highest.[2] This scenario projects carbon emissions from all anthropogenic sources to rise from 7.3 gigatons of carbon (GtC) in 1990 to 17.4 GtC by 2050 and 29.1 GtC by 2100. As argued in Cline (2004, 14), two of the six scenarios (A1T and B1) have implausible declines in carbon intensity of energy and are inconsistent with a baseline with no policy incentive to reducing carbon dioxide emissions. In addition carbon intensity of energy could well rise later this century from the more rapid exhaustion of natural gas and oil supplies than of abundant coal supplies, in view of the higher carbon intensity of energy from coal. As a result, scenario A2 should be seen more as an intermediate path among those that are realistic than as a high emissions baseline.

It is also important to ask whether the climate models available for this study have any particular bias toward over- or understatement of future climate change. The climate sensitivity parameter (S) of the model is the best gauge for this question. The average sensitivity parameter in the six GCMs applied in this study is $S = 3.3°C$ (table 4.1). In comparison, the 2007 Fourth Assessment Report of the IPCC reported that the climate sensitivity parameter "is likely to be in the range 2 to 4.5°C with a best estimate of about 3°C" (IPCC 2007a, 12). So the GCMs used are close to the standard norm for the climate sensitivity parameter.

Country-Level Climate Results: Present Day and for 2070–99

The present and future climate estimates are calculated at the level of each of the approximately 2,800 land-based cells in the standardized grid.[3] Table 4.2 reports the result of averaging these estimates at the level of 116 individual countries (68), regions (10), or subzones for the seven largest countries (38). Definitions of the multicountry regions and large-country subzones are in appendix D. Development of the estimates for agricultural land and output within each subzone of the large countries is discussed in appendix E.

Tables H.1 through H.4 in appendix H report the corresponding monthly average values for present and future temperatures and precipitation. Monthly detail is needed to implement several of the country- or region-specific Ricardian agricultural impact functions used in this study (see chapter 5).

---

2. Cumulative anthropogenic carbon emissions from 2000 through 2100, including from deforestation, were as follows, by scenario: A1B, 1,430 GtC; A1T, 986 GtC; A1F1, 2,107 GtC; A2, 1,780 GtC; B1, 901 GtC; B2, 1,081 GtC (calculated from IPCC 2001a, 801).

3. The standardized grid contains 10,800 cells (90 x 120). The mapping of base to future climate is first done at the 1° × 1° grid level, which corresponds to 180 × 360 = 64,800 cells. There are 22,156 land-based cells at that resolution.

Table 4.2   Present and future climate: Average temperature and precipitation (°C and mm per day, annual averages)

Country	Temperature		Precipitation	
	Present, 1961–90	Future, 2070–99	Present, 1961–90	Future, 2070–99
Afghanistan	13.10	18.75	0.86	0.86
Algeria	22.67	27.81	0.22	0.23
Angola	21.52	25.53	2.75	2.62
Argentina	14.65	17.89	1.63	1.66
Australia				
Southeast	16.68	20.27	1.66	1.61
Southwest	18.35	21.75	0.79	0.65
Central East	22.02	26.10	1.59	1.61
Central West	23.49	27.63	0.81	0.75
North	26.38	30.04	2.55	2.55
Bangladesh	24.46	28.13	6.42	7.04
Belgium	9.62	13.72	2.23	2.27
Brazil				
Amazon	26.04	30.38	5.97	5.84
Northeast	25.58	29.46	3.58	3.52
South	22.04	25.90	3.98	4.15
Burkina Faso	28.16	32.38	2.12	2.29
Cambodia	26.64	29.99	5.31	5.21
Cameroon	24.60	28.16	4.36	4.50
Canada				
Arctic	−15.09	−7.28	0.46	0.78
Central	−0.47	5.41	1.21	1.41
Northwest Territories	−8.88	−2.42	0.82	1.21
Pacific Coast	0.79	5.40	2.17	2.54
Southeast	−0.93	5.42	2.26	2.56
Central America	24.23	27.76	6.51	6.18
Central Europe	7.67	12.54	2.39	2.35
Chile	9.01	11.91	1.52	1.43
China				
Beijing Northeast	2.73	8.89	1.32	1.57
Central	9.49	14.48	2.03	2.43
Hong Kong Southeast	18.78	22.67	4.47	4.82
Northwest	6.06	12.08	0.37	0.44
South Central	17.50	21.27	3.59	3.95
Tibetan Plateau	−1.45	4.15	1.13	1.53
Yellow Sea	14.59	19.25	2.77	3.12
Colombia	24.31	27.81	7.25	7.44
Cuba	25.25	28.19	3.57	3.50
Democratic Republic of the Congo	23.95	27.93	4.21	4.27
Ecuador	22.15	25.36	5.52	6.01

(table continues next page)

Table 4.2   Present and future climate: Average temperature and precipitation (°C and mm per day, annual averages) *(continued)*

Country	Temperature		Precipitation	
	Present, 1961–90	Future, 2070–99	Present, 1961–90	Future, 2070–99
Egypt	22.16	26.79	0.12	0.12
Ethiopia	23.08	26.92	2.04	1.97
France	10.56	14.95	2.33	2.13
Germany	8.26	12.70	2.00	2.09
Ghana	27.15	30.87	3.23	3.27
Greece	13.86	17.96	1.78	1.47
India				
Northeast	20.54	24.54	3.51	4.23
Northwest	23.55	27.52	1.58	1.97
Southeast	26.76	30.06	3.05	3.42
Southwest	26.23	29.32	3.04	3.47
Indonesia	25.76	28.58	7.74	8.02
Iran	17.26	22.63	0.62	0.62
Iraq	20.86	26.16	0.57	0.58
Italy	12.20	16.52	2.48	2.23
Ivory Coast	26.19	29.79	3.88	3.95
Japan	10.73	14.87	4.40	4.46
Kazakhstan	5.79	12.19	0.69	0.75
Kenya	24.33	27.83	2.02	2.19
Madagascar	22.28	25.53	4.12	3.91
Malawi	21.79	25.72	3.10	3.04
Malaysia	25.35	28.27	7.95	8.14
Mali	28.24	33.01	0.85	0.87
Mexico	20.66	24.71	2.09	1.84
Morocco	17.43	21.91	0.88	0.77
Mozambique	23.44	27.28	2.82	2.80
Myanmar	22.67	26.08	5.47	5.91
Nepal	12.90	17.13	3.64	4.57
Netherlands	9.26	13.21	2.16	2.31
New Zealand	10.22	12.71	4.79	5.03
Niger	27.13	31.53	0.46	0.68
Nigeria	26.73	30.46	3.09	3.29
North Korea	5.66	11.03	2.87	3.18
Other Central Asia	10.01	15.79	0.75	0.74
Other Equatorial Africa	24.81	28.46	4.23	4.30
Other Horn of Africa	26.79	30.35	0.81	0.96
Other South America	21.61	25.90	3.04	3.15
Other Southern Africa	20.57	24.91	0.93	0.80
Other West Africa	25.77	29.29	5.24	5.32
Pakistan	19.91	24.76	0.83	0.96
Peru	19.52	23.34	4.22	4.42

(table continues next page)

Table 4.2 Present and future climate: Average temperature and precipitation (°C and mm per day, annual averages) *(continued)*

Country	Temperature Present, 1961–90	Temperature Future, 2070–99	Precipitation Present, 1961–90	Precipitation Future, 2070–99
Philippines	25.51	28.24	6.52	6.68
Poland	7.80	12.81	1.66	1.82
Portugal	14.93	18.82	2.16	1.85
Romania	8.87	14.07	1.74	1.52
Russia				
Caspian Black Sea	7.85	13.52	1.34	1.32
Far Eastern	−10.56	−2.69	1.05	1.52
North European	2.05	8.60	1.62	2.01
North Urals Siberia	−7.02	1.00	1.30	1.70
Northeast Siberia	−13.97	−5.84	0.79	1.15
South Urals Siberia	−0.25	6.79	1.33	1.62
Southeast Siberia	−5.58	1.48	1.31	1.68
Saudi Arabia	24.57	29.30	0.22	0.34
Scandinavia	1.79	6.89	1.93	2.36
Senegal	27.80	31.51	1.95	1.80
South Africa	17.72	21.89	1.31	1.20
South Korea	11.03	15.33	3.72	3.96
Southeast Europe	10.32	15.08	2.27	1.99
Spain	13.24	17.90	1.76	1.43
Sri Lanka	26.80	29.64	4.67	4.96
Sudan	26.70	30.87	1.18	1.28
Syria	17.48	22.19	0.87	0.73
Tanzania	22.25	26.01	2.88	2.91
Thailand	26.20	29.39	4.38	4.69
Turkey	11.42	16.14	1.57	1.30
Uganda	22.36	26.04	3.24	3.30
Ukraine	8.16	13.67	1.55	1.47
United Kingdom	8.51	11.76	3.13	3.37
United States				
Alaska	−5.10	1.12	1.14	1.70
Lakes and Northeast	8.26	14.17	2.54	2.63
Pacific Northwest	7.57	12.11	1.98	2.09
Rockies, Plains	6.68	12.36	1.18	1.24
Southeast	16.69	21.44	3.52	3.44
South Pacific Coast	12.11	16.56	1.22	1.36
Southwest and Plains	15.05	20.20	1.35	1.20
Uzbekistan	12.36	18.14	0.52	0.48
Venezuela	25.44	29.17	5.33	5.31
Vietnam	24.09	27.44	4.87	4.94
Yemen	23.77	27.72	0.46	0.64
Zambia	21.57	25.86	2.75	2.61
Zimbabwe	21.03	25.39	1.85	1.81

As a first step in thinking about the agricultural implications of the climate projections, it is useful to keep in mind the turning point identified by Mendelsohn et al. (2000, 558) beyond which additional warming has negative effects. They place this optimal temperature at 11.7°C in their reduced form statistical equation for process-based crop model results, and at 14.2°C in their Ricardian model based on cross-section statistical estimates. Even if the more optimistic (higher) threshold is used, it turns out that already in the present climate 62 developing countries, developing regions, or developing-country subzones are above this level, and only 25 (of which 7 are in Russia) are below it. In India, for example, all four subzones are well above the optimal level (with the lowest average annual temperature being for the Northeast at 20.54°C). In China, 3 of the 7 subzones are above the 14.2°C optimum level.

In contrast, for industrial countries, regions, or subzones, only 7 are presently at temperatures above the optimum (5 in Australia and 2 in the United States) whereas 22 are below it. Broadly, then, data on the present climate indicate that the bulk of the developing world is already at temperatures that exceed optimal levels for agriculture. For these countries, further global warming would reduce agricultural production capacity. For many countries already well above the optimal temperature level, this deterioration could be severe, because the relationship is nonlinear with the negative impact rising with the square of temperature, as discussed later. These data similarly suggest that if an initial phase of warming would benefit rather than harm agriculture, it would primarily be to the advantage of industrial countries and disadvantage of developing countries.

It is useful to consider the global nonocean averages for present and future temperatures and precipitation based on the estimates of table 4.2. For this purpose, each entry in the table can be weighted by its share in global land area or global farm area, respectively, from appendix table E.1. The results of this weighting are shown in table 4.3.

Using broadly the same climate models and the same scenario (SRES A2), the IPCC (2001a, 527) places the change in global mean temperature from 1961–90 to 2070–99 at an average of 3.0°C and a range of 1.3°C to 4.5°C. The higher warming found here for land areas, 4.95°C weighting by land area and 4.43°C by farm area, reflects the fact that realized surface warming by a given future date is expected to be greater over land than for the oceans.[4] Actual warming to date from 1950 to 1993 for land surface air temperature has been about twice that for sea surface air temperature (IPCC 2001a, 26). This is an important distinction for exercises examining agricultural impact in response to temperature change, because it means that the relevant temperature change for agriculture will be higher than the change in global mean temperature including the oceans.

---

4. "Generally, the land warms faster than the ocean, the land warms more than the ocean after forcing stabilizes, and there is greater relative warming at high latitudes" (IPCC 2001a, 528).

**Table 4.3   Global land-based climate averages and changes,
1961–90 to 2070–99**

	Land area weighting	Farm area weighting
Temperature (°C), 1961–90 (base)	13.15	16.20
Precipitation (mm per day)	2.20	2.44
Change from base to 2070–99 average:		
Temperature (°C)	4.95	4.43
Precipitation (mm per day)	0.129	0.072
Percent change (precipitation)	5.9	2.9

Table 4.3 shows that when farm area rather than land area is used for weighting, the warming is somewhat smaller. This result reflects the fact that the share of land masses in the high latitudes (primarily in the Northern Hemisphere), for example, at latitudes above 50°, is much greater than the share of these regions in global farm area, reflecting the limited feasibility of farming in these areas. When this fact is combined with the expected greater warming at high latitudes, the result is (modestly) lesser warming weighting by farm area than weighting by land area.

The change in precipitation is found to be 5.9 percent weighting by land area and 2.9 percent weighting by farm area. This result is broadly consistent with the global mean change predicted for scenario SRES A2, which is 3.9 percent with a range of 1.3 to 6.8 percent (IPCC 2001a, 542). The difference between land and farm area–weighted averages is considerably greater for precipitation than for warming. Once again this result would appear to reflect a greater share of land not currently primarily in agriculture in the future increase in precipitation than of agricultural lands. Thus, the IPCC states of future precipitation change:

> Most tropical areas have increased mean precipitation, most of the sub-tropical areas have decreased mean precipitation, and in the high latitudes the mean precipitation increases (IPCC 2001a, 528).

Considering that prime agricultural land today is in neither tropical nor high-latitude areas, this prognosis implies lesser increase in precipitation for current agricultural areas than for the global land-based means.[5]

---

5. In its color graphics of precipitation change by 2070–99, the IPCC (2001a, 550) shows increased precipitation on the order of 20 percent at latitudes higher than 60° and a patch of 20 percent or more increase across the Sahara Desert and into the Arabian Peninsula (but from minimal base precipitation). Precipitation declines on the order of 5 to 10 percent for Mexico, southern United States, the eastern half of Brazil and western half of Argentina, most of Australia, and the Mediterranean region. There is an increase of 0 to 5 percent for much of sub-Saharan Africa, most of China and Russia, and northern United States and most of Canada.

5

Country-Level Agricultural Impact Estimates

This chapter sets forth the method and results for this study's country-level estimates of the potential effect of global warming by the 2080s on agriculture. The chapter first reviews the two main families of models: Ricardian and crop models. It then specifically examines a series of agricultural impact models, beginning with estimates by Mendelsohn and Schlesinger (1999) reflecting both of the alternative schools, then turning to a series of Ricardian country or regional model estimates, and concluding with the principal set of crop model estimates (Rosenzweig and Iglesias 2006). The analysis applies detailed climate projections to the various agricultural impact models to develop a set of alternative impact estimates. It then arrives at a set of preferred estimates, applying judgmental weighting of estimates by likely reliability. With preferred estimates in hand from the array of models without taking carbon fertilization into account, the analysis then incorporates this study's preferred quantification of carbon fertilization.

Mendelsohn-Schlesinger Agricultural Response Functions

It is useful to begin the review of agricultural impact models with the two summary statistical models, reduced form and cross section, provided by Mendelsohn and Schlesinger (1999), or MS, because their two alternative models reflect, respectively, the crop model and the Ricardian model approach. The reduced form, process-based model is derived from a summary statistical estimate based on underlying results from an agronomic model of crop growth and a linear-programming model of US farms (in

Figure 5.1 Iso-production curves for the Mendelsohn-Schlesinger reduced form function

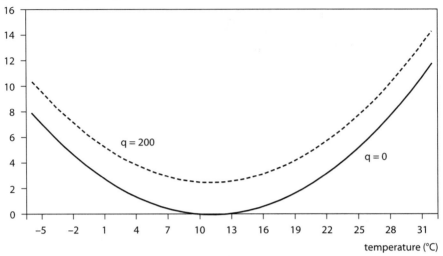

precipitation (mm per day)

temperature (°C)

Mendelsohn and Neuman 1999). It states the agricultural impact of temperature, precipitation, and atmospheric concentration of carbon dioxide as follows:

$$y = 2.16 \times [-308 + 53.7T - 2.3T^2 + 0.22P + 36.5\ln(c/350)] \quad (5.1)$$

where y is annual agricultural output in 1990 dollars per hectare of agricultural land, T is average annual temperature in degrees Celsius, P is average annual precipitation in millimeters, and c is atmospheric concentration of carbon dioxide (parts per million, or ppm).[1] Note that in the base period (broadly the present), carbon concentration is 350 ppm, so that the final term becomes 36.5 times the natural logarithm of unity, which is zero, so the carbon fertilization term drops out when examining the present influence of climate on agriculture.

Figure 5.1 shows curves corresponding to zero output and output of $200 per hectare on the basis of equation (5.1). Both curves show the optimal temperature at 11.7°C. At this temperature, output is $200 per hectare at daily precipitation of about 2.5 mm. With zero precipitation,

---

1. Mendelsohn and Schlesinger (1999) state this function as $W_a = 2.16 L_a [\ldots]$, where the elements in brackets are the same as in equation (5.1) here; W_a is agricultural output in billions of dollars, and L_a is land area. Although they do not identify the units for land area, Robert Mendelsohn has confirmed by personal communication that when both sides are divided by L_a, the result is output in dollars per hectare.

output is zero even at this optimal temperature. At higher temperatures, more precipitation is required to keep productive potential positive. For example, at average temperature of 22°C, output would be zero if precipitation were only 3 mm per day. Output of $200 per hectare would require precipitation of 5.5 mm per day at this temperature. In comparison, present-day averages for the south of Brazil are 22°C and 4 mm per day (table 4.2), placing it above the zero curve but below the $200 curve.

In principle the MS reduced form model takes account of the potential for adaptation. As the authors state, "The analysis improves upon earlier studies . . . by adding fruits and vegetables (not just cereals), including livestock, and exploring farm adaptation" (Mendelsohn and Schlesinger 1999, 363). The underlying study (Adams et al. 1999) on which the MS function is based emphasizes that the improved models used take account of the scope for shifting crop mixes from corn, wheat, and soybeans to more heat-tolerant crops such as cotton, sorghum, fruits, and vegetables. That study also further takes account of adaptation through incorporating such adjustments as changes in fertilizer, irrigation, and timing of planting and harvesting (Adams et al. 1999, 18–20). It observes in broad terms that

> a reasonable first approximation is that adaptation could potentially offset roughly half of the negative impacts of a moderate climate change. However, the evidence suggests that adjustment possibilities are smaller for larger temperature changes (p. 32).

Mendelsohn and Schlesinger (1999) also present a cross-section or Ricardian agricultural impact function. This model was an early entry in a now relatively long series of studies that trace their lineage to Mendelsohn, Nordhaus, and Shaw (1994), as noted in chapter 2.

The cross-section Ricardian function identified in Mendelsohn and Schlesinger (1999) is

$$v = r \times g \times [-475.5 + 223.2T - 7.87T^2 + 0.063P \\ - 0.000026P^2 + 480\ln(c/350)] \tag{5.2}$$

where r is the interest rate and g is a factor for the growth rate of agricultural output, set at 0.03 and 1.02, respectively.[2] In the cross-section function, the value in brackets is the capital value of land per hectare; multiplying it by the interest rate yields the estimated rental equivalent opportunity cost of land per hectare, v, in dollars per hectare. In principle this amount should be significantly smaller than the output value per hectare in the reduced form (equation 5.1), because it is only the land factor share of output rather than total output.

---

2. These parameter values were clarified in a personal communication with Mendelsohn, July 15, 2006.

Mendelsohn, Morrison, Schlesinger, and Andronova (2000), or MMSA, also present versions of equations (5.1) and (5.2) with slightly modified parameter values. However, the set of equations in this second study performs less well in predicting actual base-period agricultural productivity than the Mendelsohn and Schlesinger (1999) equations, which are applied in the estimates in appendix F.[3]

Mendelsohn-Schlesinger Estimates
for the United States

Appendix F develops the application of the MS models to obtain comprehensive country-specific estimates of the agricultural impact of climate change. Because the models are based on the United States, the results are of most direct relevance only for the United States. Nonetheless, as discussed later, the MS model will be applied as the default version for the Ricardian estimate when no region- or country-specific model is otherwise available. For the United States, the MS models when applied to the future climate estimates of the present study yield the results shown in table 5.1 for the case without carbon fertilization (see appendix F for more complete discussion).

The reduced form crop model specifies the dependent variable directly as output per hectare. However, the Ricardian model generates an estimate of land rental equivalent per hectare. For the latter, it is necessary to translate the percent change in land rental equivalent into a corresponding expected change for output. This step is ambiguous. One can certainly conceive of land value (or land rental value) changes that translate directly to corresponding proportionate changes in output potential. If a nuclear explosion were to contaminate a land area and make it unusable for decades, its land value would go to zero and so would its output potential. For less extreme changes, however, the output potential change will be only a fraction of the percentage change in land rental value. From one standpoint, it will simply be the factor share of land multiplied by the percent change in land rental value. From another standpoint, in principle compatible with the first, the percent change in output potential will be the percent change in land rental value multiplied by the ratio of net revenue to total output, because land value is the capitalized value of net revenue. The final column in table 5.1 estimates the percent change in output potential in the Ricardian model by multiplying the percent change in

---

3. For the 116 countries, regions, or subzones, the reduced form equation in Mendelsohn and Schlesinger (1999) yields negative predicted base output in 53 percent of the cases, whereas the MMSA (2000) reduced form equation produces negative base output in 63 percent of the cases. The two studies both yield 22 percent negative base output cases for the cross-section model.

Table 5.1   Impact of baseline global warming by the 2080s on US agricultural potential using the Mendelsohn-Schlesinger functions (without carbon fertilization) (percent)

Region	Farm area (millions of hectares)	Output, 2003 (billions of dollars)	Reduced form crop model	Ricardian model Land value	Ricardian model Output potential
United States	379.3	98.5	−14.8	11.5	4.7
Lakes, Northeast	74.3	30.5	9.1	35.4	14.5
Pacific Northwest	13.1	4.2	24.5	40.6	16.6
Rockies, Plains	113.3	15.1	74.6	65.8	27.0
Southeast	58.0	22.2	−67.9	−33.3	−13.6
South Pacific Coast	11.2	12.7	−5.7	—	0.04
Southwest Plains	109.1	13.8	−100.0	−27.0	−11.1

— = not available. See table F.2, note b.

land rental equivalent by the average ratio of net revenue to agricultural value added, 0.41 in the 2002 agricultural census.[4]

Both the reduced form crop model and the Ricardian model show agricultural losses for the Southeast and the Southwest Plains regions, and these losses are severe in the case of the reduced form model. There are also mild losses in the Southern Pacific Coast region. In the aggregate, there are losses of about 15 percent in the reduced form crop model but gains of about 5 percent in the Ricardian model. As reported in appendix F, the reduced form model losses are smaller (2.9 percent) when carbon fertilization is included using the MS parameter value, and the Ricardian model swings to major gains (+20 percent).

Ricardian Estimates for Developing Countries and Canada

For the Ricardian estimates used in this study, the Mendelsohn and Schlesinger (1999) cross-section model estimated for the United States provides a default model for application to climate projections for countries and regions in which no directly estimated function is available, as discussed later. More recent models estimated explicitly for several important developing countries and regions provide a preferable basis for the estimates developed in the present study for those countries and regions.

---

4. In 2003, GDP originating in agriculture was $98.5 billion (appendix table E.1). "Net cash income of operations" in 2002 was $40.5 billion (USDA 2004). On this basis, net revenue was 41 percent of output as measured by agricultural value added.

Mendelsohn, Dinar, and Sanghi (2001) provide estimates for India; Ku-rukulasuriya et al. (2006) provide estimates for Africa; and a series of studies sponsored by the World Bank provide new estimates for major Latin American countries (see appendix G).[5] For all three sets of estimates, the model structure is as follows:

$$z = \Sigma_i \, [\alpha_i T_i + \beta_i T_i^2 + \gamma_i P_i + \delta_i P_i^2] + K \qquad (5.3)$$

where z is the measure of agricultural productivity (net revenue per hectare for Africa, natural logarithm of net revenue per hectare for India, and land value per hectare for the Latin American studies), T is average temperature, P is average monthly precipitation, i refers to the season, and K is a composite variable that reflects the regression constant as well as the influence of other control variables in the particular model esti-mated.[6] The impact of business as usual global warming through the 2080s is then obtained using this equation to estimate the difference be-tween agricultural productivity using the base period (1961–90) and fu-ture period (2070–99) climate estimates of this study. Application of these models requires applying the relevant seasonal monthly averages for fu-ture temperature and precipitation from the climate models, rather than the annual averages. The effect of carbon fertilization is not incorporated in these regional Ricardian estimates and must be added subsequently to obtain the overall impact of future climate change.

It is necessary to translate the change in net revenue from climate change to the corresponding percent change in output from the base level of output. In principle the change in net revenue will be the same in ab-solute terms as the change in output.[7] In order to estimate this change as

---

5. Note that the Mendelsohn, Dinar, and Sanghi (2001) study also provides a model for Brazil. However, application of the model results in estimates of complete shutdown of agri-culture from global warming, which as in the Brazil finding with the MS functions strains credibility. In part because of ambiguities in the data (including nonavailability of average land price for the study), the more recent World Bank study for Brazil is used instead as the preferred estimate for that country, as discussed later.

6. Note, however, that in the India model, the underlying variables are expressed as differ-ences from their means (for example, $T\text{-}\check{T}$, for temperature, or $(T\text{-}\check{T})^2$, for temperature squared, where $\check{T}$ is base average temperature). This approach has the property that the co-efficient on the linear term shows the marginal impact of the climate variable (e.g., temper-ature), because the square term causes symmetric damage for either a rise or a decline in temperature and has a marginal impact of zero at the original base temperature, where the influence of an increase in temperature is shifting from positive to negative. In contrast, in the Africa and Latin America models, the levels rather than differences from means are the underlying variables.

7. That is, $NR = Q - \Sigma_i X_i$, where NR is net revenue per hectare and X_i is the amount of pur-chased input i per hectare (mainly hired labor and fertilizer). With such inputs held constant, a yield shock from climate change translates directly into the same change in net revenue: $\Delta NR = \Delta Q$.

a percent of output, it is necessary to know the base level of output that corresponds to the base level of net revenue.

India

Table 5.2 reports the results of applying the Mendelsohn, Dinar, and Sanghi (2001) model for India to the base and 2080s climate variables identified in the present study. The model applies seasonal monthly climate data (see appendices G and H). The table first reports the levels and change in the dependent variable, which is the logarithm of net revenue per hectare. It then identifies the corresponding percent change from the base level of net revenue.[8] The final column restates the change as a percent of base output.[9]

The results for India are sobering, with reductions in output potential ranging from about 30 to 35 percent in the southern regions to about 60 percent in the northern regions. As discussed later, this model does not include the favorable effect of carbon fertilization. Even after inclusion of carbon fertilization effects, however, the losses would be severe.[10]

Africa

The World Bank has recently carried out a massive farm survey in Africa to examine the relationship between agricultural productivity and climate

---

8. Given an initial actual net revenue or land value of q_0 and base level model-estimated logarithm z_0, the implied value of the missing constant is $K = ln(q_0) - z_0$. With the change in logarithm resulting from change in temperature and precipitation estimated as $z_1 - z_0$, the absolute level changes from q_0 to $q_1 = exp(K + z_1)$. The proportionate change is then $(q_1 - q_0)/q_0$. For moderate changes, this proportionate change will be approximately equal to $z_1 - z_0$.

9. A rough estimate for India is that average net revenue per hectare in the estimation period amounts to two-thirds of output per hectare. This estimate is obtained as follows: According to Dinar et al. (1998, 98), average net revenue in the India sample was 1,424.7 rupees of 1980 per hectare. The data referred to the period 1966–86. Total farm area in India amounted to about 170 million hectares. In 1976, the midpoint of the period, agriculture accounted for 47 percent of GDP, or $43.7 (World Bank 1978, 80). By 1982, agriculture's share of GDP was down to 33 percent, amounting to $49.8 billion (World Bank 1984, 222). Taking the average of these two estimates, and using the 1980 exchange rate (7.86 rupees per dollar), agricultural value added in the base period was 367 billion rupees of 1980, or 2,160 rupees per hectare. Average net revenue was thus 1,425 / 2,160 = 66 percent of agricultural output. Correspondingly, for a given estimate of the percent change in net revenue, the appropriate estimate for percent change in output will be only two-thirds as large.

10. The counterintuitive greater losses in the higher latitude regions appear to stem from the following influences. First, the increase in temperatures in the northern regions is greater than that in the southern regions, even though the base temperatures are higher in the south. Second, the impact of changes in precipitation turns out to be positive in the south but negative in the north.

Table 5.2 Impact of global warming by the 2080s on Indian agricultural productivity[a] using the Mendelsohn-Dinar-Sanghi model[b]

Region	Present climate	Implied constant K for other variables	Future climate	Change in log	Percent change Net revenue	Output
Northeast	2.1006	9.3625	−0.3408	−2.441	−91.3	−60.9
Northwest	−2.3678	4.8941	−4.3992	−2.031	−86.9	−57.9
Southeast	−4.5516	2.7103	−5.1900	−0.633	−46.9	−31.3
Southwest	−4.3051	2.9568	−5.1085	−0.803	−55.2	−36.8

a. Logarithm of net revenue per hectare.
b. Mendelsohn, Dinar, and Sanghi (2001). See appendix G.

(see appendix G). A summary analysis estimates cross-section Ricardian functions relating net revenue per hectare to linear and quadratic terms for seasonal temperature and precipitation. Once again nonclimate variables have the effect of shifting the net revenue estimate by a constant K. Application of the base and future climate variables provides the basis for estimating the change in net revenue from climate change (excluding the effect of carbon fertilization and changes in water runoff, a variable in these cross-Africa functions).

Table 5.3 shows the results of applying the World Bank Ricardian functions for Africa to the base and future climates, again using seasonal monthly climate data (see appendix G for model parameters and appendix H for country-level averages of the underlying grid-level monthly climate data, although the actual estimates are calculated at the much more detailed standard grid level). It then expresses the change in net revenue per hectare as a percent of the all-Africa average base level of output per hectare.[11] Even though average net revenue and output per hectare will

---

11. Once again it is necessary to estimate the relationship of base net revenue per hectare to base output. As reported in table 5.4, for all of the African countries considered, total dryland farm area is 193.4 million hectares, and total irrigated farm area 13.44 million hectares. Agricultural value added for the region is a total of $100.2 billion. The World Bank sample showed average net revenue per hectare for irrigated land was four times as large as that for dryland. Using this same ratio, agricultural GDP can be estimated to have averaged $405 per hectare for dryland and $1,622 per hectare for irrigated land. That is, $13.44 \times 10^6 \times q_d \times 4 + 193.4 \times 10^6 \times q_d = \$100.2 \times 10^9$. Solving for output per dryland hectare, $q_d = \$405$, and output per irrigated hectare is four times as much, or $1,622. From the sample, net revenue was an average of $319 per hectare for dryland and $1,261 per hectare for irrigated land. Net revenue is thus a relatively high 78 percent of agricultural GDP per hectare. The high ratio likely reflects substantial incidence of the use of family labor relative to hired labor and purchased inputs in a relatively low-income region.

Table 5.3 Impact of climate change by the 2080s on African agriculture, World Bank Ricardian models (without carbon fertilization)

Country/region	Net revenue per hectare estimate excluding nonclimate variables (2005 dollars)					Change as percent of base output/hectare, Africa average		
	Base		Future					
	Dryland	Irrigated	Dryland	Irrigated: A	Irrigated: B	Dryland	Irrigated: A	Irrigated: B
Algeria	-133	-739	-403	86	-637	-66.6	50.8	6.3
Angola	-130	4,485	-237	4,736	4,059	-26.3	15.5	-26.2
Burkina Faso	-431	4,298	-498	5,095	4,638	-16.5	49.1	20.9
Cameroon	57	8,383	-21	8,258	7,870	-19.1	-7.7	-31.6
Democratic Republic of the Congo	118	1,832	95	2,731	2,208	-5.5	55.4	23.2
Egypt	-164	-993	-367	-126	-781	-50.1	53.5	13.1
Ethiopia	-212	1,992	-339	1,724	1,118	-31.4	-16.5	-53.9
Ghana	-170	3,637	-182	3,454	2,963	-3.0	-11.3	-41.6
Ivory Coast	-96	4,905	-111	4,151	3,702	-3.6	-46.5	-74.2
Kenya	-305	626	-272	1,320	963	8.3	42.8	20.8
Madagascar	31	6,824	-52	7,196	6,558	-20.5	22.9	-16.4
Malawi	-152	7,249	-289	7,687	7,083	-33.6	27.0	-10.2
Mali	-481	1,457	-670	1,922	1,265	-100.0	28.6	-11.9
Morocco	60	-1,370	-117	-739	-1,458	-43.7	38.9	-5.5
Mozambique	-187	5,905	-311	6,511	5950	-30.6	37.4	2.8
Niger	-485	131	-664	1,168	720	-100.0	64.0	36.3
Nigeria	-245	5,797	-300	6,130	5,768	-13.7	20.5	-1.8

(table continues next page)

Table 5.3 Impact of climate change by the 2080s on African agriculture, World Bank Ricardian models (without carbon fertilization) *(continued)*

| Country/region | Net revenue per hectare estimate excluding nonclimate variables (2005 dollars) | | | | | Change as percent of base output/hectare, Africa average | | |
| | Base | | Future | | | | | |
	Dryland	Irrigated	Dryland	Irrigated: A	Irrigated: B	Dryland	Irrigated: A	Irrigated: B
Other Equatorial Africa	240	1,767	247	1,872	1,409	1.6	6.5	–22.0
Other Horn of Africa	–388	–887	–439	–395	–772	–100.0	30.3	7.1
Other Southern Africa	–201	1,010	–413	864	142	–52.5	–9.0	–53.5
Other West Africa	162	14,028	98	13,120	12,690	–15.6	–56.0	–100.0
Senegal	–396	5,822	–482	5,578	4928	–100.0	–15.1	–55.2
South Africa	33	1,046	–175	1,083	403	–51.5	2.3	–39.6
Sudan	–383	1,683	–498	2,348	1838	–100.0	41.0	9.5
Tanzania	–185	6,313	–251	6,807	6,296	–16.3	30.4	–1.1
Uganda	–79	1,102	–86	1,502	1,024	–1.7	24.6	–4.8
Zambia	–211	4,549	–408	4,668	3,938	–48.5	7.4	–37.7
Zimbabwe	–164	2,676	–376	3,069	2,421	–52.4	24.2	–15.7

Irrigated: A = model including Egypt
B = model excluding Egypt

Note: Base average net revenue per hectare: dryland, $319; irrigated, $1,261 (Kurukulasuriya et al. 2006).
Base output per hectare: dryland, $405; irrigated, $1,622 (see text).

Source: Author's calculations. See appendix G.

vary among countries, because the parameters of the models are uniform across all countries in the region, it is appropriate that estimated net revenue changes be compared with the regional average rather than country-specific output per hectare.

For irrigated agriculture, variant A is from the model reported in Kurukulasuriya et al. (2006) for all observations including those in Egypt, which alone accounts for 58 percent of the observations for irrigated agriculture. The authors note that Egypt may be atypical because of the massive availability of irrigation from the Nile River; indeed, there are no dryland farms at all in the sample for Egypt. They therefore also report the key marginal parameters for temperature and precipitation separately for the full model including Egypt and for a model excluding Egypt, designated here as A and B, respectively (see appendix G). Table 5.3 reports estimates for model B by applying the differences in these marginal parameters to the change in temperature and precipitation and adding the result to the estimated change in net revenue in model A.[12]

There is a predominant pattern of large negative changes from business as usual warming (excluding carbon fertilization) in dryland African agriculture. The median change is –31 percent. In contrast, for variant A of the irrigated agriculture model (including Egypt), the median change is +24.4 percent. However, when variant B of the irrigated agriculture model is applied (excluding Egypt in the parameter estimation), negative results also dominate irrigated agriculture, with the median change at –11.1 percent.

One pattern that stands out in table 5.3 is the dispersion of results. There is a high frequency of severely adverse effects for dryland agriculture, as five of the 28 countries or regions have complete shutdown. Another six have reductions in agricultural capacity by about half or more. However, four countries have only modest declines averaging about 3 percent, and two countries or regions have modest increases. Even so, the dominant pattern is of serious loss.

A second pattern is that several countries show major gains for irrigated agriculture if the model heavily influenced by Egypt and its Nile water is used (variant A), but the pattern shifts to dominant losses even in irrigated agriculture if the function omitting the Egypt observations is applied (variant B).

Because the results differ substantially between dryland and irrigated agriculture (even when variant B is used), to obtain meaningful estimates it is necessary to weight the two types of agriculture. Table 5.4 reports the

---

12. That is, the full model A yields the estimates shown in the second and fourth columns of table 5.5. The future net revenue estimate for model B is obtained by adding the following value to that in the fourth column of the table for model A: $\Delta y_B - \Delta y_A = (\eta_B - \eta_A) \Delta T + (\theta_B - \theta_A) \Delta P$, where T is temperature (degrees Celsius), P is precipitation (mm per month), y is net revenue per hectare, Δ refers to change from climate change, η is the marginal parameter for temperature, and θ is the marginal parameter for precipitation. The values for ΔT and ΔP are taken from the present and future annual averages shown in table 4.2.

Table 5.4 Weighted average impact of global warming by the 2080s on the African agriculture
(percent and millions of 2005 dollars)

Country/region	Dryland (without carbon fertilization)	Irrigated (without carbon fertilization)	Irrigated share of cropland		Weighted average		Base output (millions of dollars)
			Area	Value	Without carbon fertilization	With carbon fertilization	
Algeria	-66.6	6.3	7.0	27.2	-46.7	-38.7	6,657
Angola	-26.3	-26.2	7.0	27.2	-26.3	-15.2	1,188
Burkina Faso	-16.5	20.9	0.0	0.0	-16.5	-4.0	1,298
Cameroon	-19.1	-31.6	2.0	9.2	-20.3	-8.3	5,499
Democratic Republic of the Congo	-5.5	23.2	1.0	4.8	-4.1	10.2	3,292
Egypt	-50.1	53.5	100.0	100.0	53.5	76.5	13,189
Ethiopia	-31.4	-53.9	0.0	0.0	-31.4	-21.2	2,748
Ghana	-3.0	-41.6	3.0	13.3	-8.2	5.6	2,748
Ivory Coast	-3.6	-74.2	1.0	4.8	-7.0	7.0	3,574
Kenya	8.3	20.8	19.0	53.7	15.0	32.3	2,302
Madagascar	-20.5	-16.4	1.0	4.8	-20.3	-8.3	1,587
Malawi	-33.6	-10.2	2.0	9.2	-31.5	-21.2	651
Mali	-100.0	-11.9	31.0	69.0	-39.0	-29.9	1,645
Morocco	-43.7	-5.5	2.0	9.2	-40.1	-31.1	7,436

Mozambique	-30.6	2.8	5.0	20.7	-23.6	-12.1	1,122
Niger	-100.0	36.3	15.0	46.6	-36.1	-26.5	1,094
Nigeria	-13.7	-1.8	3.0	13.3	-12.1	1.1	15,180
Other Equatorial Africa	1.6	-22.0	1.0	4.8	0.5	15.6	1,429
Other Horn of Africa	-100.0	7.1	1.0	4.8	-94.8	-94.1	20
Other Southern Africa	-52.5	-53.5	1.0	4.8	-52.5	-45.4	619
Other West Africa	-15.6	-100.0	5.0	20.7	-33.2	-23.2	1,832
Senegal	-100.0	-55.2	10.0	35.5	-84.0	-81.6	1,105
South Africa	-51.5	-39.6	11.0	38.0	-47.0	-39.0	6,395
Sudan	-100.0	9.5	4.0	17.1	-81.1	-78.3	6,944
Tanzania	-16.3	-1.1	0.0	0.0	-16.3	-3.7	4,629
Uganda	-1.7	-4.8	6.0	24.0	-2.5	12.1	2,016
Zambia	-48.5	-37.7	3.0	13.3	-47.1	-39.1	1,000
Zimbabwe	-52.4	-15.7	5.0	20.7	-44.7	-36.4	3,018
Total					-18.6	-6.3	100,215
Excluding Egypt					-29.5	-18.9	
Median					-28.9	-18.2	

Sources: Table 5.3 using non-Egypt irrigated model B except for Egypt; World Bank (2006).

share of farm area under irrigation and the corresponding estimate of the share of total crop value from irrigated farming in each country.[13] In table 5.4, the with-Egypt irrigated function is applied only for Egypt; for all others the without-Egypt function is used (variant B in table 5.3).

For each country or region, the weighted average impact of climate change is calculated by weighting the dryland and irrigated estimates by their respective value shares in the base period. This estimate excludes the carbon fertilization effect. When this estimate is aggregated across all African countries and regions by weighting by base period agricultural output, the result is that African agricultural capacity would decline by an estimated 18.6 percent by the 2080s, before taking account of carbon fertilization. Excluding Egypt, the decline would be about 30 percent. A comparable set of estimates including carbon fertilization is obtained by applying a uniform 15 percent enhancement of yields from this effect by the 2080s, as discussed above. The result is a still substantial aggregate decline of 6.3 percent in the aggregate and about 19 percent excluding Egypt.

These averages mask greater declines in the majority of countries in the region. The weighted averages are buoyed by the highly favorable results for Egypt, which has the second largest output base in the continent, and an unusually small net decline for Nigeria, which has the largest output base. This masking is evident in the fact that the median changes in agricultural capacity are almost identical to the output-weighted average changes when Egypt is excluded.

Latin America

In another recent study coordinated by the World Bank, farm sample survey data were compiled and used to estimate Ricardian functions for the impact of climate on land value per hectare. These studies also used relatively standardized versions of equation (5.3) above. All included equations for land value per hectare. Some included equations for net revenue per hectare, and some distinguished between small- and large-farm equations.

Appendix table G.3 reports the coefficients estimated in these equations for Argentina, Brazil, Chile, and Ecuador. The equations shown there are applied to the detailed grid-level climate projection data of this study (averages of which are shown at the country level in appendix H) to estimate the percent change in land value from business as usual global warming by the 2080s. The results of this calculation are shown in the third column of table 5.5. Difficulties in interpretation of variables or data values in the source studies precluded application here of the equations estimated in this series for Colombia and Venezuela.

---

13. The African average net revenue per hectare in irrigated farming is about four times as high as that for dryland farming. The irrigated value shares are correspondingly higher than area shares.

Table 5.5 **Impact of global warming by the 2080s on agricultural potential in major Latin American countries (without carbon fertilization), World Bank studies** (percent)

Country	Implied by underlying study: Land value	Basis	Model application in present study: Land value	Average Land value	Average Output potential
Argentina	−17.9	A	1.4	−8.2	−4.1
Brazil	−22.0	A	2.1	−10.1	−5.0
Amazon	n.a.		−76.0	−49.0	−24.5
Northeast	n.a.		−18.0	−20.0	−10.0
South	n.a.		10.0	−6.0	−3.0
Chile	−3.6	B	−86.0	−44.8	−22.4
Colombia	−34.1	B	n.a.	−34.1	−17.0
Ecuador	−6.9	A	−100.0	−53.5	−26.8
Venezuela	−75.4	A	n.a.	−75.4	−37.7

n.a. = not available

A = average of 2060 and 2100 results in underlying study
B = application of marginal temperature and precipitation parameters in underlying study to climate change estimated in present study

Source: See text and appendix G.

The underlying studies themselves included either outright estimates of the impact of future climate change (Argentina, Brazil, Ecuador, and Venezuela) or parametric results indicating the impact that could be expected from alternative amounts of warming (2.5°C and 5°C) and change in precipitation (±10 percent; the cases of Chile and Colombia). The studies used three climate models: the Parallel Climate Model (PCM), Center for Climate System Research (CCSR), and Climate Crisis Coalition (CCC), from Washington et al. (2000), Emori et al. (1999), and Boer, Flato, and Ramsden (2000), respectively. However, they did not report the emissions scenarios assumed or the climate projections of these models.

It is possible to take account of the climate impact estimates of the studies themselves as well as the estimates obtained when applying the present study's climate estimates to the models in these studies. For the four studies reporting direct impacts (labeled "A" in table 5.5), the simple average agricultural impact estimate is taken across the three climate models and the two benchmark years 2060 and 2100 as the central estimate for 2080 comparable to the estimates of the present study. In cases where there are both small-farm and large-farm estimates, the average of both is used. In the other two studies without direct impact projections, the parametric effects of changes in temperature and precipitation are applied to the present study's estimate of climate change (table 4.2) to obtain the implied climate impact from the underlying study (cases labeled "B" in table 5.5).

The resulting estimates show relatively large divergence between the impact estimates in the underlying Latin American studies and the corresponding estimates of the present study using their models. There is no systematic direction of the difference, as the underlying studies show more severe effects than the calculations in this study for Argentina and Brazil but less severe for Chile and Ecuador. The divergences could arise because of divergent future climate estimates, differences between the large- and small-farm estimates (the models applied here are either the aggregate model or a weighted average), and differences in regional detail. In Brazil, in particular, the underlying study does not distinguish among regions, whereas the estimates here differentiate among three geographical zones.

Because of the fairly large divergences, the most prudent approach would seem to be to take a simple average of the impact estimates indicated (directly or implied) in the underlying studies and the impact estimates obtained here by applying the present study's climate projections to the Ricardian equations taken from these studies. This average estimate is shown in the next to last column of table 5.5.

Once again it is necessary to translate the percent change in land value from the models into corresponding change in output potential. Following the discussion for US estimates above, the land factor share or ratio of net revenue to value added is the fraction appropriate to apply for this purpose, with the caveat that it could understate the loss in output potential in extreme cases in which the land becomes essentially unusable. For Latin America, this ratio is set at 50 percent, intermediate between the US ratio (41 percent) and the ratio for India (67 percent) in view of the likely intermediate factor share of land at an intermediate stage of development. The final column in table 5.5 applies this fraction to arrive at the impact on potential output.

Canada

Reinsborough (2003) has prepared Ricardian estimates for the impact of climate change on agriculture in Canada. She emphasizes that this approach "presents an upper bound on the benefits of climate change" because it "assumes perfect adjustment to climate change and no costs other than change in land value" (pp. 22, 25). She estimates farmland value per hectare as a function of seasonal temperature, temperature squared, precipitation, and precipitation squared (for January, April, July, and October), as well as control variables. When she applies the estimated coefficients to a postulated climate change of 2.8°C temperature increase and 8 percent increase in precipitation, she finds a negligible change in farmland values.[14]

Preliminary subsequent work by Mendelsohn and Reinsborough (2007) confirms that there is a statistically significant difference between Ricar-

---

14. A total rise of only about $1 million for the whole of Canada (Reinsborough 2003, 32).

dian function estimates for Canada and those for the United States. On this basis, it would be misleading to use the default MS Ricardian estimates in appendix F for Canada. The approach adopted later will instead simply place the Canadian estimates in the Ricardian family at zero, based on the Reinsborough (2003) results. Because Russia is located in a similar latitude range as Canada, the preferred estimates developed later set climate impact effects at zero for Russia as well, because once again application of the default MS function could be seriously misleading.

It should be emphasized that if instead the default US-based MS Ricardian model estimates were used, large gains in agricultural potential from global warming would be identified for Canada and Russia (see appendix F).[15] Because the Reinsborough (2003) estimates are directly for Canada, however, they should be seen as strictly dominating the default MS estimates for that country. Note moreover that the zero-impact results in the Canadian study are much more consistent with the estimates for Canada from the Rosenzweig and Iglesias (2006) crop models, discussed later.

Sensitivity to Climate Models

The spirit of this study is to apply a "consensus" projection of the business as usual climate to the agricultural response functions to obtain a central estimate of the implications of global warming for agriculture. It is fair to ask, however, whether this approach masks an extreme degree of variability that would be found if each of the climate models were applied individually for this task. Appendix I examines the degree of dispersion of future temperature and precipitation estimates among the six climate models in the IPCC Data Distribution Centre (listed in table 4.1).

To examine the corresponding dispersion of estimates for agricultural impact, it is useful to consider the results of the standard default MS Ricardian model when applied to each of the underlying climate models separately. Table 5.6 reports these results for 30 major countries or regions to provide a sense of the range of dispersion. Each of the countries in the table is in category "a" in appendix table F.2, the category in which it is

---

15. The case of Russia is more ambiguous, and application of the Canadian zero-impact result to Russia (rather than the default MS model) rests on the proposition that given its latitudinal location it resembles Canadian conditions much more than those of the United States. The US-based MS Ricardian function would instead place the impact on Russia at a remarkable 152 percent rise in agricultural capacity even without carbon fertilization, and applying that estimate would boost the estimated global impact in table 5.8 by 0.86 percentage point. However, such a large contribution from Russia would surely raise questions of political economy and in particular the question of "Dutch disease." As a major energy exporter, Russia could well have such a strong exchange rate that its firms would not have much incentive to make the country a major agricultural exporter.

Table 5.6 Dispersion of Mendelsohn-Schlesinger Ricardian model estimates across climate models (without carbon fertilization) (percent change in land rental equivalent)

Country	CCSR	HadCM	GFDL	ECHAM	CSIRO	CGCM	Consensus estimate	Coefficient of variation
Angola	-100.0	-89.5	-67.5	-100.0	-63.4	-83.1	-84.1	0.42
Argentina	-20.5	-17.0	-9.8	-11.6	-15.1	-15.7	-14.8	0.57
Brazil, Southern	-100.0	-100.0	-67.1	-100.0	-86.8	-89.7	-99.2	0.32
Chile	18.7	16.8	18.2	16.8	18.2	19.7	18.2	0.14
China, Central	26.4	23.5	23.5	28.9	29.2	23.5	27.1	0.24
China, South Central	-47.3	-34.8	-22.2	-29.3	-26.2	-32.5	-31.4	0.61
Colombia	-100.0	-100.0	-100.0	-100.0	-100.0	-100.0	-100.0	0.00
Germany	31.2	28.8	28.3	32.2	26.6	24.7	30.6	0.22
Madagascar	-95.9	-77.8	-74.1	-97.0	-70.8	-80.6	-81.6	0.30
Malawi	-100.0	-100.0	-68.3	-100.0	-58.1	-76.1	-84.8	0.50
Mexico	-100.0	-80.8	-60.3	-68.9	-53.8	-52.8	-71.8	0.59
Morocco	-68.9	-32.9	-23.2	-44.5	-31.6	-35.3	-38.5	0.91
Mozambique	-100.0	-100.0	-100.0	-100.0	-100.0	-100.0	-100.0	0.00
New Zealand	6.0	10.5	11.7	11.9	10.3	11.3	10.0	0.48
Peru	-95.9	-100.0	-57.1	-86.3	-57.0	-59.8	-78.1	0.60
Poland	33.2	35.6	32.7	38.4	33.6	32.3	37.2	0.15
Portugal	-27.0	-12.4	-11.0	-23.2	-10.1	-10.2	-14.7	1.07
Romania	16.1	24.2	22.1	24.8	23.7	22.8	24.8	0.32
Russia, Caspian Black Sea	33.8	41.0	33.9	41.9	40.1	40.0	41.1	0.21
South Africa	-42.4	-39.5	-32.3	-43.5	-30.5	-39.6	-37.7	0.32
Syria	-75.1	-38.1	-26.5	-39.2	-39.3	-37.0	-41.9	0.88
Tanzania	-100.0	-100.0	-77.2	-100.0	-69.8	-77.8	-95.4	0.36
Turkey	-7.7	2.8	5.8	4.1	3.4	5.3	3.5	4.89
Uganda	-100.0	-100.0	-85.2	-99.9	-74.3	-74.7	-94.9	0.32
United Kingdom	26.9	18.4	22.8	25.4	21.1	18.5	23.4	0.35
US Lakes and Northeast	25.9	32.9	32.8	36.9	36.1	33.3	35.4	0.26
US Southeast	-64.6	-34.8	-23.9	-22.6	-31.2	-31.0	-33.3	0.99
Venezuela	-100.0	-100.0	-100.0	-100.0	-100.0	-100.0	-100.0	0.00
Zambia	-100.0	-99.9	-69.1	-100.0	-67.8	-90.5	-91.3	0.39

Note: For climate models, see table 4.1.

possible to compare the change in land rental equivalent directly against the model's prediction for the base period. The table considers the case without carbon fertilization.

It is evident in table 5.6 that there is relatively close agreement among the underlying climate models in terms of the resulting agricultural impacts estimated for each country when applied to the MS cross-section model. The US Lakes-Northeast region, for example, generates estimates lying in a relatively narrow range, from an increase in land rental equivalent of about 26 percent to an increase of about 36 percent. The next to last column, labeled "consensus," is the central estimate using the average of the six climate models.[16] The final column reports the coefficient of variation for the country.[17] The median value for the coefficient of variation is 0.34, indicating in rough terms that typically the variability of the estimates as measured by the standard deviation is some ± 17 percent of the average estimate.[18]

The central message of the experiment reported in table 5.6 is that the estimates here should be relatively robust with respect to variation among climate models. All six models tend to agree on whether the agricultural impact will be substantially positive in a particular region (e.g., Germany or Poland) or strongly negative (e.g., Colombia or Mozambique). For some countries and regions, alternative impact estimates in this study based on alternative agricultural-economic models are considerably different from those in appendix tables F.1 and F.2. The relatively close adherence of the various climate model estimates when applied to the same impact model (in the case of table 5.6, the MS Ricardian model) suggests that in estimating country-specific impacts, variability across the agricultural-economic models is more important than variability across the climate models. This diagnosis also tends to support the use of the consensus climate model approach adopted for this study and the focus on differing results from differing agricultural-economic models rather than from differing climate models.

Rosenzweig et al. Crop Model Results

Rosenzweig and Iglesias (2006) provide a query-based database that returns estimates of the impact of prospective global warming, under alter-

---

16. The entries in appendix table F.2 correspond to those in the final column of table 5.6 after shrinkage to take account of the ratio of net revenue to output.

17. The coefficient of variation is calculated as the square root of the sum of squared residuals of each of the six estimates from the average of the six, divided by the average (and reported in absolute value).

18. The coefficient of variation is increasingly misleading as the average value approaches zero. The high coefficient of variation for Turkey reflects this fact.

native climate scenarios and using alternative GCMs, on four major crops: wheat, rice, coarse grains (maize, barley, and others), and soybeans. The underlying research was developed in the 1990s by a team of agricultural scientists from 18 countries, who estimated compatible crop models at 125 agricultural sites using consistent climate change scenarios (see Rosenzweig et al. 1993, as discussed above; and Parry, Rosenzweig, and Livermore 2005). The process-based dynamic crop growth models incorporate the effects of change in temperature, precipitation, and solar radiation; the effect of carbon fertilization from increased atmospheric concentrations of carbon dioxide; and crop management, particularly with respect to timing of planting and extent of fertilization and irrigation. The estimates are for three levels of adaptation: 1) no adaptation; 2) level 1 (L1): shifts in planting dates by less than one month, shifts to other available varieties and crops, and increased irrigation using existing systems; and 3) level 2 (L2): more intensive adaptations involving higher costs, including change in date of planting by more than one month; installation of new irrigation systems; and development of new varieties.

The GCMs and climate scenarios in the query system include three models with results for equilibrium carbon concentrations of 555 ppm (double preindustrial levels) and two "transient" model variants for expected conditions by the 2080s. For the transient model used here (HadCM3, Hadley Centre for Climate Prediction and Research Coupled Model 3), the IS95a scenario is used, which is the same as the IS92a "business as usual" scenario in the IPCC's Second Assessment Report of 1995.[19] This scenario has a modestly lower path of rising emissions than the SRES A2 scenario in the Third Assessment Report of 2001, used for the projections in the first part of this study (see table 4.2). Thus, by 2040 fossil fuel and industrial process emissions stand at 12.66 gigatons of carbon equivalent (GtC) in IS92a and 15.01 GtC in SRES A2; by 2080 the comparison is 17.0 versus 22.97 GtC, respectively (IPCC 2001a, 801).

The equilibrium and transient models tend to generate relatively similar results at 555 ppm equilibrium and 731 ppm transient warming.[20] This is presumably because ocean thermal lag means the ultimate equilibrium warming associated with any given atmospheric concentration of carbon is greater than will be observed at the date this concentration is first attained (see Cline 1992, 92).

---

19. Rosenzweig and Iglesias (2006) also report results for Hadley model HadCM2. However, these results show much greater divergence from the results of the other three models used here (GISS, GFDL, and UKMO) than do the results for HadCM3. The HadCM3 results, being more representative, are thus chosen for the analysis here. (For the regions shown in table 5.7, the sum of squared residuals of percent deviation from the average estimate from the other three models is 11,414 for HadCM2 but only 3,116 for HadCM3.)

20. See the color maps on the methodology page in Rosenzweig and Iglesias (2006).

Table 5.7 reports the results compiled in the Rosenzweig-Iglesias database for the impact of global warming by the 2080s on yields of the four major grains and oilseeds, again interpreting the equilibrium 555 ppm results as proxies for realized impact by the 2080s. These estimates are all for the moderate level of adaptation (L1) and full carbon fertilization effects. Analysis of the difference between results with and without carbon fertilization indicates that the Rosenzweig-Iglesias estimates place the carbon fertilization impact at about +17 percent by the 2080s.[21] This impact is close to the 15 percent identified above as the proper target for carbon fertilization by this period on the basis of the recent free air concentration enrichment (FACE) field experiments.

Synthesis of Preferred Estimates

The two basic frameworks discussed above (Ricardian statistical models, on the one hand, and crop models on the other) provide the basis for identifying a set of preferred estimates that synthesize the alternative model results. In the first group five studies are from the same family of models and even share key authors.[22] The first of these, and the default model for this framework, is Mendelsohn and Schlesinger (1999). This set of estimates, designated source 1, comprises the cross-section estimates in appendix table F.2. As noted earlier, this model was estimated using data for the United States. Although the model provides a basis for estimation for other countries in the absence of statistical studies specific to those countries, climate responses elsewhere could be substantially different from those for the United States, and the ranges in temperature (especially) could extend beyond those included in the US database on which the models were estimated. This is especially so for the tropics and other latitudes not represented in the United States.

The second study within the first framework is the set of estimates for Africa developed in the World Bank study (Kurukulasuriya et al. 2006) and applied here with results shown in table 5.4. The third set of estimates

---

21. The Rosenzweig and Iglesias (2006) results are reported as percent change in yield from the base period. If we call this "a" (expressed as a proportion) for results with carbon fertilization and "b" without, the median for the ratio $(1+a)/(1+b)$ across the regions shown in table 5.7 is 1.159 for GISS, 1.154 for GFDL, and 1.179 for UKMO (using comparisons for the L0 adaptation levels only, because results are not reported without carbon fertilization for the L1 adaptation cases for these three models). For the HadCM3 model, with L1 adaptation, this ratio has a median of 1.208. Note that these implied enhancement ratios are broadly consistent with the crop-specific ratios reported above in the summary of Rosenzweig et al. (1993).

22. Robert Mendelsohn is coauthor of three of the four studies and a project coordinator for the fourth (the World Bank project on Latin America). All of the Ricardian estimates, moreover, trace their origins to Mendelsohn, Nordhaus, and Shaw (1994).

Table 5.7   Rosenzweig-Iglesias agricultural impact estimates for the 2080s, four major grains and oilseeds (percent change in yield)

Region	HadCM3	GISS	GFDL	UKMO	Average
Africa LICX	−13	−16	−26	−21	−19.0
Africa LICM	−13	−21	−21	−26	−20.3
Africa MICX	−14	−1	4	−12	−5.8
Africa MICM	−13	−13	−13	−18	−14.3
Africa OilX	−13	−7	−12	−17	−12.3
Argentina	5	−3	−7	−10	−3.8
Australia	−7	6	6	6	2.8
Brazil, similar	−25	−12	−7	−21	−16.3
Canada	−1	24	25	2	12.5
China, similar	−2	8	2	3	2.8
Egypt, similar	−13	−17	−13	−32	−18.8
Europe	5	8	2	3	4.5
Far East Asia HMICX	−1	−24	−16	−20	−15.3
Far East Asia HMICM	0	4	2	−2	1.0
Far East Asia LI	−3	−12	−11	−23	−12.3
India	−13	−4	−13	−27	−14.3
Indonesia	−1	−14	−6	1	−5.0
Japan	−2	14	10	7	7.3
Kenya	−9	−14	−14	−14	−12.8
Latin America HICX	−27	−14	−9	−25	−18.8
Latin America HICM	−16	−15	−11	−12	−13.5
Latin America MLI	−16	−17	−8	−27	−17.0
Mexico	−17	−27	−20	−31	−23.8
Northeast Asia MLI	−16	−20	−20	−25	−20.3
Northeast Asia OilX	−16	−10	−15	−20	−15.3
New Zealand	8	29	24	14	18.8
Nigeria	−19	−6	−16	−6	−11.8
Pakistan	−18	−29	−5	−50	−25.5
Former Soviet Union, Eastern Europe	−16	16	5	−7	−0.5
Thailand	−4	−19	−8	−24	−13.8
Turkey	−12	−5	−15	−15	−11.8
United States	−5	5	−2	−13	−3.8

CM = calorie importers; CX = calorie exporters; HI = high income; HMI = high and middle income; LI = low income; MI = middle income; MLI = middle and low income; OilX = oil exporters; GFDL = Geophysical Fluid Dynamics Laboratory; GISS = Goddard Institute for Space Studies; HadCM3 = UK Hadley Centre for Climate Prediction and Research Coupled Model 3; UKMO = UK Meterological Office

Note: All estimates are for "level 1" adaptation and include full carbon fertilization effect. The four major grains are wheat, rice, maize, and soybeans.

Source: Calculated from Rosenzweig and Iglesias (2006).

in the same Ricardian family is the series of recent World Bank–supported studies on Latin America, with results of the models as applied here reported in table 5.5. The fourth source is for India, based on Mendelsohn, Dinar, and Sanghi (2001) and with results as applied here reported in table 5.2. The fifth source is the Reinsborough (2003) study for Canada, whose finding of zero impact of climate change is applied to both Canada and its latitudinal peer Russia.

In the second framework, the estimates come from a different conceptual approach, which uses crop models developed on the basis of agricultural science rather than statistical regressions across climate regions of large countries and which directly calculates the effects of reasonable levels of adaptation rather than assuming that cross-section regressions capture adaptation. The Rosenzweig-Iglesias estimates provide the sole basis for the crop model estimates for all countries except the United States. For the United States, the reduced form crop model function by Mendelsohn and Schlesinger (1999) is available as an alternative model synthesizing this school, and its estimates (table 5.1) are given equal weight with the Rosenzweig-Iglesias estimates for the United States.

The synthesis of preferred estimates then follows two alternative procedures. For those countries for which the Ricardian estimates are available from models specifically estimated for the country or region in question, the Ricardian estimates and the crop model estimates are given equal weight. This set of countries includes the United States, Canada, Africa, most of Latin America, and India. Russia is also treated in this fashion, for the reasons discussed above. This first category of preferred estimates encompasses about half of the total number of countries and 35 percent of global agricultural production.

The second alternative approach applies to those countries without specific regionally based Ricardian models, for which the default US model (MS cross-section, appendix table F.2) must be applied. Because of the potential misleading results when the US model is applied to other countries (as illustrated by the case of Canada), less weight is given to the Ricardian estimate than to the crop model estimate in these countries.[23] For these countries, the weight is set at one-third for the default MS Ricardian estimates and two-thirds for the Rosenzweig-Iglesias crop model estimates.

These are the preferred estimates for the case with no carbon fertilization. The corresponding set of estimates including carbon fertilization then simply applies a 15 percent yield increase to the estimates without

---

23. As discussed above, the Reinsborough (2003) Ricardian model estimated directly for Canada shows virtually zero impact of future global warming on agricultural potential as proxied by farmland value. In contrast, the MS cross-section Ricardian model for the United States shows a remarkable doubling or more of Canadian agricultural potential from future global warming (appendix table F.2).

carbon fertilization, based on the FACE studies as discussed above.[24] In practice, the preferred estimates accept the underlying Mendelsohn-Schlesinger, Mendelsohn-Dinar-Sanghi, World Bank Africa, World Bank Latin America, and Rosenzweig-Iglesias estimates for the non–carbon fertilization case but apply this study's own preferred measure of the boost from carbon fertilization rather than accepting the corresponding estimates in the underlying studies.[25]

Table 5.8 reports the results of the preferred estimates. The table first shows farm area, output per hectare, and corresponding total output for each country or region for 2003. These output estimates serve as the basis for weighting to obtain regional and global aggregates. Column D then reports the preferred framework 1 estimate in the Ricardian statistical model family, as just discussed. Column E reports the source or basis for each of these estimates. Column F shows the crop model–based estimates. For all countries but the United States, these are the Rosenzweig and Iglesias estimates from table 5.7 converted to magnitudes excluding carbon fertilization (by removing a uniform 17.5 percent boost, the average for the four climate models in the Rosenzweig-Iglesias estimates). As noted, for the United States the crop model estimates are an average of these adjusted Rosenzweig-Iglesias estimates and the MS reduced form estimates (from appendix table F.1). Column G reports the geographical grouping that is the source of the Rosenzweig-Iglesias estimate for the country in question.

Column H reports the preferred estimate for agricultural impact without carbon fertilization, following the procedure just discussed (equal weight for Ricardian and crop models where the regional or country Ricardian model is available—indicated as 1 in column I; one-third and two-thirds weight, respectively, where the general default Ricardian model must be used—indicated as 2 in column I). The corresponding preferred estimate including carbon fertilization is reported in column J. This estimate includes the effect of a uniform boost of 15 percent in yield from carbon fertilization. These two respective percentage changes in agricultural productivity are then applied to each country's base output to estimate the implied absolute change in output potential, reported in columns K and L. Aggregating these changes in potential output and comparing the

---

24. With a uniform yield increase, the with–carbon fertilization estimates are a strict transformation of the without–carbon fertilization estimates because the expansion factors out of the detailed calculations regardless of the level of aggregation. Thus, with q as average output per hectare (for example), and with $q = \Sigma q_i \, \varphi_i$ where φ_i is the weight applied to the disaggregated components of the aggregate in question, then the estimate q' including carbon fertilization will uniformly be $1.15 \times q$, because $\Sigma \, 1.15 \, q_i \, \varphi_i = 1.15 \, \Sigma q_i \, \varphi_i$. For its part, q expressed as an index with value of 1 for base period productivity is simply $q = 1 + d/100$ for the future period, where d is the estimate of the percent change in productivity from climate change without including carbon fertilization.

25. Note that the World Bank–sponsored studies for Africa and Latin America do not estimate carbon fertilization effects.

Table 5.8   Preferred estimates of impact of baseline global warming by the 2080s on world agriculture

Country	Farm area (1,000 hectares) (A)	Output per hectare (2003 dollars) (B)	Output (millions of 2003 dollars) (C)	Ricardian Estimate (percent) (D)	Ricardian Basis[a] (E)	Crop models Estimate (percent) (F)	Crop models Grouping[b] (G)	Preferred estimates Without carbon fertilization (percent) (H)	Preferred estimates Basis[c] (I)	Preferred estimates With carbon fertilization (percent)[d] (J)	Change in output Without carbon fertilization (K)	Change in output With carbon fertilization (L)
Afghanistan	7,827	313	2,448	-9.5	1	-32.1	24	-24.7	2	-13.4	-604	-327
Algeria	8,459	787	6,653	-46.7	2	-25.3	5	-36.0	1	-26.4	-2,394	-1,756
Angola	3,300	360	1,187	-26.3	2	-25.3	5	-25.8	1	-14.7	-306	-174
Argentina	172,106	83	14,256	-4.1	3	-18.1	6	-11.1	1	2.2	-1,581	320
Australia	455,723	29	13,059	-55.1	1	-12.6		-26.6	2	-15.6	-3,471	-2,033
Southeast	192,824	16	3,147	-11.6	1	-12.6	7	-12.2	2	0.9	-385	29
Southwest	84,778	14	1,212	-15.3	1	-12.6	7	-13.5	2	-0.5	-163	-6
Central East	22,955	146	3,357	-45.5	1	-12.6	7	-23.4	2	-11.9	-787	-401
Central West	84,838	14	1,213	-80.9	1	-12.6	7	-35.1	2	-25.4	-426	-308
North	70,327	59	4,131	-100.0	1	-12.6	7	-41.4	2	-32.6	-1,711	-1,348
Bangladesh	8,429	1,355	11,421	-14.3	1	-25.3	15	-21.7	2	-9.9	-2,475	-1,133
Belgium	1,428	2,114	3,019	2.2	1	-11.1	12	-6.7	2	7.3	-202	220
Brazil	353,611	84	29,540	-5.1	3	-28.7		-16.9	1	-4.4	-4,976	-1,292
Amazon	41,593	29	1,215	-24.5	3	-28.7	8	-26.6	1	-15.6	-323	-190
Northeast	95,062	48	4,574	-10.0	3	-28.7	8	-19.4	1	-7.3	-886	-332
South	216,956	109	23,751	-3.0	3	-28.7	8	-15.9	1	-3.2	-3,767	-770
Burkina Faso	6,830	190	1,296	-16.5	2	-32.1	2	-24.3	1	-13.0	-315	-168
Cambodia	3,807	378	1,438	-53.5	1	-14.0	14	-27.1	2	-16.1	-389	-232
Cameroon	7,160	768	5,496	-20.3	2	-19.8	3	-20.0	1	-8.0	-1,100	-441
Canada	67,504	254	17,146	0.0	5	-4.3		-2.2	1	12.5	-364	2,150
Arctic	0	0	0	0.0	5	-4.3	9	-2.1	1	12.6	0	0
Central	44,401	254	11,268	0.0	5	-4.3	9	-2.1	1	12.6	-240	1,414
Northwest Territories	0	0	0	0.0	5	-4.3	9	-2.1	1	12.6	0	0
Pacific Coast	13,121	254	3,330	0.0	5	-4.3	9	-2.1	1	12.6	-71	418
Southeast	9,980	254	2,533	0.0	5	-4.3	9	-2.1	1	12.6	-54	318

(table continues next page)

Table 5.8 Preferred estimates of impact of baseline global warming by the 2080s on world agriculture (continued)

Country	Farm area (1,000 hectares) (A)	Output per hectare (2003 dollars) (B)	Output (millions of 2003 dollars) (C)	Impact without carbon fertilization				Preferred estimates			Change in output (millions of 2003 dollars)	
				Ricardian		Crop models		Without carbon fertilization (percent) (H)	Basis[c] (I)	With carbon fertilization (percent)[d] (J)	Without carbon fertilization (K)	With carbon fertilization (L)
				Estimate (percent) (D)	Basis[a] (E)	Estimate (percent) (F)	Grouping[b] (G)					
Central America	7,624	1,429	10,892	-12.3	1	-29.4	22	-23.7	2	-12.3	-2,586	-1,340
Central Europe	11,563	1,150	13,294	7.3	1	-11.1	12	-5.0	2	9.3	-664	1,231
Chile	26,502	246	6,517	-22.4	3	-26.4	21	-24.4	1	-13.1	-1,590	-851
China	153,956	1,381	212,550	3.8	1	-12.6		-7.2	2	6.8	-15,340	14,241
Beijing Northeast	38,907	1,040	40,480	22.1	1	-12.6	10	-1.1	2	13.7	-457	5,547
Central	31,600	845	26,702	16.3	1	-12.6	10	-3.0	2	11.5	-811	3,073
Hong Kong Southeast	13,599	2,829	38,471	-3.8	1	-12.6	10	-9.7	2	3.9	-3,722	1,491
Northwest	9,436	774	7,308	17.2	1	-12.6	10	-2.7	2	11.9	-199	868
South Central	19,250	997	19,197	-18.8	1	-12.6	10	-14.6	2	-1.8	-2,808	-349
Tibetan Plateau	1,226	788	966	39.9	1	-12.6	10	4.8	2	20.5	46	198
Yellow Sea	39,938	1,989	79,426	-2.7	1	-12.6	10	-9.3	2	4.3	-7,390	3,415
Colombia	50,706	186	9,438	-17.0	3	-29.4	22	-23.2	1	-11.7	-2,188	-1,100
Cuba	3,788	285	1,078	-56.3	1	-30.9	20	-39.3	2	-30.2	-423	-325
Democratic Republic of the Congo	7,800	422	3,289	-4.1	2	-25.3	5	-14.7	1	-1.9	-484	-64
Ecuador	12,356	176	2,176	-26.8	3	-30.9	20	-28.8	1	-18.1	-627	-394
Egypt	3,751	3,516	13,188	53.5	2	-30.9	11	11.3	1	28.0	1,494	3,696
Ethiopia	11,047	253	2,794	-31.4	2	-31.1	1	-31.3	1	-20.9	-873	-585
France	29,898	1,176	35,152	2.3	1	-11.1	12	-6.7	2	7.3	-2,339	2,583
Germany	19,098	881	16,822	13.8	1	-11.1	12	-2.9	2	11.7	-483	1,967
Ghana	6,331	434	2,745	-8.2	2	-19.8	3	-14.0	1	-1.1	-384	-30
Greece	3,875	2,400	9,299	-1.2	1	-11.1	12	-7.8	2	6.0	-726	560

India	170,115	777	132,140	-49.2	4	-27.0		-38.1	1	-28.8	-50,391	-38,129
Northeast	64,870	777	50,389	-60.9	4	-27.0	16	-43.9	1	-35.5	-22,143	-17,906
Northwest	37,528	777	29,151	-57.9	4	-27.0	16	-42.5	1	-33.8	-12,382	-9,867
Southeast	42,767	777	33,220	-31.3	4	-27.0	16	-29.1	1	-18.5	-9,682	-6,151
Southwest	24,950	777	19,381	-36.8	1	-27.0	16	-31.9	1	-21.7	-6,184	-4,205
Indonesia	33,700	1,051	35,413	-15.3	1	-19.1	17	-17.9	2	-5.6	-6,330	-1,967
Iran	17,088	883	15,086	-30.9	1	-27.9	25	-28.9	2	-18.2	-4,356	-2,746
Iraq	4,591	370	1,697	-67.8	1	-27.9	25	-41.1	2	-32.2	-697	-547
Italy	19,607	1,648	32,303	0.1	2	-11.1	12	-7.4	2	6.5	-2,387	2,101
Ivory Coast	6,900	518	3,571	-8.8	1	-19.8	3	-14.3	1	-1.5	-511	-52
Japan	4,762	9,032	43,009	0.4	1	-8.7	18	-5.7	2	8.4	-2,464	3,618
Kazakhstan	21,671	110	2,380	65.6	2	-15.3	29	11.4	2	28.1	271	669
Kenya	5,162	446	2,300	15.0	2	-25.7	19	-5.4	1	8.8	-123	203
Madagascar	3,550	447	1,587	-20.3	2	-32.1	2	-26.2	1	-15.1	-416	-240
Malawi	2,440	267	651	-31.5	2	-31.1	1	-31.3	1	-21.0	-204	-137
Malaysia	7,585	1,368	10,374	-11.6	1	-27.9	13	-22.5	2	-10.9	-2,336	-1,130
Mali	4,700	350	1,644	-39.0	2	-32.1	2	-35.6	1	-25.9	-585	-426
Mexico	183,839	136	25,043	-35.9	1	-35.1	23	-35.4	2	-25.7	-8,856	-6,428
Morocco	9,283	801	7,434	-51.0	2	-27.0	4	-39.0	1	-29.9	-2,899	-2,219
Mozambique	4,435	253	1,123	-23.6	2	-19.8	3	-21.7	1	-10.0	-244	-112
Myanmar	10,611	386	4,095	-67.5	1	-25.3	15	-39.3	2	-30.1	-1,607	-1,234
Nepal	3,294	728	2,399	-0.9	1	-25.3	15	-17.3	2	-4.8	-414	-116
Netherlands	2,239	4,568	10,230	1.2	1	-11.1	12	-7.0	2	6.9	-719	708
New Zealand	15,640	254	3,979	4.5	2	1.1	26	2.2	2	17.5	87	697
Niger	4,500	243	1,092	-36.1	2	-32.1	2	-34.1	1	-24.2	-373	-265
Nigeria	33,000	460	15,181	-12.1	1	-24.9	27	-18.5	2	-6.3	-2,809	-953
North Korea	2,700	2,222	6,000	6.3	2	-14.0	14	-7.3	2	6.6	-440	394
Other Central Asia	4,383	605	2,652	13.3	1	-15.3	29	-5.9	2	8.2	-156	218
Other Equatorial Africa	2,989	478	1,429	-94.8	2	-25.3	5	-60.1	1	-54.1	-859	-773
Other Horn of Africa	1	20,118	20	-1.1	2	-32.1	2	-16.6	1	-4.1	-3	-1

(table continues next page)

Table 5.8 Preferred estimates of impact of baseline global warming by the 2080s on world agriculture *(continued)*

Country	Farm area (1,000 hectares) (A)	Output per hectare (2003 dollars) (B)	Output (millions of 2003 dollars) (C)	Ricardian Estimate (percent) (D)	Ricardian Basis[a] (E)	Crop models Estimate (percent) (F)	Crop models Grouping[b] (G)	Without carbon fertilization (percent) (H)	Basis[c] (I)	With carbon fertilization (percent)[d] (J)	Without carbon fertilization (K)	With carbon fertilization (L)
Other South America	23,818	118	2,808	-70.7	1	-29.4	22	-43.0	2	-34.4	-1,207	-967
Other Southern Africa	14,066	44	620	-66.7	2	-27.0	4	-46.9	1	-38.9	-291	-241
Other West Africa	4,372	419	1,833	-33.2	2	-32.1	2	-32.7	1	-22.6	-599	-414
Pakistan	22,120	856	18,935	-17.9	1	-36.6	28	-30.4	2	-20.0	-5,762	-3,786
Peru	35,382	171	6,058	-39.1	1	-26.4	21	-30.6	2	-20.2	-1,852	-1,221
Philippines	10,700	1,054	11,280	-14.3	1	-27.9	13	-23.4	2	-11.9	-2,639	-1,342
Poland	19,325	239	4,610	16.7	1	-15.3	29	-4.7	2	9.5	-219	440
Portugal	5,189	713	3,697	-6.6	1	-11.1	12	-9.6	2	4.0	-355	147
Romania	13,940	490	6,834	11.2	1	-15.3	29	-6.6	2	7.4	-450	508
Russia	250,182	87	21,643	0.0	5	-15.3		-7.7	1	6.2	-1,658	1,340
Caspian Black Sea	49,157	87	4,252	0.0	5	-15.3	29	-7.7	1	6.2	-326	263
Far Eastern	11,868	87	1,027	0.0	5	-15.3	29	-7.7	1	6.2	-79	64
North European	46,332	87	4,008	0.0	5	-15.3	29	-7.7	1	6.2	-307	248
North Urals Siberia	11,230	87	971	0.0	5	-15.3	29	-7.7	1	6.2	-74	60
Northeast Siberia	12,742	87	1,102	0.0	5	-15.3	29	-7.7	1	6.2	-84	68
South Urals Siberia	61,495	87	5,320	0.0	5	-15.3	29	-7.7	1	6.2	-407	329
Southeast Siberia	57,358	87	4,962	0.0	5	-15.3	29	-7.7	1	6.2	-380	307
Saudi Arabia	4,046	2,654	10,737	-9.8	1	-27.9	25	-21.9	2	-10.2	-2,351	-1,093
Scandinavia	22,742	397	9,027	55.4	1	-11.1	12	10.9	2	27.5	981	2,483
Senegal	2,506	441	1,104	-84.0	1	-19.8	3	-51.9	1	-44.7	-573	-493
South Africa	15,712	407	6,395	-47.0	2	-19.8	3	-33.4	1	-23.4	-2,134	-1,495
South Korea	1,877	8,707	16,344	0.2	1	-14.0	14	-9.3	2	4.3	-1,525	698
Southeast Europe	13,243	949	12,566	5.0	1	-15.3	29	-8.6	2	5.1	-1,084	638
Spain	42,181	716	30,191	-4.5	1	-11.1	12	-8.9	2	4.8	-2,691	1,434

Sri Lanka	1,916	1,808	3,465	-9.5	1	-25.3	15	-20.1	2	-8.1	-697	-282
Sudan	16,653	417	6,939	-81.1	2	-31.1	1	-56.1	1	-49.5	-3,892	-3,435
Syria	5,421	912	4,945	-25.2	1	-27.9	25	-27.0	2	-16.0	-1,334	-792
Tanzania	10,764	430	4,634	-16.3	2	-32.1	2	-24.2	1	-12.8	-1,122	-595
Thailand	19,367	738	14,295	-25.3	1	-26.6	30	-26.2	2	-15.1	-3,739	-2,156
Turkey	28,523	935	26,682	1.6	1	-24.9	31	-16.2	2	-3.6	-4,312	-956
Uganda	7,200	280	2,015	-2.5	2	-31.1	1	-16.8	1	-4.3	-338	-86
Ukraine	33,457	207	6,935	15.3	1	-15.3	29	-5.2	2	9.0	-361	625
United Kingdom	16,528	760	12,564	10.5	1	-11.1	12	-3.9	2	10.5	-495	1,315
United States	379,343	260	98,537	4.7	1	-16.5		-5.9	1	8	-5,791	8,120
Alaska	365	62	23	0.0	1	-9.0	e	-4.5	1	10	-1	2
Lakes, Northeast	74,276	411	30,515	14.5	1	-4.5	e	5.0	1	21	1,526	6,332
Pacific Northwest	13,117	320	4,198	16.6	1	3.2	e	9.9	1	26	417	1,109
Rockies, Plains	113,276	133	15,077	27.0	1	28.3	e	27.6	1	47	4,164	7,050
Southeast	58,046	383	22,214	-13.7	1	-43.0	e	-28.3	1	-18	-6,294	-3,906
South Pacific Coast	11,170	1,135	12,673	0.0	1	-11.9	e	-5.9	1	8	-752	1,036
Southwest Plains	109,094	127	13,836	-11.1	1	-59.0	e	-35.1	1	-25	-4,851	-3,503
Uzbekistan	4,827	721	3,482	-5.5	1	-15.3	29	-12.1	2	1	-421	38
Venezuela	30,071	114	3,416	-37.5	3	-26.4	21	-31.9	1	-22	-1,091	-742
Vietnam	8,895	969	8,616	-17.2	1	-14.0	14	-15.1	2	-2	-1,300	-202
Yemen	1,669	973	1,625	-20.2	1	-32.1	24	-28.2	2	-17	-458	-283
Zambia	5,289	189	997	-47.1	2	-32.1	2	-39.6	1	-31	-395	-305
Zimbabwe	3,350	901	3,018	-44.7	2	-31.1	1	-37.9	1	-29	-1,144	-863
World	3,097,935	380	1,175,860	-10.1		-18.9		-15.9		-3.2	-186,510	-38,107
median				-9.8		-19.8		-16.7		-4.2	

a. 1 = on the basis of Mendelsohn-Schlesinger (appendix table F.2); 2 = World Bank Africa (table 5.4); 3 = World Bank Latin America (table 5.5); 4 = Mendelsohn-Dinar-Sanghi India (table 5.2); 5 = Reinsborough (2003); see text.

b. Number refers to grouping in table 5.7.

c. 1 = average, Ricardian and crop model; 2 = 1/3 weight Ricardian, 2/3 weight crop model.

d. Equals without–carbon fertilization estimate adjusted for 15 percent yield increase.

e. Equals average between Mendelsohn-Schlesinger (appendix table F.1) and Rosenzweig-Iglesias (table 5.7) adjusted for non–carbon fertilization.

results with aggregated base output provides the basis for obtaining the percent change in agricultural potential at the global (table 5.8) and regional levels (discussed later). As discussed in chapter 3, these output effects represent direct supply impact before taking into account induced effects from price changes and from adjustments in international trade.

The global result in the preferred estimates is that business as usual climate change by the 2080s would reduce world agricultural production capacity by about 16 percent if carbon fertilization is omitted and by about 3 percent if it is included. A 16 percent reduction would be severe and would potentially cause major price increases because of the inelasticity of demand for food. These price increases would need to be taken into account in estimating resulting global welfare losses.

Even if the moderate global reduction of 3 percent assuming carbon fertilization were the outcome, the large disparity of results across countries would mean much more serious losses for many countries and regions. Generally, the developing countries would tend to fare much worse than the industrial countries, as examined later.

There are 21 countries, regions, or subzones of large countries in which production capacity falls by more than one-third without carbon fertilization and 7 in which it does so even with carbon fertilization. If the threshold is set at a loss of 20 percent or greater, there are 53 countries and regions with severe losses without carbon fertilization and 29 even with carbon fertilization.

For the United States, there would be moderate results overall but sharp disparities among regions. Without carbon fertilization, there would be a loss of 5.9 percent for the United States, but this outcome masks dispersion between gains as high as 28 percent in the Rockies and Plains and losses in the range of 30 percent in the Southeast and Southwest Plains.[26] For the US results including carbon fertilization, the corresponding estimates are an overall average gain of 8 percent, with impacts as favorable as +47 percent in the Rockies and Plains but as unfavorable as –18 percent in the Southeast and –25 percent in the Southwest Plains.

India would face a major loss on the order of 30 percent even with carbon fertilization. The loss would be about 35 percent in the Northeast and Northwest. In the key case of China, the aggregate gains would be about 7 percent assuming carbon fertilization but losses of 7 percent if carbon fertilization failed to materialize. Moreover, in the case without carbon fertilization, losses would be as high as 15 percent in the South Central region, which accounts for about 140 million people (appendix E and ERS 2006a).

---

26. The Rockies-Plains gains are probably overstated, moreover, by using land area rather than output value to aggregate from the standard grid level up to the region. This would tend to give substantial weight to supposed gains from warming in the cold mountainous areas even though their topography constrains agricultural potential.

Figures 5.2 and 5.3 portray the preferred results graphically. The substantially more favorable results when carbon fertilization is included (figure 5.3) are evident in most regions. These maps also underscore the concentration of damage in the latitudes closer to the equator and of gains in latitudes closer to the poles. With the exception of New Zealand, the Southern Hemisphere is nearly uniform in experiencing losses, reflecting the paucity of land masses in the latitudes south of about 35°S. Losses are also predominant in the Northern Hemisphere below about 35°N, but a much smaller fraction of total land area lies between the equator and 35°N than in the corresponding zone in the Southern Hemisphere.

The underlying components shown in table 5.8 for the preferred estimates provide a basis for a broad comparison between results from the Ricardian family and those from the crop model family. As discussed above, only those countries or regions with specific Ricardian function estimates are given full equal weight to the crop model estimates, so it is most useful to limit the comparison to these countries and regions (indicated by 1 for the basis for the preferred estimates in column I of table 5.8).

Figure 5.4 plots the percent change in agricultural potential (without carbon fertilization) for the 47 regions for which a regionally or country-specific Ricardian estimate exists, showing the Ricardian estimate on the vertical axis and the crop model (Rosenzweig-Iglesias for all but the United States) estimate on the horizontal axis. The scale of the two axes immediately confirms one major pattern: The crop model results show considerably less dispersion than the Ricardian results. The wider dispersion of the Ricardian estimates is confirmed by their standard deviation, which is 28 percentage points versus 12.1 percent for the crop model estimates. One underlying reason seems to be that the Rosenzweig-Iglesias crop model findings tend to be linear with regard to the magnitude of climate change, whereas at least the models in the Ricardian family are nonlinear.[27]

The pattern of the scatter diagram indicates that there is a reasonable degree of agreement between the two sets.[28] Given the figure scale, complete agreement would place all observations along the 17.5° line. The agreement is far from complete. Nonetheless there is a clear upward slope in the scatter, meaning that high estimates in one set are also high in the other, and the large negative estimates in one set also tend to be large negative estimates in the other. The two sets of estimates yield comparable

---

27. Thus, Parry, Rosenzweig, and Livermore (2005, 2136) state that: "Without the counteracting direct CO_2 effects, crop production responds approximately linearly to temperature increases across the suite of scenarios."

28. The simple correlation coefficient between the two sets of estimates is 0.38. A regression of the Ricardian estimates on the crop model estimates yields a statistically significant coefficient of 0.73 (t-statistic of 2.3). Note that the observation of greatest disagreement is that for Egypt, with 53 percent gain in the Ricardian estimate but 31 percent loss in the crop model estimates.

Figure 5.2 Impact on agricultural productivity without carbon fertilization (percent)

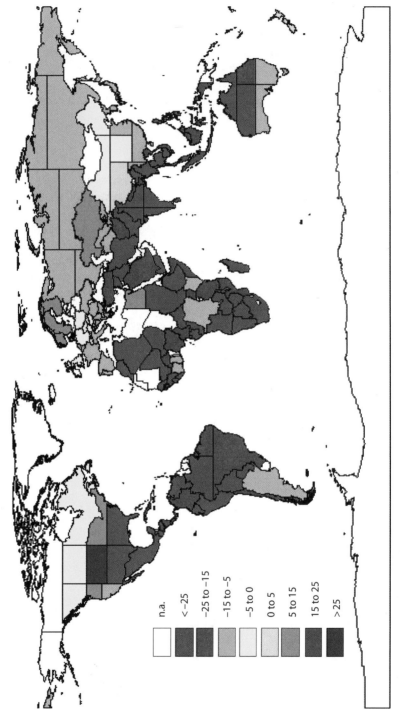

n.a.
< –25
–25 to –15
–15 to –5
–5 to 0
0 to 5
5 to 15
15 to 25
> 25

Note: In both maps, n.a. refers to "not applicable" for Alaska, Northern Canada, and Antarctica and "not available" otherwise.

Figure 5.3   Impact on agricultural productivity with carbon fertilization (percent)

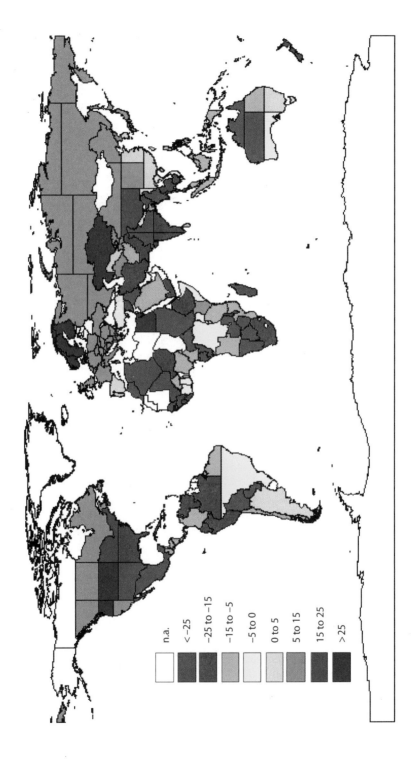

n.a.

< –25

–25 to –15

–15 to –5

–5 to 0

0 to 5

5 to 15

15 to 25

> 25

Figure 5.4   Percent change in agricultural capacity by the 2080s in 47 countries and regions (without carbon fertilization)

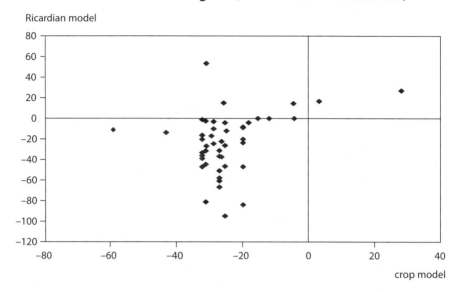

central results, although the Ricardian estimates show modestly milder effects than the crop model results. The median impact for the Ricardian estimates is –21.3 percent; that for the crop models is –27 percent. The corresponding average impacts are –23.4 and –25 percent, respectively.

Broadly, then, for the subset of countries and regions for which the Ricardian estimates are based on data for the countries in question, the two sets of underlying estimates tend to show similar patterns, with the median and average Ricardian losses only modestly smaller than those of the crop model estimates. The greater difference is that in crop model estimates the disparities between the winners and losers would not be as extreme as in the Ricardian estimates. The two approaches show wider divergence in the averages once the full set of countries is considered, after including those for which the Ricardian estimates must be based on the default US parameters (appendix table F.2). This conclusion is evident in table 5.8, which shows that the global output-weighted impact is an average of –10 percent for the Ricardian estimates versus –18.9 percent for the crop model estimates, and the two respective global medians are –9.8 and –19.8 percent. The implication is that the subset of less reliable (default-based) Ricardian estimates tends to understate global losses. For example, the large positive estimates in this subset may be an overstatement of gains, such as those for Kazakhstan (66 percent) and Scandinavia (55 percent).

Table 5.9 restates the preferred results in terms of aggregates for the Rosenzweig-Iglesias regions. This grouping of estimates facilitates comparison of the framework 1 Ricardian estimates against the framework 2

Table 5.9   Change in agricultural capacity by regional aggregates (percent)

Region[b]	Without carbon fertilization			With carbon fertilization[a]		
	Ricardian	Crop model	Preferred	Ricardian	Crop model	Preferred
Africa LICX	−52.6	−31.1	−41.8	−45.5	−20.7	−33.1
Africa LICM	−26.1	−32.1	−29.1	−15.0	−21.9	−18.4
Africa MICX	−28.3	−19.8	−24.2	−17.5	−7.8	−12.8
Africa MICM	−52.2	−27.0	−39.6	−45.0	−16.1	−30.5
Africa OilX	−28.4	−25.3	−32.2	−17.7	−14.1	−22.0
Argentina	−4.1	−18.1	−11.1	10.3	−5.8	2.2
Australia	−55.1	−12.6	−26.6	−48.3	0.6	−15.6
Brazil, similar	−5.0	−28.7	−16.8	9.3	−18.0	−4.4
Canada	0.0	−4.3	−2.1	15.0	10.1	12.6
China, similar	3.6	−12.6	−7.2	19.2	0.6	6.7
Egypt, similar	53.5	−30.9	11.3	76.5	−20.5	28.0
Europe	5.1	−11.1	−5.7	20.8	2.3	8.4
Far East Asia HMICX	−13.0	−27.9	−23.0	0.0	−17.1	−11.4
Far East Asia HMICM	−5.7	−14.0	−11.3	8.5	−1.1	2.0
Far East Asia LI	−22.2	−25.3	−24.3	−10.5	−14.1	−12.9
India	−49.2	−27.0	−38.1	−41.6	−16.1	−28.9
Indonesia	−15.3	−19.1	−17.9	−2.6	−7.0	−5.6
Japan	0.4	−8.7	−5.7	15.4	5.0	8.4
Kenya	15.0	−25.7	−5.4	32.3	−14.6	8.8
Latin America HICX	−36.6	−30.9	−32.3	−27.0	−20.5	−22.1
Latin America HICM	−31.9	−26.4	−28.3	−21.7	−15.3	−17.6
Latin America MLI	−21.3	−29.4	−25.8	−9.5	−18.8	−14.7
Mexico	−35.9	−35.1	−35.4	−26.3	−25.4	−25.7
Northeast Asia MLI	−13.8	−32.1	−26.1	−0.9	−21.9	−15.0
Northeast Asia OilX	−25.0	−27.9	−26.9	−13.7	−17.1	−15.9
New Zealand	4.5	1.1	2.2	20.2	16.2	17.5
Nigeria	−12.1	−24.9	−18.5	1.1	−13.6	−6.3
Pakistan	−17.9	−36.6	−30.4	−5.6	−27.1	−20.0
Former Soviet Union, Eastern Europe	8.1	−15.3	−6.7	24.3	−2.6	7.3
Thailand	−25.3	−26.6	−26.2	−14.1	−15.6	−15.1
Turkey	1.6	−24.9	−16.2	16.8	−13.6	−3.6
United States	4.7	−16.5	−5.9	20.4	−3.9	8.2
World						
Median of regions	−14.5	−25.5	−23.6	−1.7	−14.4	−12.1
Total	−10.0	−18.9	−15.9	3.5	−6.8	−3.2
Developing countries						
Median of regions	−21.3	−27.0	−25.8	−9.5	−16.1	−14.7
Total	−16.9	−22.5	−21.0	−4.5	−10.8	−9.2
Industrial countries						
Median of regions	2.4	−9.9	−5.7	17.8	3.6	8.4
Total	1.9	−11.9	−6.3	17.2	1.3	7.8
Economies in transition (former Soviet Union, Eastern Europe)	8.1	−15.3	−6.7	24.3	−2.6	7.3

a. Equals without carbon fertilization result plus effect of uniform 15 percent yield increase.
b. See table 5.7.

Source: Table 5.8.

crop model estimates. The table shows them individually along with the preferred regional estimates.

Several important findings are evident in table 5.9. First, at the global level and weighting by base output, the two sets of underlying estimates once again tend to show more severe effects in the crop model estimates than in the Ricardian estimates. In the case without carbon fertilization, global output capacity would fall by about 10 percent in the Ricardian model–based estimates and about 19 percent in the crop model estimates (the same as in table 5.8). The corresponding median changes show a somewhat wider divergence as well as larger damages for both, at about −15 and −26 percent, respectively. In the results including carbon fertilization, the differences persist, with a global average gain of 4 percent for the Ricardian models but a loss of 7 percent for the crop model estimates and corresponding median impacts across the various regions at −2 and −14 percent, respectively.

Second, once again there is less dispersion between severe negative effects and large positive effects in the crop model results than in the Ricardian results. In the groupings of table 5.9 the simple average impact for the worst quintile (6 groupings) is −44 percent for the Ricardian estimates (without carbon fertilization) versus −33 percent for the crop model estimates. Conversely, the most favorable quintile of results shows an average of +15 percent for the Ricardian estimates but −8 percent for the crop model estimates.

Third, in both sets of results most countries and regions would experience larger losses than would be seen if attention focused solely on global aggregates, as indicated by the differences between the average and median estimates already noted. For the 32 regions, in the Ricardian-based estimates the median losses are about 50 percent larger than the global average in the case without carbon fertilization. With carbon fertilization there are losses for the median region (1.7 percent) but a slight gain for the global aggregate (3.5 percent). The median losses are also higher than the global averages in the crop model estimates but to a lesser degree (multiples of 1.35 and 2 for the without and with carbon fertilization cases, respectively), reflecting the previous point about dispersion of results in the two sources.

Fourth, and in this same vein, both sets of estimates confirm that developing countries would fare substantially worse than industrial countries. In the case including carbon fertilization, for developing countries the median change in productive potential is a decline of about 16 (crop model) to 10 percent (Ricardian). In contrast, for industrial countries, the corresponding medians show an increase of about 4 (crop model) to 18 percent (Ricardian).

Finally, the detailed preferred results of table 5.8 can be aggregated into an alternative grouping of developing and industrial countries based on more usual geographical regions than in the Rosenzweig-Iglesias analysis in order to consider further the differences in impact between the two sets

Table 5.10   Agricultural impact by major regions: Developing and industrial countries

Country/region	Base output (billions of 2003 dollars)	Population (millions)	Change in agricultural output potential preferred estimates (percent)	
			Without carbon fertilization	With carbon fertilization
Developing countries	838	5,202	−19.7	−7.7
Excluding Europe	745	4,807	−21.0	−9.1
Africa	73	660	−27.5	−16.6
Nigeria	15	136	−18.5	−6.3
South Africa	6	46	−33.4	−23.4
Asia	500	3,362	−19.3	−7.2
China	213	1,288	−7.2	6.8
India	132	1,064	−38.1	−28.8
Indonesia	35	215	−17.9	−5.6
Middle East North Africa	61	280	−21.2	−9.4
Algeria	7	32	−36.0	−26.4
Egypt	13	68	11.3	28.0
Iran	15	66	−28.9	−18.2
Latin America	111	506	−24.3	−12.9
Argentina	14	37	−11.1	2.2
Brazil	30	177	−16.9	−4.4
Mexico	25	102	−35.4	−25.7
Europe	93	395	−9.4	4.1
Poland	5	38	−4.7	9.5
Russia	22	143	−7.7	6.2
Turkey	27	71	−16.2	−3.6
Industrial countries	338	846	−6.3	7.7
Australia	13	20	−26.6	−15.6
Canada	17	32	−2.2	12.5
Germany	17	83	−2.9	11.7
United Kingdom	13	59	−3.9	10.5
United States	99	291	−5.9	8.2
World	1,176	6,049	−15.9	−3.2
Population-weighted			−18.2	−6.0

Source: Table 5.8.

of countries. In addition, it is possible to obtain overall weighted results using population weights to examine how the implications differ from global averages weighting by agricultural production. Table 5.10 presents these alternative aggregations.

At the most aggregate level, the comparison between narrowly defined developing countries and industrial countries is the same in tables 5.9 and 5.10. Namely, including carbon fertilization, output-weighted agricultural potential rises for industrial countries by a preferred estimate of 7.7 percent, whereas for developing countries defined as excluding developing Europe it falls by 9.1 percent. The additional regional information in table 5.10 shows that in the preferred estimate (and including carbon fertilization), output potential falls by about 17 percent in Africa excluding North Africa, by 7 percent in Asia, 9 percent in the Middle East and North Africa, and 13 percent in Latin America. In contrast, for developing Europe it rises by 4 percent, the same broad range as the 7 percent in table 5.9 for the former Soviet Union and Eastern Europe.[29]

These results indicate that Africa (excluding Egypt and other North Africa) and Latin America are the two developing regions most vulnerable to global warming. This finding is consistent with the IPCC (1996) pattern noted in the survey above. Asia on average is less vulnerable, but this masks the divergence between more favorable results for China in particular and more unfavorable results for India, reflecting in part the difference in their latitudes.

At the world level the aggregates are again the same as in tables 5.8 and 5.9. Weighting by output, global agricultural potential falls by about 16 percent without carbon fertilization and 3 percent with carbon fertilization. Table 5.10 also reports the global impact weighting by population rather than output. In this case, output potential falls by a weighted average of 18 percent without carbon fertilization and by about 6 percent with carbon fertilization. The greater decline in output potential weighting by population reflects the predominance of more severe adverse effects in developing countries in contrast to milder losses or even gains in industrial countries.

Comparison to Estimates in the Model-Source Studies

The analysis above has applied models developed by other authors to detailed future climate data as calculated in this study to obtain estimates of the impact of global warming on agricultural potential. The authors of these models have in some cases provided their own estimates of global warming impact, so it is important to compare their results with those here.

---

29. Developing Europe in table 6.1 shares Russia, Poland, Romania, Southeastern Europe, and Ukraine with former Soviet Union and Eastern Europe in table 5.10. It adds Turkey and Central Europe but drops Kazakhstan, Uzbekistan, and other Central Asia, which are reallocated to Asia.

Mendelsohn, Morrison, Schlesinger, and Andronova

The Mendelsohn and Schlesinger (1999) models used in appendix tables F.1 and F.2 were not used by their authors to calculate the impact of global warming on world agriculture, but a subsequent study by Mendelsohn, Morrison, Schlesinger, and Andronova (MMSA; 2000) made such estimates. The models in MMSA are almost identical to the reduced form and cross-section models in Mendelsohn and Schlesinger (1999). The only substantial difference is that in the cross-section model the MMSA coefficient for carbon fertilization is 43 percent larger than the corresponding coefficient in the MS version (equation 5.2 above). With the benefit of hindsight in view of the recent FACE agronomic results, this increase appears to have been ill-advised.

Applying their models, MMSA arrive at a very benign prognosis of the impact of global warming by 2100 for the world as a whole.[30] They state:

> The aggregate impacts are projected to be beneficial in every scenario relative to the current climate and carbon dioxide levels. . . . With the Ricardian model, benefits climb for the first 2°C of warming and then they decline. . . . With the reduced-form model, warming benefits climb through 1°C and then just begin to decline at 2°C. Warming begins to be harmful between 1 and 2°C. The overall magnitude of the market impacts [including forestry, coastal resources, energy, and water] is small in all cases, being less than 0.16% of world GDP. Thus, these initial results imply that global warming over the next century is not a serious threat to the world economy, and is likely to be a small benefit (Mendelsohn, Morrison, Schlesinger, and Andronova 2000, 560).

MMSA find small global net losses in the other market sectors they include, and their conclusion just cited is entirely attributable to their estimate that there would be global gains from agriculture, amounting to $297 billion at 1990 prices in the cross-section model and $171 billion in the reduced form model, against a global economy of $172 trillion by 2100 in the central case. Chapter 6 of this study suggests that by 2085 global agricultural demand is likely to expand by a multiple in the range of 2.7 to 3.7 times the 2005 level. With world agricultural output at about $1.2 trillion in 2003 (appendix E), by 2085 world agricultural output would be on the order of $3.8 trillion. The potential gain from global warming of about $300 billion estimated by MMSA in their Ricardian model would

---

30. It should be noted that nowhere in their study do MMSA report the paradox encountered in the present study when applying both the reduced form and cross-section models: A high incidence of negative base period agricultural productivity is calculated when these US-based models are applied to the temperature and precipitation averages for other countries. Correspondingly, they do not report how they address this problem or whether they use the approach applied here of considering the change in output per hectare from climate change against an estimate of base period actual productivity, even where the predicted base level is negative.

thus represent a favorable impact of 8 percent of world agricultural output potential.

The results in the present study using the same underlying MS models are much less favorable (appendix tables F.1 and F.2). Thus, even including the MS carbon fertilization estimates, their reduced form model is estimated here to generate a global loss of 13 percent in agricultural potential, rather than a sizable gain. One key source of the difference is that the climate model MMSA use (University of Illinois) generates 2°C mean global warming by 2100, whereas the suite of climate models used for the present study places mean global warming at 3°C by the 2080s. Because their models find improvement at up to 1 to 2°C warming, it is no coincidence that using 2°C mean warming does not show damage and in fact shows small gains.[31] The other likely source of the difference in aggregate results is from carbon fertilization. The MMSA version of the cross-section model would appear to overstate the carbon fertilization effect. When applied to the 2080s climate, the MMSA carbon fertilization parameter boosts land rental equivalent by 46 percent above levels it would otherwise have reached, which globally would correspond to an increase in output potential by about half as much or 23 percent, well above the 15 percent adopted in the present study (see chapter 3). In short, the basic sources of the difference between the benign global effects in MMSA and the more adverse ones in the present study using the same basic models would seem to be the use of lower expected future warming and higher carbon fertilization in the MMSA study than in the present study.[32]

In contrast to the divergence in global aggregate estimates, for the pattern of regional and country winners and losers there is more similarity between the results here in appendix F using the MS models and those in MMSA. Both identify Canada and Russia as large beneficiaries (MMSA place Russia's agricultural gains at $124 billion to $351 billion at 1990 prices and Canada's gains at $19 billion to $49 billion). This same pattern of large gains in Canada and Russia is found for the MS reduced form and Ricardian estimates shown in appendix F, but as noted above, for the main estimates of this study the zero impact findings of Reinsborough (2003) are instead applied, for both countries. The strong MMSA gains for

---

31. Although it is not quite that simple: As discussed above, the relevant warming over land areas significantly exceeds the global mean, so the land areas even in MMSA should show warming higher than 2°C.

32. It is also possible that the coarser grid specification in the MMSA climate model than that in this study contributes to the difference. With grids of 4° latitude and 5° longitude, instead of 2° latitude and 3° longitude used in this study, their grid areas are 3.2 times as large as those in this study. Even so, simple back-of-the-envelope application of the functions in equations (5.1) and (5.2) to the much more aggregative country climate averages shown in table 4.2 generates results broadly similar to the detailed results of this study built up from the grid level, so grid size seems unlikely to account for much of the difference between the MMSA results and those in this study.

China ($39 billion to $65 billion) and the United States ($17 billion to $35 billion) are in the same direction, although larger, than the results from application of the MS models in appendix F of the present study.

For developing countries, the MMSA results generally parallel those found here. In the reduced form model, India and Brazil both experience large losses (by $86 billion and $106 billion annually, respectively). The reduced form model in MMSA gives severe losses for Africa ($131 billion) and Latin America as a whole ($49 billion). However, the Ricardian (cross-section) model in MMSA shows gains even for these two regions, in contrast to the results here. The MMSA finding of positive results for the cross-section function in all regions is in sharp contradiction to the cross-section findings in the present study in appendix table F.2. This divergence may in particular reflect the much stronger carbon fertilization effect used in MMSA than in the estimates here. Overall, nonetheless, it is fair to say that there is much more agreement between the MMSA findings and those here, especially using the reduced form rather than Ricardian cross-section model, on the differential effects among countries (including the broad pattern of losses in Africa and Latin America, in particular, in contrast to more favorable results in industrial countries) than on the severity of the losses and the overall global balance of results.

Mendelsohn, Dinar, and Sanghi

The model used for India is from Mendelsohn, Dinar, and Sanghi (2001). In that study, however, the authors focus on how the level of development affects the climate sensitivity of agriculture. They do not include specific calculations of the impact of prospective global warming on agriculture.

An earlier study by the same authors does provide impact estimates for India. Sanghi, Mendelsohn, and Dinar (1998, 107) develop a Ricardian model for Indian agriculture and calculate that benchmark global warming (2 × CO_2) would reduce net revenue by 12.3 percent. However, their calculation applies 2°C rise in temperature and 7 percent rise in precipitation for benchmark climate change. Instead, it is evident from table 4.2 that the consensus estimate from the six climate models considered in the present study would place climate change by the 2080s at much greater warming—a rise of 3.6°C for annual average temperature across the four subzones. Although the corresponding estimate in the present study for precipitation is also higher (at 17 rather than 7 percent), in the model in question the favorable impact of higher precipitation is much smaller than the unfavorable impact of higher temperatures.[33] One reason the authors

---

33. The 7 percent boost in precipitation raises average net revenue by 14.4 rupees per hectare (at 1980 prices) whereas the 2°C increase in temperature reduces net revenue by 208 rupees per hectare (Sanghi, Mendelsohn, and Dinar 1998, 98).

apply much less warming than used in the present study may be that they have implicitly assumed the change for India is the same as the global average, whereas the increase for land areas would tend to be greater than the global average including the oceans (as emphasized above).

World Bank Studies

Africa. In the recent World Bank study on Africa (Kurukulasuriya et al. 2006), the authors do not apply their models to a postulated future climate with global warming, so once again there is no basis for direct comparison with the results of the present study. Qualitatively, however, the study appears to conclude that global warming has a neutral effect on Africa because gains for irrigated agriculture approximately offset losses in dryland agriculture. In particular, they find that for a 1°C temperature increase, the models calculate a "slight and insignificant *increase* [emphasis added] in net revenue across African farms . . ." (p. 13).

The use of 1°C warming as the gauge makes this finding essentially irrelevant to the question of effects by the end of this century. In particular, by the 2080s the simple average rise in annual average temperature for the African countries and regions shown in table 4.2 is 4°C. Even within the confines of the minimal 1°C warming, the result is misleading because it depends on applying the with-Egypt function for irrigated farming. As discussed above, the without-Egypt function shows a negative rather than positive response to warming, and Egypt's atypical access to the Nile River (and its atypical 100 percent irrigated farming in contrast to only about 6 percent for Africa as a whole) would surely counsel use of the without-Egypt function to assess the impact on irrigated agriculture outside Egypt, as is done here.

Perhaps more fundamentally, the "irrigation compensation" message in the World Bank study does not come to grips with the problem that less water may be available for irrigation in a hotter and drier future. Thus, IPCC (2001b, 289) finds that

> Africa is the continent with the lowest conversion factor of precipitation to runoff . . . . Although the equatorial region and coastal areas of eastern and southern African are humid, the rest of the continent is dry subhumid to arid. The dominant impact of global warming is predicted to be a reduction in soil moisture in subhumid zones and reduction in runoff.

Indeed, the question of water availability for future irrigation poses a problem for the applicability of the Ricardian models that do not evaluate irrigated agriculture separately (the MS cross-section model in particular), because one of the prime reasons farms can adjust in hotter and drier climates is through increased irrigation. To the extent that the US-based MS function implicitly relies on greater irrigation as the vehicle for benign effects of warming, it will give an unduly optimistic picture of future agricultural prospects in those areas where irrigation would be increasingly constrained because of adverse effects on water availability.

In a related study using the World Bank Africa surveys, Kurukulasuriya and Mendelsohn (2006) apply alternative climate models to each country. They find that by the end of this century, and excluding carbon fertilization, Africa as a whole could experience agricultural impacts ranging from annual losses of $48 billion if the future climate were "hot and dry" to annual gains of $97 billion if it were "mild and wet" (p. 7). The effects are not uniform across countries, and the hotter and drier regions of Africa fare the worst in all scenarios. The African estimates in the present study suggest, however, that this wide range, and especially its average of +$25 billion, are likely to be misleading and that instead the best guess using a consensus climate model is that large losses would predominate.

Latin America. The discussion above of the recent World Bank–sponsored studies for Latin America, and the estimates presented in table 5.5, directly address the climate impact estimates contained in that set of studies in comparison with the corresponding results obtained using their models with the climate assumptions of the present study.

Rosenzweig-Iglesias

The most relevant study from the Rosenzweig-Iglesias set of research for comparison with results here is that by Parry, Rosenzweig, and Livermore (2005). They confirm their earlier finding

> that climate change is likely to reduce global food potential and that risk of hunger will increase in the most marginalized economies. . . . [C]limate change scenarios excluding the direct physiological effects of CO_2 predict decreases in simulated yields in many cases, while the direct effects of increasing atmospheric CO_2 mitigate the negative effects primarily in mid and high latitudes. . . . At low latitudes crops are grown nearer the limits of temperature tolerance and global warming may subject them to higher stress. In many mid and high latitude areas, increasing temperatures may benefit crops, otherwise limited by cold temperatures and short growing seasons in the present climate (pp. 2127–28).

Citing their estimates from the early 1990s, they report that under conditions by 2060 as predicted by three climate models (GISS, GFDL, and UKMO), with level 1 adaptation (discussed above), global warming would boost cereal production by an average of about 8 percent for developed countries, reduce it by 11 percent in developing countries, and reduce global production by about 3 percent (Parry, Rosenzweig, and Livermore 2005, 2129, figure 2). Revisiting their estimates in light of the IPCC scenarios in the 2001 Third Assessment Report, they find that in the SRES A2 scenario (the one used in the climate estimates of this study) the number of people globally at risk of hunger would increase by about 550 million above the no climate change reference level of 800 million, although this outcome is more attributable to a rise in global population to a level (15 billion) higher than in their reference scenario than to a decline in yields.

In broad terms the results using the Rosenzweig-Iglesias model query system in the present study are similar to those in Parry, Rosenzweig, and Livermore (2005). This similarity is to be expected because the calculations here directly apply the results for the specified scenarios in Rosenzweig and Iglesias (2006) with the minor modification that the carbon fertilization effect by the 2080s is curbed from an average 17.5 percent boost in yields to 15 percent.

6

Dynamic Considerations

The analysis in this study uses current production (or population) for country weights in obtaining global estimates for the impact of climate change on agriculture. This approach tends to understate the future losses, because it is likely that by late in this century the business as usual baseline for agricultural output would have shown a much larger share for developing and low latitude countries than is the case at present. So from this standpoint the losses may be understated.

In contrast, it might be argued that dynamic considerations will typically shrink the relative importance of losses from climate change, because technological change can be expected to raise yields by far more than global warming reduces them. Comfort from the prospect of rising yields from technological change may nonetheless fail to take into account the fact that rising demand for agricultural products may run a close race with technological change, so that yield losses to climate change could still do damage that more than exceeds any excess supply trends in the baseline. Moreover, an important additional factor must be incorporated into the dynamic analysis: the likely diversion of agricultural land to production of biomass for ethanol.

This chapter seeks to arrive at some ballpark estimates of the net effect of these divergent influences. Define the ratio of demand or supply in 2085 to the level in 2005 as λ for each of several dimensions. Consider first population. The United Nations (2006) projects population in 2050 at 9.08 billion in its medium case, compared with 6.46 billion in 2004. Population grows at a pace of 0.42 percent per year in the decade 2040–2050 in this case. In its high case, the United Nations projects world population in 2050 at 10.65 billion, with annual growth at 0.93 percent in the decade 2040–2050. If these two respective levels and rates are used for projection to 2085, the resulting global population in 2085 is 10.52 billion in the

Figure 6.1   Income elasticity of demand for food, tobacco, and beverages and purchasing power parity (PPP) income per capita

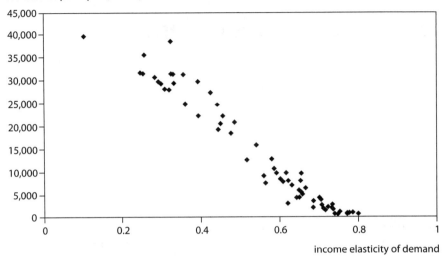

PPP income per capita (dollars)

income elasticity of demand

medium case and 14.72 billion in the high case. The expansion factor from current levels to 2085 for population is thus $\lambda_N = 1.63$ in the medium case and 2.28 in the high case. In broad terms, global agricultural output will need to double, approximately, to keep up with population growth over this period.

Also, demand will increase from rising per capita incomes. Figure 6.1 shows the relationship of the income elasticity of demand for food, beverages, and tobacco (as calculated by ERS 2006b) to purchasing power parity (PPP) GDP per capita (World Bank 2006) for 64 countries. There is a clear inverse relationship between per capita income and income elasticity of food, which amounts to a strong form of Engel's law (which states that food expenditure rises less than proportionately with rising income).[1] If the regression equation relating the two is applied to global average PPP GDP per capita for 2004 ($6,329), the resulting global income elasticity for food at present is 0.655.[2] Even if per capita income grew at 1 percent per year through 2045 (the midpoint of the period considered), the global income elasticity would still be relatively high at 0.612.

Assuming that per capita income grows at 1 percent annually over the next 80 years, and that the average income elasticity is 0.612, then rising

---

1. A weak form would be any income elasticity less than unity.

2. A simple regression yields the following results: $\theta = 0.744$ (100.1) $- 1.4 \times 10^{-5}$ (−34.7) y^*, adjusted $R^2 = 0.95$ (t-statistics in parentheses), where θ is income elasticity of food demand and y^* is PPP per capita GDP in dollars.

income per capita should boost demand for food by a factor of $\lambda_y = 1.63$, coincidentally the same as the medium population expansion factor.[3]

Total demand for food at unchanged real prices would thus rise by a factor that is the multiple of the expansion factor for population and the expansion factor for per capita income, or $\lambda^D = \lambda_N \lambda_y = 1.63 \times 1.63 = 2.66$ for the medium population growth case and $2.28 \times 1.63 = 3.72$ for the high population growth case.

On the supply side, one positive influence and two negative influences can be identified. The positive influence is secular rise in yield from technological change. The negative influences are diversion of agricultural land from food production to the production of energy crops and (certainly by 2085) the impact of global warming.

For land diversion to biomass, a recent study of future energy technologies by the International Energy Agency states the following (IEA 2006, 289):

> Conventional biofuel production requires about 1% of all arable land and yields about 1% of global transportation fuels. If 100% of the fuel requirements for world transport were derived from conventional biofuels, the land requirement would reach 1.4 gigahectares, an amount equivalent to all of the world's arable land. For this reason, even if large existing portions of pasture land could be converted to cropland, competition among conventional biofuel production and food production appears to be inevitable.

The study also notes that sugarcane ethanol is already (more than) competitive with oil at $60 per barrel, that grain ethanol (e.g., from maize) would be competitive in relatively large volumes by 2030, and that lignocelluloic ethanol from such crops as switch grass would be competitive in large volumes by 2050. On this basis, it seems reasonable to expect that about one-third or more of agricultural land would be devoted to ethanol by the middle of this century. This means that from the standpoint of diversion of land to biomass for energy, the agricultural supply expansion factor for other crops from the present to the 2080s would be less than unity, at perhaps $\lambda_B = 0.7$.

To examine the prospects for rising agricultural yields from technological change, it is useful to review the record of the past few decades for the major crops and the major producers. Table 6.1 first presents estimates of production of the four most important grains, for the 21 largest-producing countries. The data are annual averages for 2001–04.

By identifying the principal world producers of each major crop, table 6.1 provides a basis for focusing the analysis of trends in agricultural yields on the most important producing countries for each product in

---

3. That is, demand for food per capita would rise at the rate of income growth per capita multiplied by the income elasticity of demand for food, or $1\% \times 0.612$. The expansion factor is thus $\lambda_y = 1.00612^{80} = 1.629$.

Table 6.1   Production of four major crops, by major producers and world, 2001–04 annual average (million metric tons)

Country	Rice	Wheat	Maize	Soybeans	Four crops, wheat-equivalent	Rank
United States	9.7	55.0	256.8	76.4	335.1	1
China	174.6	90.7	120.5	16.2	331.1	2
India	128.7	69.9	13.1	6.5	182.8	3
Brazil	11.1	4.6	41.9	45.9	89.2	4
Argentina	0.8	14.2	15.1	30.8	55.9	5
Indonesia	52.0	0.0	10.3	0.7	47.7	6
France	0.1	35.2	15.3	0.2	47.4	7
Russia	0.5	44.3	2.0	0.4	46.6	8
Canada	0.0	21.6	9.0	2.3	30.7	9
Bangladesh	37.6	1.5	0.1	0.0	29.8	10
Vietnam	34.3	0.0	2.8	0.2	28.1	11
Pakistan	6.8	19.0	2.0	0.0	25.7	12
Germany	0.0	22.1	3.7	0.0	25.0	13
Thailand	25.9	0.0	4.3	0.3	23.0	14
Turkey	0.4	19.6	2.5	0.1	22.0	15
Australia	1.0	20.7	0.4	0.1	21.7	16
Mexico	0.2	0.0	20.2	0.1	18.9	17
Myanmar	22.6	0.1	0.7	0.1	17.7	18
Philippines	13.7	0.0	4.7	0.0	13.9	19
South Africa	0.0	2.0	9.4	0.2	9.6	20
Japan	10.8	0.8	0.0	0.2	9.1	21
Subtotal	530.9	421.2	534.7	180.8	1,411.0	
Top 5	427.2	295.0	454.7	175.8	994.0	
World	589.4	589.5	647.6	188.8	1,716.1	
Shares (percent):						
21 countries	90.1	71.4	82.6	95.8	82.2	
Top 5	72.5	50.0	70.2	93.1	57.9	

Note: Weights: wheat = 1.0, rice = 0.75, maize = 0.78, and soybeans = 0.95.

Source: United Nations FAOSTAT database.

question. The table also shows several important patterns itself, however. First, it reveals substantial concentration in production. The top five producing countries account for about 70 percent of world output of both rice and maize and a surprisingly high 93 percent of world production of soybeans. Wheat production is somewhat less concentrated, but even for this product the top five producers account for half of world output.

Second, the United States and China are approximately tied for first place in agricultural production. This calculation is based on a consolidated wheat-equivalent total of output for the four crops, weighting by average world prices in 2002–05.[4]

Third, again using the consolidated wheat-equivalent, world output is approximately 1.7 billion metric tons for the four major grains, or about 264 kg per person annually (723 grams per day).[5]

Fourth, dietary differences are evident in the table, with heavy reliance on rice in Asia and much greater reliance on wheat and maize in the Western Hemisphere and Europe.

With this rough summary of global agricultural production in hand, relative country weights in production of key commodities can be applied to country-specific estimates of the pace of technological change to arrive at broad aggregates for technological change in global agriculture. Table 6.2 reports average annual yield increases for these crops in each of their major producing countries for 1961–83 and 1984–2005. These rates are estimated using statistical regressions of the logarithm of yield per hectare on time and thus avoid distortion by choice of endpoints.[6]

For each crop, the weighted average pace of increasing yield is obtained by weighting the production shares of the respective countries in the set of major producers examined. The countries are selected for each crop based on the top producing countries shown in table 6.1.

In order to obtain an overall rate of yield increase for the four crops, the weighted averages for each commodity are in turn weighted by the share of the product in global wheat-equivalent production as indicated in table 6.1. The result is a central estimate that these agricultural yields rose at an annual rate of 2.81 percent in 1961–83 and decelerated to an annual increase of 1.57 percent during 1984–2005. This trend is consistent with the stylized fact that globally the green revolution has slowed down somewhat since its heyday in the 1960s.

The final element is now in place for comparing the expansion of agricultural demand through late in the 21st century against the corresponding prospective expansion in supply. Assuming that the pace of increasing yields continues at its rate of the past two decades, or 1.57 percent,

---

4. Average prices in this period, per metric ton, were $132.5 for wheat, $98.8 for rice, $103.7 for maize, and $125.9 for soybeans (IMF 2006).

5. Note that the corresponding "food quantity" estimates in the Food and Agriculture Organization (FAO) data are substantially smaller. For the United States, for example, the FAO estimate under this concept is a total of 692 grams per person per day for four grains (rice, wheat, maize, and soybeans) and three meat types (bovine, chicken, and pig). For India, the corresponding total is only 472 grams (UN FAOSTAT database). The difference from the higher cereal production total reflects primarily the high ratio of grains to meat production for feedgrains, as discussed later.

6. All of the estimates are statistically significant at the 95 percent level or above except for wheat in Australia in both periods.

Table 6.2   Average annual increase in yields per hectare (percent)

Crop/country	1961–83	1984–2005
Wheat		
Argentina	1.19	1.56
Australia	0.21	1.02
Canada	2.09	1.53
China	5.88	1.82
France	3.10	0.98
India	3.70	1.94
United States	1.73	0.83
Weighted average	3.46	1.49
Rice		
Bangladesh	1.10	2.71
China	2.96	0.95
India	1.59	1.50
Indonesia	3.76	0.61
United States	0.87	1.13
Vietnam	0.86	2.95
Weighted average	2.28	1.38
Maize		
Argentina	3.12	3.72
Brazil	1.43	3.47
China	4.63	1.47
Mexico	2.60	2.33
United States	2.12	1.58
Weighted average	2.77	1.83
Soybeans		
Argentina	3.68	1.16
Brazil	2.64	2.45
India	3.46	1.27
United States	0.98	1.34
Weighted average	2.08	1.62
Four crops, wheat-equivalent weights:		
Major producers	2.81	1.57

Source: Calculated from United Nations FAOSTAT database.

then the supply expansion factor from rising yields from 2005 to 2085 amounts to $\lambda_q = (1.0157)^{80} = 3.48$.

In the absence of any influence of global warming, the prospective late-century demand expansion factors would thus be $\lambda^D = 1.63 \times 1.63 = 2.66$ from population (medium case) and rising per capita income, respectively; or $\lambda^D = 2.28 \times 1.63 = 3.72$, for the high population case. In com-

Table 6.3 Meat consumption per capita (kilograms per person per year)

	Beef	Pork	Poultry	Mutton	Total
Industrial countries	21	25	24	2	72
Developing countries	5	11	7	1	24
Memorandum:					
Feed/meat ratio	7	4	2	4	4.1

Source: WorldWatch Institute (1998).

parison, the supply expansion factor would be $\lambda^S = 0.7 \times 3.48 = 2.44$, taking account of the diversion of land area to energy crops (the first factor) and expected increase in yields (the second).

As it turns out, in the central case there is a moderately unfavorable balance between expansion of potential demand (by a factor of 2.66) and expansion of potential supply (2.44), a divergence of almost 10 percent. So even on relatively optimistic grounds, it would be a mistake to be complacent about a sizable loss in future global yields from global warming from levels they would otherwise reach, on grounds that technological change will flood the market with agricultural goods in any event.

There are significant grounds, moreover, for a less optimistic projection. The first reason is that population growth at the high variant would set the ex ante expansion factor at considerably higher for demand (3.72) than for supply (2.44). The second reason is that just as yield increases have slowed down in the past 20 years, they might be expected to slow further in the next eight decades, mainly because the high rates of increase in the developing countries would tend to ease toward rates in the United States, Canada, and other industrial countries as best practices are adopted. If average annual yield increases eased to 1 percent, the yield expansion factor by 2085 would be only 2.22 instead of 3.48, placing the supply expansion factor at only 1.55 after taking account of diversion of land to biomass for energy. In this case, potential demand expansion at unchanged real prices would be almost twice as great as supply expansion at constant prices, even with no loss from global warming.

A third reason why the central calculations may be too optimistic is that they do not explicitly allow for a dietary shift toward meat. Table 6.3 reports estimates of average consumption of meat per capita in industrial and developing countries, along with the feed/meat ratio indicating the number of kilograms of grains required to produce one kilogram of the meat in question. Overall, on average industrial-country consumers eat three times as much meat per capita as developing-country consumers, and it requires four kilograms of grains to produce one kilogram of meat.

In 2004, average PPP income per capita stood at $31,009 for high-income countries and $4,726 for developing (low- and middle-income) countries (World Bank 2006). As a first approximation, then, approximately a sevenfold rise in real per capita income ($31,009 / $4,726 = 6.56) might be expected to generate a threefold rise in per capita consumption of meat (72/24, from table 6.3), with some attendant reduction in direct consumption of grains (likely especially rice). Correspondingly, if on average developing countries' real per capita incomes were to rise at 1 percent annually over the next eight decades, for an increase by a factor of 2.22, their meat consumption per capita could be expected to rise by a factor of approximately 1.6.[7]

These specific calculations somewhat surprisingly give almost an identical increase in demand for meat in developing countries as that obtained for all food applying the estimated income elasticity of 0.612, which in turn would have the implausible implication that rising income would not shift the composition of demand toward meat. So the main calculations of this chapter may not be seriously biased from this standpoint, but if there is a bias, it still seems likely that it is toward an understatement of the rise in demand for crop production because of a failure to take special account of shifting demand toward grain-intensive meat.

In short, the principal uncertainties in the estimates of expansion factors above are all on the side of downside risk to the late century balance between potential agricultural demand and supply. These considerations reinforce the main conclusion that future technological change is no panacea for addressing concerns about the adverse impact of global warming.

---

7. With $c = y^\gamma$ where c is per capita meat consumption, y is real PPP income per capita, and h and d refer to high-income and developing countries, respectively, then $c_h/c_d = 3$ when $y_h/y_d = 6.56$ implies that $\gamma = 0.58$ and thus that a rise in developing-country income per capita (y_d) by a factor of 2.22 would boost per capita consumption of meat in developing countries by the factor $2.22^{0.58} = 1.59$.

7

Conclusion

This study has applied what might be called a consensus estimate by six climate models of changes in temperature and precipitation by 2070–99, by averaging their results as converted to a standardized grid size of 2° latitude by 3° longitude. Models relating agricultural impact to temperature and precipitation (mostly of the Ricardian variety) have then been applied to these changes at the standardized grid level and averaged to obtain agricultural impacts at the level of more than 100 countries, regions, or subzones within the largest countries. Projections of agricultural impact from a suite of alternative crop models and climate models have also served as the second framework for examining future agricultural impact of unabated global warming.

The two central results of these estimates are, first, that at least modest global agricultural damage can be expected from business as usual climate change by late in this century, with losses about 15 percent greater if the carbon fertilization effect fails to materialize; and second, the damages will be disproportionately concentrated in developing countries. The diagnosis of damage suggests that it would be a risky strategy to do nothing about global warming on grounds that some studies have estimated that there would be global agricultural gains rather than losses for the first few degrees of warming. The magnitude of global land surface warming by the 2080s under business as usual warming would be 4.4°C (weighting by farm area), and precipitation would rise only 2.9 percent (table 4.3). This combination would go far beyond optimal temperatures in the low latitudes and also in the mid-latitudes.

Table 7.1 presents an overview of the aggregate estimates of this study. The estimate for global productive capacity change including carbon fertilization is a decrease of about 3 percent. This reduction probably understates potential losses, however. If the carbon fertilization effect (already

Table 7.1 Summary estimates for impact of global warming on world agricultural output potential by the 2080s (percent)

	Without carbon fertilization	With carbon fertilization
Global		
Output-weighted	−15.9	−3.2
Population-weighted	−18.2	−6.0
Median by country	−23.6	−12.1
Industrial countries	−6.3	7.7
Developing countries[a]	−21.0	−9.1
Median	−25.8	−14.7
Africa	−27.5	−16.6
Asia	−19.3	−7.2
Middle East North Africa	−21.2	−9.4
Latin America	−24.3	−12.9

a. Excluding Europe.

Source: Tables 5.8 to 5.10.

constrained to a 15 percent increase in these estimates, lower than in some earlier estimates) failed to materialize, the losses would be estimated at about 16 percent. The Ricardian models probably err in the direction of optimism by implicitly counting on availability of more water for irrigation under circumstances in which there could easily be less water. Neither the Ricardian nor the crop models deal explicitly with increased damage from pests or more frequent and more severe extreme weather events (floods and droughts).

For several reasons, then, a prudent range for impact on global agricultural capacity by the 2080s could thus easily involve greater damage than the direct preferred estimates in this study and could perhaps lie in the range of reductions of 10 to 25 percent. Even if global productive potential were cut by only 3 percent, the results find an inequitable distribution of the effects, driven by the fact that the poor countries tend to be located in lower latitudes, where temperatures are already at or above optimal levels. On average developing countries would suffer losses of 9 percent, and median losses for these countries would amount to 15 percent. Confirming previous studies, the results here indicate that the losses would be most severe in Africa (estimated here at 17 percent average loss and 18 percent median loss in agricultural capacity) and Latin America (13 percent average and 16 percent median loss). The losses would be much larger if the benefits from carbon fertilization failed to materialize (averaging about 21 percent for all developing countries, 28 percent for Africa, and 24 percent for Latin America).

In terms of geopolitics, the results here are particularly important for the cases of China and India. China is already the second-largest emitter of carbon dioxide (after the United States but ahead of the European Union), and its cooperation will surely be crucial to effective action against global warming. Although the central estimate in this study finds China a modest gainer in agriculture under business as usual (increase in agricultural capacity by about 7 percent with carbon fertilization), the estimate turns to a loss (7 percent reduction in agricultural capacity) if carbon fertilization effects do not materialize or are offset by excluded damages. For India, there is no ambiguity: Prospective losses are massive (on the order of 30 to 40 percent).

For Australia, one of the two steadfast opponents of the principal international initiative to date against global warming (the Kyoto Protocol), the results also suggest that a more positive position on global warming abatement would be in its long-term interests. The estimates for Australia indicate losses of around 16 percent even with carbon fertilization (with potentially much larger losses suggested by the Ricardian estimates). As for the United States, the other principal opponent, although the estimates show an aggregate gain of 8 percent in the case with carbon fertilization, they indicate a comparable loss (6 percent) if carbon fertilization is excluded. Moreover, regional losses are pronounced: by about 30 to 35 percent in the Southeast and in the Southwest Plains, if carbon fertilization is excluded (and about 20 to 25 percent if it is included; table 5.8).

For an initial phase of modest global warming, average impacts on agriculture are ambiguous and may be benign globally on average, but it would be a serious mistake to infer from such a diagnosis that little should be done to curb climate change. This study has sought to sharpen analysis of agricultural impacts by bringing to bear rigorous and detailed estimates available for regional climate change and quantitative models of agricultural impact. The new estimates in this study strongly suggest that by late in the present century the global effects under business as usual global warming would turn malignant for agriculture globally and that the damages would be the most severe and begin the soonest where they can least be afforded: in the developing countries. Moreover, it would be a serious mistake to downplay the risks of future agricultural losses from global warming on grounds that technological change, for example in new seed varieties, will offset any negative climatic effects. A close look at the pace of yield increases in the past two decades, combined with attention to the prospective rise in global food demand and the conversion of a substantial portion of agricultural land from food to energy crops, suggests that there is little margin for complacency about erosion in agricultural potential from global warming.

Finally, it should be emphasized that the estimates of this study understate potential damages from another crucial standpoint: They take a snapshot of time at the 2080s, yet baseline damages could be expected to continue to grow throughout the following two centuries before atmospheric concentrations of carbon eventually would begin to decline once again from mixing into the deep ocean (Cline 1992). Even if carbon emissions collapsed after the 2080s back to well below today's levels, the delay of some three decades for ocean thermal lag means that the warming and impacts estimated in this study would substantially underestimate the eventual equilibrium warming and damages.

APPENDICES

Appendix A
Standardizing Global Grids
of Climate Change Data

This appendix describes a technique for standardizing global grids in order to compare climate data produced by different global circulation models (GCMs). The data of various climate modeling centers, including changes in average temperature and precipitation, are available through the Data Distribution Centre of the Intergovernmental Panel on Climate Change (IPCC).[1] Every climate modeling center chooses a grid for its unique GCM, and the resolution in latitude and longitude varies greatly across GCM grids. To compare current observed climate (the 1961–90 average) and future climate simulations from multiple sources, the observed and model output data must be scaled to a standard grid (G). The task is to link the standard grid to the grid of observed data and the grids of six GCMs. This task is accomplished through pair-wise mapping to G from each of the other seven grids, resulting in one representation of current global climate and six representations of future global climate scaled to the same grid. Mapping to G from the grid of the CCSR/NIES climate model (M_{CCSR}; Emori et al. 1999) will serve as an example of the standardization process.

G is defined to have 90 latitudes and 120 longitudes; it comprises 10,800 cells, each with dimension $2° \times 3°$, spanning the $180° \times 360°$ of the globe. Each cell is identified by two values, $LatID_G \in [1, 90]$ and $LngID_G \in [1, 120]$. The cell with $LatID_G = 1$ and $LngID_G = 1$ is just below the North Pole and bordered on its west side by the prime meridian, with $LatID_G$ in-

---

1. The database is available at http://ipcc-ddc.cru.uea.ac.uk (accessed on June 23, 2006). The Web site is maintained for the IPCC by the Climate Research Unit, University of East Anglia, United Kingdom.

creasing southward and $LngID_G$ increasing eastward. M_{CCSR} has 32 latitudes and 64 longitudes; its cells are 5.625° × 5.625°, and the cell with identifiers $LatID_M = 1$ and $LngID_M = 1$ also falls alongside the North Pole and prime meridian. With G and M_{CCSR} now defined, a subgrid is created specifically for this pair of grids. The subgrid has a finer resolution than both G and M_{CCSR} and its subcells can be repeated some number of times to exactly fill both a cell in G and a cell in M_{CCSR}.

The dimensions of a subcell are determined by the greatest common divisor (GCD) of the dimensions of a G cell and an M_{CCSR} cell. In the direction of latitude:

$$\text{height of subcell} = \text{GCD } (2, 5.625) = 0.125°$$

and similarly for longitude:

$$\text{width of subcell} = \text{GCD } (3, 5.625) = 0.375°.$$

Thus the greatest common subcell is 0.125° × 0.375°. Some additional simple calculations characterize the relationship of the subgrid to G and to M_{CCSR} and allow for systematic identification of each unique subcell. Let r_G be the number of rows of subcells in a row in G, c_G be the number of columns of subcells in a column in G, r_M be the number of rows of subcells in a row in M_{CCSR}, and c_M be the number of columns of subcells in a column in M_{CCSR}. These ratios are calculated as follows:

$$r_G = \frac{\text{height G cell}}{\text{GCD (height G cell, height M cell)}} = \frac{2}{0.125} = 16$$

$$c_G = \frac{\text{width G cell}}{\text{GCD (width G cell, width M cell)}} = \frac{3}{0.375} = 8$$

$$r_M = \frac{\text{height M cell}}{\text{GCD (height G cell, height M cell)}} = \frac{5.625}{0.125} = 45$$

$$c_M = \frac{\text{width M cell}}{\text{GCD (width G cell, width M cell)}} = \frac{5.625}{0.375} = 15$$

Thus there are 1,382,400 (= 16 × 90 × 8 × 120 = 45 × 32 × 15 × 64) subcells in the subgrid.

Each unique subcell is defined by a $LatID_M$, $LngID_M$, LatSubID, and LngSubID. The SubID values are determined in reference to the cells in M_{CCSR}, so LatSubID ∈ [1, r_M = 45] and LngSubID ∈ [1, c_M = 15]. LatSubID and

LngSubID describe the position of a unique subcell out of 675 (= 45 × 15) possible subcells within an M_{CCSR} cell. Thus $LatID_M$, $LngID_M$, $LatSubID$, and $LngSubID$ together define a unique subcell within the entire M_{CCSR} grid. A pair of equations takes this four-part subcell address as the input and returns the two-part address of a G cell, completing the initial mapping between G and M_{CCSR}. The mapping is expressed as two piece-wise functions, one for latitude and one for longitude:

$LatID_G(LatID_M, LatSubID) =$

$$
\begin{cases}
(LatID_M - 1)\left(\dfrac{r_M}{r_G}\right) + (LatSubID)\left(\dfrac{1}{r_G}\right) \\
\qquad\qquad if \left\lfloor (LatID_M - 1)\left(\dfrac{r_M}{r_G}\right) + (LatSubID)\left(\dfrac{1}{r_G}\right)\right\rfloor \\
\qquad\qquad - (LatID_M - 1)\left(\dfrac{r_M}{r_G}\right) + (LatSubID)\left(\dfrac{1}{r_G}\right) = 0 \\[2em]
1 + \left\lfloor (LatID_M - 1)\left(\dfrac{r_M}{r_G}\right) + (LatSubID)\left(\dfrac{1}{r_G}\right)\right\rfloor \\
\qquad\qquad if \left\lfloor (LatID_M - 1)\left(\dfrac{r_M}{r_G}\right) + (LatSubID)\left(\dfrac{1}{r_G}\right)\right\rfloor \\
\qquad\qquad - (LatID_M - 1)\left(\dfrac{r_M}{r_G}\right) + (LatSubID)\left(\dfrac{1}{r_G}\right) \neq 0
\end{cases}
$$

$LngID_G(LngID_M, LngSubID) =$

$$
\begin{cases}
(LngID_M - 1)\left(\dfrac{c_M}{c_G}\right) + (LngSubID)\left(\dfrac{1}{c_G}\right) \\
\qquad\qquad if \left\lfloor (LngID_M - 1)\left(\dfrac{c_M}{c_G}\right) + (LngSubID)\left(\dfrac{1}{c_G}\right)\right\rfloor \\
\qquad\qquad - (LngID_M - 1)\left(\dfrac{c_M}{c_G}\right) + (LngSubID)\left(\dfrac{1}{c_G}\right) = 0 \\[2em]
1 + \left\lfloor (LngID_M - 1)\left(\dfrac{c_M}{c_G}\right) + (LngSubID)\left(\dfrac{1}{r_G}\right)\right\rfloor \\
\qquad\qquad if \left\lfloor (LngID_M - 1)\left(\dfrac{c_M}{c_G}\right) + (LngSubID)\left(\dfrac{1}{c_G}\right)\right\rfloor \\
\qquad\qquad - (LngID_M - 1)\left(\dfrac{r_M}{r_G}\right) + (LngSubID)\left(\dfrac{1}{c_G}\right) \neq 0
\end{cases}
$$

where ⌊ ⌋ is the operator returning only the integer portion of its argument.

A change in temperature (dT) and precipitation (dP) from base period 1961–90 to the period 2070–99, simulated by the CCSR/NIES model, is associated with each cell in the M_{CCSR} grid. With the mapping from cells in M_{CCSR} to subcells and then to cells in G completed, it is possible to represent the model-derived changes in climate variables over the standard grid. A simple average of the climate data in the 128 (= 16 × 8) subcells within a G cell is computed, associating a dT and a dP based on the CCSR/NIES simulations with each G cell. Because of the curvature of the earth's surface, the area of a subcell of fixed degree dimensions is greater near the equator than near the poles; the area increases with the absolute value of latitude. However, the difference in the area of a subcell with $LatSubID = 1$ and a subcell with $LatSubID = 45$ within a given cell is insignificant. Therefore, the average of climate data over the subcells within a G cell does not need to be weighted by area. The expressions for dT and dP are simply:

$$\sum_{LatSubID,\ LngSubID=1}^{r_G,c_G} \frac{dT}{r_G \times c_G} \quad \text{and} \quad \sum_{LatSubID,\ LngSubID=1}^{r_G,c_G} \frac{dP}{r_G \times c_G}.$$

In the case of M_{CCSR}, $r_G = 16$ and $c_G = 8$.

The same method is implemented with the five additional GCMs for which data are available and with the observed 1961–90 data, all distributed by the IPCC. The GCMs are ECHAM4/OPYC3, HadCM3, CSIRO-Mk2, GFDL-R30, and CGCM2, along with CCSR/NIES (see table 4.1 for full names of these models). Unlike the other GCM grids, in the grid of the HadCM3 model the equator bisects a row of cells rather than falling on the boundary of two rows. The standardization method can still be applied after shifting and renumbering the latitudes of the HadCM3 grid to correct the inconsistency. For all grids, the standardization does become slightly unreliable very near the poles. The latitude lines in all of the grid systems are infinitesimally closer together as the absolute value of latitude climbs into the 80s, and some of the grids reach 1° or 2° closer to 90° than others. However, these polar areas are not included in the economic impact analysis because of the absence of any land that would be economically relevant under plausible levels of warming. Potentially habitable land is easily captured within the domain of the standardization method.

Appendix B
Mapping Grid Cells to Countries

This study's database of 1961–90 and 2070–99 climates is based on a grid of 2° latitude × 3° longitude cells (standard grid G). Matching these cells with national borders is done using the publicly available Global Population Distribution Database (Li 1996).[1] This database was created for geographic analysis of global population but also includes a table that maps 1° × 1° cells to countries. In cases where parts of more than one country (or a combination of land and ocean) are contained in the same cell, the database assigns the cell proportionally—for example, 32 percent of a cell to Argentina, 9 percent to Brazil, and 59 percent to Uruguay. Data on the proportional share of each cell in the total area of a given country are also included—for example, that same cell contains 0.122 percent of Argentina's land area, 0.011 percent of Brazil's, and 3.695 percent of Uruguay's.

Description of the Global Population Distribution Database

The database consists of three datasets compiled in dBase IV format.[2] The first dataset contains global population in 1990 on a 1° × 1° grid.

1. The work was supported by Environment Canada and the United Nations Environment Program—Global Resource Information Database (UNEP GRID) and conducted at Environment Canada. The second dataset in this source, "GridCtry," is used here for country assignment. The dataset is distributed by the United States Geological Survey EROS Data Center, which is the North American base of the UNEP GRID. The data and information are available at http://grid2.cr.usgs.gov/globalpop/1-degree/description.php3 and http://grid2.cr.usgs.gov/metadata/unep/grid/gridctry.html.

2. This description of the national population grid database is the same as that provided by its creators but is reformatted for readability.

The second, used for this study, defines the relationship between grid cells and countries. The third dataset contains data on rural population distribution.

Definition of Grid Code Number

Grid code number = $(j * 1000) + i$

- j: row number starting at 1 for 90°S to 89°S latitude to 180 for 89°N to 90°N latitude
- i: column number starting at 1 for 180°W to 179°W longitude to 360 for 179°E to180°E longitude.

The latitude and longitude of the center of the grid cell are given by

$$latitude = (j - 91) + 0.5$$
$$longitude = (i - 181) + 0.5$$

Dataset 2 (GridCtry.dbf): Relationship Between Grid Cells and Countries

Fields:

- Grid   Grid code number
- Cover-Id   Cover ID number
  - "0":   All covered by sea
  - "1":   Entirely contained in one country
  - "2":   Shared by two countries
  - "3":   Shared by three countries
  - "4":   Shared by four countries
  - "10":   Shared by one country and ocean
  - "20":   Shared by two countries and ocean
  - "30":   Shared by three countries and ocean
  - "40":   Shared by four countries and ocean
- UNCode2   United Nations standard ISO country codes
- Country   Country/region name
- Rate-in-Country (%)   Percentage of the area of a country contained in each grid cell
- Rate-in-Grid (%)   Percentage of the area of the grid cell occupied by country or ocean

Number of records:	25,540
Number of cells:	12,200
Total number of countries:	217

Mapping from 1° Cell Assignments to National Climate Data

The first step is to convert the cell-to-country data in the GridCtry dataset in terms of latitude and longitude into the present study's standardized grid structure. Following the equations in the definitions above, the grid code numbers are first broken into column number i and row number j.

Example: Grid code number = 139189

In Excel, RIGHT ([cell containing 139189],3) = 189 = i.
That is, the three rightmost characters of the grid code number give the column number i.
LEFT ([cell containing 139189],3) = (139189 − 189) ÷ 1,000 = 139 = j.
That is, the three leftmost characters of the grid code number equal the row number j.

Next, i and j are converted into degrees to obtain the coordinates of the midpoint of each cell using the given equations.

Example: Grid code number = 139189

i = 189 => midpoint longitude = $(i - 181) + 0.5 = 8.5°E$
j = 139 => midpoint latitude = $(j - 91) + 0.5 = 48.5°N$

Returning to the standardized 2° × 3° grid (G), each latitude value (representing the midline through a 2° tall row of cells) is assigned two corresponding latitude values (representing the midlines through the two 1° tall rows of cells contained in the 2° tall row). This is done in Access by creating a table of the latitude values in G with two entries for each value. Consider the first three rows of grid G. They are centered at the 89°, 87°, and 85° latitudes, respectively. The corresponding latitude cells in the Environment Canada (E) grids will be centered at 89.5° and 88.5° for the first, 87.5° and 86.5° for the second, and 85.5° and 84.5° for the third. Therefore, rather than 89, 87, 85, the table contains 89, 89, 87, 87, 85, 85, and so on, with the first instance of each value assigned a "1" and the second instance of each number assigned a "2." The midpoint latitude values for the 1° cells contained within the G cells can then be easily generated.

G	Instance	E
89	1	If "1", 89 + 0.5; otherwise if "2", 89 − 0.5 = 89.5
89	2	If "1", 89 + 0.5; otherwise if "2", 89 − 0.5 = 88.5
87	1	If "1", 87 + 0.5; otherwise if "2", 87 − 0.5 = 87.5
87	2	If "1", 87 + 0.5; otherwise if "2", 87 − 0.5 = 86.5
85	1	If "1", 85 + 0.5; otherwise if "2", 85 − 0.5 = 85.5
85	2	If "1", 85 + 0.5; otherwise if "2", 85 − 0.5 = 84.5

The same is done for longitude, but this time fitting three columns of 1° cells from E into each column in G.

G	Instance	E
1.5	1	If "1", 1.5 − 1; if "2", 1.5; otherwise if "3", 1.5 + 1 = 0.5
1.5	2	If "1", 1.5 − 1; if "2", 1.5; otherwise if "3", 1.5 + 1 = 1.5
1.5	3	If "1", 1.5 − 1; if "2", 1.5; otherwise if "3", 1.5 + 1 = 2.5
4.5	1	If "1", 4.5 − 1; if "2", 4.5; otherwise if "3", 4.5 + 1 = 3.5
4.5	2	If "1", 4.5 − 1; if "2", 4.5; otherwise if "3", 4.5 + 1 = 4.5
4.5	3	If "1", 4.5 − 1; if "2", 4.5; otherwise if "3", 4.5 + 1 = 5.5
7.5	1	If "1", 7.5 − 1; if "2", 7.5; otherwise if "3", 7.5 + 1 = 6.5
7.5	2	If "1", 7.5 − 1; if "2", 7.5; otherwise if "3", 7.5 + 1 = 7.5
7.5	3	If "1", 7.5 − 1; if "2", 7.5; otherwise if "3", 7.5 + 1 = 8.5

With the 1961–90 and 2070–99 climate data organized in 2° × 3° cells and the correspondence of each 1° cell to a unique 2° × 3° cell, it is possible to fill a 1° × 1° grid with the temperature and precipitation data by adding four columns (two climate variables: temperature, T, and precipitation, P, for each of two periods: 1961–90 base and 2070–99 future) to a table containing the latitude and longitude information from the previous exercise. Note that the base period climate data are actuals, and the future climate data are the base values plus the average changes in temperature and precipitation from base to 2070–99 across six GCMs, for the harmonized grid G (see appendix A). Now the components are in place to create a table with the following fields:

1° Lat	Latitude coordinate of midpoint
1° Lng	Longitude coordinate of midpoint
2080s T	Future temperature in a given 1° cell (six-model average)
2080s P	Future precipitation in a given 1° cell (six-model average)
6190 T	Base temperature in a given 1° cell (observed)
6190 P	Base precipitation in a given 1° cell (observed)
UNCode2	United Nations numerical country code
Country	Name of the country
Rate in Country	Percent of the country's total area contained in the cell

Note that if a cell contains more than just one country, say, two countries and the ocean, there will be multiple records for this cell, specifically three records in this example. The first six fields will be the same for all three records, but the last three will be different.

The final step is to query the above table to calculate base and future T and P for each country (or, for the largest countries, each subzone) as a weighted average of the T and P in the component cells, with the weights equal to the shares of the component cells in a country's land area. For example, for any country, say, Germany, baseline T = sum (baseline T * rate in country * 0.01), summed over all cells that contain some portion of Germany. The result is temperature and precipitation, for the 1961–90 base period and 2070–99 future period, in about 220 countries, islands, and territories.

Appendix C
Calculating the Geographical
Area of the Grid Cell

For purposes such as estimating global average land surface changes in temperature and precipitation, it is necessary to know the area of the cells of the grid used in the climate projection. Each cell is an isosceles trapezoid with parallel top and bottom and sides sloping slightly inward poleward. Considering that the distance from pole to pole along any longitudinal line is πR where R is the earth's radius (6,378.17 km), in a grid with vertical resolution of $v°$ and hence $180/v = N$ rows, the height of each trapezoid will be a constant $h = (\pi R)/N$.[1]

The average width of each cell will be the circumference of the circle around the earth's surface perpendicular to the earth's axis at the average latitude of the cell in question, divided by the number of columns. With grid horizontal resolution of $k°$, there are $360/k = M$ columns. At the equator, cell width is $(2\pi R)/M = w_e$. It can be shown that at latitude of degree α (North or South), the circumference of the latitudinal circle around the

---

1. Approximately. Because h as calculated in this way is the length of the vertical side of the trapezoid rather than the height, or the hypotenuse rather than the height of the right triangle having base equal to one-half the difference between cell width at the equatorward side of the cell and that at the poleward side, true height h^* would be slightly smaller. However, the difference is minimal. For example, in the standard grid of this study (90 rows × 120 columns), cell height h is 222.64 km. Cell width is 334 km at the equator, 289.2 km at 30° latitude, and 167 km at 60° latitude. At this resolution, true cell height is $h^* = 222.62$ km at 30° latitude and 222.58 km at 60° latitude, extremely close to the approximation h. Because this study's calculation of country area in each cell area is at a finer 1° × 1° resolution level (see appendix B), any bias is even smaller.

earth's surface is $(\cos \alpha)(2\pi R)$. Correspondingly, the average width of the grid cell in row i will be $w_i = (\cos Lat_i)(2\pi R)/M$, where Lat_i is the latitude coordinate in degrees of the midpoint of row i. Using the radian rather than the degree cosine operator, and converting α degrees to $\alpha(\pi/180)$ radians, regardless of the cell longitude the area of the cell in row i and column j of the grid is then hw_i in square kilometers, or

$$area_{i,j} = 2\pi^2 R^2 \cdot \cos\left(\frac{\pi}{180} Lat_i\right) \cdot \frac{1}{N \cdot M}$$

The total area covered by all the cells is of course the total surface area of the earth, approximately 510,000,000 square kilometers. Summing down through each row and scaling up this sum by the total number of columns, the earth's area can be expressed as

$$area_{N,M} = M \cdot \sum_i^N 2\pi^2 R^2 \cdot \cos\left(\frac{\pi}{180} Lat_i\right) \cdot \frac{1}{N \cdot M}$$

$$= \sum_i^N 2\pi^2 R^2 \cdot \cos\left(\frac{\pi}{180} Lat_i\right) \cdot \frac{1}{N}$$

Appendix D
Definitions of Countries, Regions, and Subzones

This study estimates agricultural outcomes in 116 countries, regions, and subzones (CRSs). Seventy of the most populous countries are each included individually. A region is two or more countries that are smaller (in population terms) and are grouped by geographic proximity, with consideration also given to similarity of climate and economy. There are a total of ten regions composed of 39 countries. Seven countries with large land area and thus great agricultural significance are broken up into multiple subzones. These countries, with their respective number of subzones, are Australia (5), Brazil (3), Canada (5), China (7), India (4), Russia (7), and the United States (7). The subzones are determined by climate, though their boundaries are primarily formed by straight latitude and longitude lines for simplicity. Table D.1 shows the subzones of the seven large countries, indicating their minimum and maximum coordinates for midpoints of grid cells at 1° resolution. For longitudes, positive figures are degrees east of the prime meridian, 0 to 180; negative figures are degrees west of the prime meridian, 0 to –180. For latitudes, positive figures are degrees north of the equator, 0 to 90; negative figures are degrees south of the equator, 0 to –90. Box D.1 lists the countries that constitute regional aggregates treated as single CRSs.

Table D.1   Subzones of largest countries

Country/subzone	Latitude range	Longitude range
Australia		
Southeast	−29.5 to −43.5	140.5 to 153.5
Southwest	−29.5 to −37.5	114.5 to 139.5
Central East	−19.5 to −28.5	140.5 to 153.5
Central West	−19.5 to −28.5	112.5 to 139.5
North	−11.5 to −18.5	113.5 to 140.5
Brazil		
Amazon	−15.5 to 5.5	−73.5 to −50.5
Northeast	−15.5 to 1.5	−49.5 to −34.5
Southern	−33.5 to −16.5	−60.5 to −39.5
Canada		
Arctic	67.5 to 82.5	−140.5 to −61.5
Central	49.5 to 59.5	−113.5 to −95.5
Northwest Territories	60.5 to 66.5	−140.5 to −61.5
Pacific Coast	48.5 to 59.5	−138.5 to −105.5
Southeast	41.5 to 59.5	−94.5 to −52.5
China		
Beijing Northeast	38.5 to 53.5	112.5 to 134.5
Central	28.5 to 37.5	100.5 to 111.5
Hong Kong Southeast	21.5 to 27.5	112.5 to 121.5
Northwest	38.5 to 49.5	73.5 to 111.5
South Central	18.5 to 27.5	97.5 to 111.5
Tibetan Plateau	25.5 to 37.5	74.5 to 99.5
Yellow Sea	28.5 to 37.5	112.5 to 122.5
India		
Northeast	22.5 to 35.5	77.5 to 97.5
Northwest	22.5 to 34.5	68.5 to 76.5
Southeast	8.5 to 21.5	77.5 to 89.5
Southwest	8.5 to 21.5	69.5 to 76.5
Russia		
Caspian Black Sea	41.5 to 52.5	31.5 to 54.5
Far Eastern	43.5 to 75.5	−179.5 to 179.5
North European	53.5 to 80.5	19.5 to 54.5
North Urals Siberia	61.5 to 81.5	55.5 to 95.5
Northeast Siberia	62.5 to 81.5	96.5 to 141.5
South Urals Siberia	49.5 to 60.5	55.5 to 95.5
Southeast Siberia	42.5 to 61.5	96.5 to 141.5
United States		
Alaska	51.5 to 71.5	−178.5 to −130.5
Lakes and Northeast	38.5 to 49.5	−95.5 to −67.5
Pacific Northwest	42.5 to 48.5	−124.5 to −114.5
Rockies and Plains	38.5 to 48.5	−113.5 to −96.5
Southeast	24.5 to 37.5	−95.5 to −75.5
South Pacific Coast	32.5 to 41.5	−124.5 to −114.5
Southwest Plains	25.5 to 37.5	−113.5 to −96.5

Box D.1   Multicountry regions

Central America
  Costa Rica
  Guatemala
  El Salvador
  Honduras
  Nicaragua
  Panama

Central Europe
  Austria
  Hungary
  Switzerland
  Czech Republic
  Slovakia

Other Central Asia
  Turkmenistan
  Tajikistan
  Kyrgyzstan

Other Equatorial Africa
  Republic of the Congo
  Gabon
  Equatorial Guinea
  Central African Republic

Other Horn of Africa
  Somalia
  Djibouti

Other South America
  Bolivia
  Paraguay

Other Southern Africa
  Namibia
  Botswana

Other West Africa
  Guinea
  Guinea Bissau
  Liberia
  Sierra Leone

Scandinavia
  Norway
  Sweden
  Finland
  Denmark

Southeastern Europe
  Albania
  Bosnia and Herzegovina
  Bulgaria
  Croatia
  Macedonia
  Serbia and Montenegro
  Slovenia

Appendix E
Estimating Farm Area and
Agricultural Output by
Country, Region, and Subzone

Agricultural Output

The value of agricultural output in 2003 in millions of US dollars is obtained by multiplying the dollar value of country GDP (at market prices, not purchasing power parity [PPP]) by the percent of GDP reported as originating in the agricultural sector, as estimated by the World Bank (2005, table 4.2). The exception is for member countries of the Organization for Economic Cooperation and Development (OECD), for which more precise estimates appear to exist in OECD (2005) and are used here.[1] For multicountry regions, country-level agricultural output value from the same sources is aggregated to obtain the regional total. For subzones within the large countries, attribution of output value is developed as described below.

Geographical Versus Farm Land Area

The geographical land area of each country, region, or subzone is obtained from the mapping methodology described in appendix B. Farmland area

---

1. For the United States, for example, World Bank (2005) reports agricultural output at 2 percent of GDP in 2003. The OECD (2005) places it at 0.9 percent. The latter is closer to the value reported in US national accounts, $88 billion or 0.80 percent in 2003 (BEA 2006, table 1.3.5).

can be much smaller than geographical area, because of land in forests, mountains, deserts, and other nonfarm areas. The preferred source for this study's estimate of farm area is the set of country agricultural censuses compiled by the Food and Agriculture Organization (FAO 2006a). For each country, the most recent available agricultural census is used for the estimate of land area in farms, typically reported together with the number of farms and distribution by farm size. For numerous countries, census estimates are not available. Instead, FAO estimates of "arable land" plus land in "permanent crops" (e.g., fruit trees) are used (FAO 2005). For the 49 individual countries (table 4.2 in chapter 4) for which both sets of FAO data are available, the median ratio of farm area to total land area is 32.5 percent. The median ratio of arable land plus permanent crop land to farm land area is 96.6 percent, although there is wide variation (from 8 percent to around 200 percent), reflecting differences in the data sources. For the large agricultural countries, arable land plus permanent crop land tends to be considerably smaller than farmland area, with the ratio of the former to the latter being about 11 percent in Australia; 20 percent in Argentina, Brazil, and New Zealand; and 47 percent in the United States (but 66 percent in France and 77 percent in Canada).

The approach adopted here is simply to accept the larger of the two estimates (farm land, from the census, or arable land plus land in permanent crops) as the best estimate of the relevant farm area in each country. Output per hectare of farm area is then simply the estimate of total agricultural output at the country level divided by the estimate of farm area for the country in question. For multicountry regions, aggregates across the member countries are obtained for farm area and agricultural output.

Subzone Farm Area and Output

Subzone data for farm area and output for the larger countries are relatively accessible for Australia, Brazil, China, and the United States but not for Canada, India, and especially Russia.

For Australia, the Australian Bureau of Statistics (ABS 2005) provides data on farm area and value of agricultural products sold by province, and for all the provinces there is an obvious mapping to the specific geographical subzone (although for two provinces, the amounts are divided evenly between the zones they straddle).

For Brazil, data on farm area and output are available by major geographical region from the agricultural census of 1995–96 (IBGE 2006). With minor reallocations, these regions correspond to the subzones used here (see appendix D).

For China, a special compilation by the US Department of Agriculture (ERS 2006a) provides data on production (in 2003) and cultivated area (in 1996) by province, and for almost all provinces there is an obvious mapping to the specific geographical subzone (although for one province the amounts are divided evenly between the two zones it straddles).

For the United States, the agricultural census of 2002 provides state-level data on farm area and value of agricultural products sold (USDA 2004). The states map relatively clearly into the subzones used here.[2]

In all four countries, the proportional distributions of farm area or output data from the source in question across the subzones is applied to the country total farm area and output estimate from this study to obtain the subzone farm area and output estimates.

For Canada, Statistics Canada (2007) reports farm area by province from the 2001 agricultural census. The provinces broadly conform to subzones used here (but Alberta is divided evenly between Canada Southeast and Canada Pacific Coast). Because the census reports zero farms or farm area above latitude 60°N, farm area and output for this study's subzones Canada Arctic and Canada Northwest Territories are set to zero. In the absence of data on output in each province, it is assumed that the percentage distribution across provinces is identical for output and farm area.

For India, the US Department of Agriculture (ERS 2006b) indicates that almost the entire land area of the country is in cropland. Accordingly, the direct estimate of the land area in each subzone from the mapping of grid cells in this study provides the basis for the proportional distribution of farm land, and the corresponding hectare amounts are obtained by applying these proportions to the census estimate of India's total farm area (FAO 2006a). Land area is once again used as a proxy for output, which, as for Canada, results in a uniform estimate of output per hectare for each subzone.

Subnational data are least available for Russia. In this case, a rough approximation is made by applying broad ranges for the density of permanent crops plus arable land indicated in a country mapping summary by the FAO (2006b). These ranges are wide, and the point estimate chosen for each region is set within the respective range such that the aggregate farm land area for Russia as a whole equals a target estimate.[3] This estimate in turn is set at twice the FAO (2005) estimate for arable land plus permanent crops. Arable land and permanent crops are placed at only 7 percent of total land area, so even the doubling to include pasture (approximately the relationship in the United States) leaves a relatively low estimate for the amount of farm land in Russia.

---

2. Note, however, that Colorado, Kansas, and Utah are each divided evenly between subzones US Rockies and Plains and US Southwest and Plains (see table 4.2); Missouri between Lakes and Northeast and US Southeast; and Oklahoma between US Southeast and US Southwest and Plains.

3. The resulting fractions of total land area in farms for the subzones used in this study are as follows: Caspian Black Sea, 55 percent; Far Eastern, 5 percent; North European, 20 percent; North Urals Siberia, 5 percent; Northeast Siberia, 5 percent; South Urals Siberia, 25 percent; and Southeast Siberia, 15 percent.

Estimates

Table E.1 reports the resulting estimates of farm area and agricultural output by country, region, and subzone, as well as total land area for each. Global land area for the countries and regions covered amounts to 12.2 billion hectares (122 million square kilometers), or 90 percent of world land area excluding Antarctica. Global farm area is 3.1 billion hectares, or an average of 25.3 percent of land area. Global agricultural output in 2003 amounted to $1.18 trillion at market (not PPP) prices, or about 3.4 percent of gross world product (World Bank 2005).

Table E.1 Estimated land area, farm area, and agricultural output by country, region, and subzone

Country	Land area (square kilometers)	Farm area (thousands of hectares)	Agricultural output (millions of 2003 dollars)
Afghanistan	646,852	7,827	2,448
Algeria	2,327,529	8,459	6,653
Angola	1,248,180	3,300	1,187
Argentina	2,780,661	172,106	14,256
Australia	7,708,510	455,723	13,059
Southeast	1,098,924	192,824	3,147
Southwest	1,338,364	84,778	1,212
Central East	867,483	22,955	3,357
Central West	2,014,612	84,838	1,213
North	2,389,127	70,327	4,131
Bangladesh	129,387	8,429	11,421
Belgium	30,280	1,428	3,019
Brazil	8,490,639	353,611	29,540
Amazon	4,197,232	41,593	1,215
Northeast	2,198,314	95,062	4,574
Southern	2,095,093	216,956	23,751
Burkina Faso	275,847	6,830	1,296
Cambodia	183,343	3,807	1,438
Cameroon	472,157	7,160	5,496
Canada	9,661,335	67,502	17,130
Arctic	1,508,491	0	0
Central	1,501,539	44,401	11,268
Northwest Territories	2,280,775	0	0
Pacific Coast	1,262,141	13,121	3,330
Southeast	3,108,390	9,980	2,533
Central America	515,167	7,624	10,892
Central Europe	339,537	11,563	13,294
Chile	696,064	26,502	6,517
China	9,327,628	153,956	212,550
Beijing Northeast	1,690,517	38,907	40,480
Central	1,245,571	31,600	26,702
Hong Kong Southeast	413,221	13,599	38,471
Northwest	2,059,567	9,436	7,308
South Central	876,867	19,250	19,197
Tibetan Plateau	2,122,810	1,226	966
Yellow Sea	919,076	39,938	79,426
Colombia	1,150,119	50,706	9,438
Cuba	99,191	3,788	1,078
Democratic Republic of the Congo	2,342,369	7,800	3,289
Ecuador	251,465	12,356	2,176
Egypt	993,927	3,751	13,188
Ethiopia	1,255,693	11,047	2,794

(table continues next page)

Table E.1   Estimated land area, farm area, and agricultural output by country, region, and subzone *(continued)*

Country	Land area (square kilometers)	Farm area (thousands of hectares)	Agricultural output (millions of 2003 dollars)
France	547,593	29,898	35,152
Germany	353,963	19,098	16,822
Ghana	239,178	6,331	2,745
Greece	119,247	3,875	9,299
India	3,178,371	170,115	132,140
Northeast	1,212,010	64,870	50,389
Northwest	701,158	37,528	29,151
Southeast	799,042	42,767	33,220
Southwest	466,161	24,950	19,381
Indonesia	1,790,779	33,700	35,413
Iran	1,632,056	17,088	15,086
Iraq	439,564	4,591	1,697
Italy	309,442	19,607	32,303
Ivory Coast	328,290	6,900	3,571
Japan	371,752	4,762	43,009
Kazakhstan	2,696,406	21,671	2,380
Kenya	585,548	5,162	2,300
Madagascar	583,818	3,550	1,587
Malawi	117,522	2,440	651
Malaysia	322,252	7,585	10,374
Mali	1,257,004	4,700	1,644
Mexico	1,954,523	183,839	25,043
Morocco	405,424	9,283	7,434
Mozambique	791,186	4,435	1,123
Myanmar	661,318	10,611	4,095
Nepal	144,959	3,294	2,399
Netherlands	35,879	2,239	10,230
New Zealand	250,607	15,640	3,979
Niger	1,199,476	4,500	1,092
Nigeria	903,383	33,000	15,181
North Korea	124,520	2,700	6,000
Other Central Asia	865,104	4,383	2,652
Other Equatorial Africa	1,250,451	2,989	1,429
Other Horn of Africa	657,929	1	20
Other South America	1,486,556	23,818	2,808
Other Southern Africa	1,406,604	14,066	620
Other West Africa	437,205	4,372	1,833
Pakistan	874,102	22,120	18,935
Peru	1,303,836	35,382	6,058
Philippines	263,289	10,700	11,280
Poland	316,800	19,325	4,610
Portugal	87,696	5,189	3,697

(table continues next page)

Table E.1   Estimated land area, farm area, and agricultural output by country, region, and subzone *(continued)*

Country	Land area (square kilometers)	Farm area (thousands of hectares)	Agricultural output (millions of 2003 dollars)
Romania	235,076	13,940	6,834
Russia	16,661,998	250,182	21,643
Caspian Black Sea	893,762	49,157	4,252
Far Eastern	2,373,557	11,868	1,027
North European	2,316,608	46,332	4,008
North Urals Siberia	2,245,991	11,230	971
Northeast Siberia	2,548,377	12,742	1,102
South Urals Siberia	2,459,814	61,495	5,320
Southeast Siberia	3,823,889	57,358	4,962
Saudi Arabia	1,959,654	4,046	10,737
Scandinavia	1,071,983	22,742	9,027
Senegal	198,062	2,506	1,104
South Africa	1,233,256	15,712	6,395
South Korea	88,574	1,877	16,344
Southeastern Europe	393,549	13,243	12,566
Spain	503,679	42,181	30,191
Sri Lanka	57,846	1,916	3,465
Sudan	2,520,578	16,653	6,939
Syria	186,136	5,421	4,945
Tanzania	943,187	10,764	4,634
Thailand	513,578	19,367	14,295
Turkey	779,877	28,523	26,682
Uganda	240,138	7,200	2,015
Ukraine	614,704	33,457	6,935
United Kingdom	222,153	16,528	12,564
United States	9,373,250	379,343	98,537
Alaska	1,448,880	365	23
Lakes and Northeast	1,787,870	74,276	30,515
Pacific Northwest	603,722	13,117	4,198
Rockies and Plains	1,776,216	113,276	15,077
Southeast	1,555,232	58,046	22,214
South Pacific Coast	716,632	11,170	12,673
Southwest Plains	1,484,698	109,094	13,836
Uzbekistan	477,177	4,827	3,482
Venezuela	910,829	30,071	3,416
Vietnam	316,715	8,895	8,616
Yemen	420,297	1,669	1,625
Zambia	764,834	5,289	997
Zimbabwe	387,668	3,350	3,018
Total	122,294,308	3,097,935	1,175,860

Appendix F
Country-Level Results with the Mendelsohn-Schlesinger Functions

The Mendelsohn-Schlesinger models discussed in chapter 5 can be applied to the climate data for the countries, regions, and subzones examined in this study to estimate the impact of global warming on world agricultural production. For the carbon fertilization term, the concentration of atmospheric carbon dioxide used for 2070–99 is the 2085 estimate of 734.5 parts per million (ppm) indicated in IPCC (2001a, 807) for scenario SRES A2. That is, by that time atmospheric concentration would approximately double from its 1990 level of 350 ppm.

For application in comparison with recent output, it is necessary to change the scale of the Mendelsohn-Schlesinger (1999), or MS, functions to take account of price changes since 1990. The US GDP deflator for the farm sector has fallen from 155.4 in 1990 to 115.8 in 2003 (with 2000 = 100). Nominal values comparable to the 2003 base year for production thus need to be reduced to 0.745 times the values obtained directly with the MS functions.

Reduced Form Results

It turns out that the reduced form function generates a high incidence of *negative* estimated output per hectare as a function of temperature and precipitation even for *today's* climate. Of the 116 countries, regions, and subzones examined in this study, 62 show a negative figure when equation (5.1) of chapter 5 is applied to their climate values for the 1961–90 base period averages. For the United States, in contrast, the function performs relatively well.[1]

For the reduced form model, the approach adopted in this study is to assume that the changes in output per hectare predicted by the MS function are accurate, even if the base-level averages are not for numerous countries. This is equivalent to adding a country-specific constant to the equation for each country that makes the predicted average output the same as the observed average output. It is evident from equation (5.1) that if such a constant is added for a given country, there is no change in the predicted impact on agricultural output for the country. Because the derivative of a constant is zero, the change in output per hectare will remain the same:[2]

$$dy = 2.16 \times [53.7dT - 4.6dT + 0.22dP + 36.5\frac{dc}{c}] \qquad \text{(F.1)}$$

The analysis here further compares the change in predicted output per hectare not against the base-level predicted output but against the base-level actual output per hectare. This approach makes it possible to consider the results for those countries in which the MS function predicts negative base-level output, rather than discarding those cases, and is consistent with the notion that the change can be correct even if a country-specific constant shift factor is missing in the equation.

Table F.1 reports the results of applying the changes in temperature and precipitation from the base period (1961–90) to the future period (2070–99) to the reduced form MS equation (5.1).[3] The predicted change is expressed as a percent of 2003 actual output per hectare. Where a decline exceeds the base level of output, the proportionate change is constrained to –100 percent. This occurs in 30 of the 116 countries, regions, and subzones for the estimates without carbon fertilization and in 29 in the estimates with carbon fertilization. Of these cases, only six are in developed countries: all

---

1. US agricultural GDP in 1990 was $85 billion (CEA 1994). US agricultural land area is 938.3 million acres, or 379.9 million hectares (USDA 2004, 227). This means that farm output was $224 per hectare. When equation (5.1) is applied to the 1961–90 base climate data for the United States at the standardized G grid level of this study, and then aggregated to the US subzones (see table 5.1), the weighted average output per hectare weighting by farmland area (excluding Alaska) amounts to $204 at 1990 prices, close to the 1990 agricultural GDP per hectare of farm land.

2. Note that for the same reason, the term 350 for present atmospheric concentration drops out of the derivative. That is, $ln\,(c/350) = ln\,c - ln\,350$, and $ln\,350$ is a constant. Also note that in equation (F.1) the parameter on carbon fertilization has been reduced, as discussed above.

3. With the adjustment scalar of 0.745 to take into account the decline in agricultural prices from 1990 to 2003.

Table F.1 **Impact of climate change by 2070–99 on agricultural output: Mendelsohn-Schlesinger reduced form model**

(output per hectare, millions of 2003 dollars)

Country/region	Actual, 2003	Present	Model-predicted[a] Future Without CF	Model-predicted[a] Future With CF	Model-predicted change as percent of actual base Without CF	Model-predicted change as percent of actual base With CF
Afghanistan	313	6	−165	−122	−54.8	−40.9
Algeria	787	−422	−917	−875	−62.9	−57.6
Angola	360	1	−369	−326	−100.0	−90.8
Argentina	83	95	−25	19	−100.0	−92.1
Australia	29				−100.0	−100.0
Southeast	16	101	−94	−51	−100.0	−100.0
Southwest	14	−62	−296	−253	−100.0	−100.0
Central East	146	−191	−562	−519	−100.0	−100.0
Central West	14	−414	−848	−804	−100.0	−100.0
North	59	−463	−912	−869	−100.0	−100.0
Bangladesh	1,355	218	−98	−54	−23.3	−20.1
Belgium	2,114	282	288	331	0.3	2.3
Brazil	84				−100.0	−100.0
Amazon	29	17	−531	−488	−100.0	−100.0
Northeast	48	−247	−710	−666	−100.0	−100.0
South	109	107	−228	−184	−100.0	−100.0
Burkina Faso	190	−723	−1,283	−1,239	−100.0	−100.0
Cambodia	378	−134	−559	−515	−100.0	−100.0
Cameroon	768	−51	−421	−377	−48.1	−42.5
Canada	254				167.0	184.1
Arctic	0	−2,626	−1,253	−1,210	0.0	0.0
Central	254	−415	16	60	170.1	187.2
Northwest Territories	0	−1,481	−589	−545	0.0	0.0
Pacific Coast	254	−173	173	217	136.3	153.5
Southeast	254	−341	150	193	193.6	210.7
Central America	1,429	262	−153	−110	−29.0	−26.0
Central Europe	1,150	247	297	341	4.4	8.2
Chile	246	151	159	203	3.4	21.1
China	1,381				1.7	4.9
Beijing Northeast	1,040	−171	141	184	30.0	34.2
Central	845	152	206	250	6.4	11.6
Hong Kong Southeast	2,829	390	178	221	−7.5	−6.0
Northwest	774	−118	9	53	16.4	22.0
South Central	997	306	140	184	−16.6	−12.2
Tibetan Plateau	788	−564	−78	−34	0.0	0.0
Yellow Sea	1,989	323	190	234	−6.6	−4.5

(table continues next page)

Table F.1   Impact of climate change by 2070–99 on agricultural output: Mendelsohn-Schlesinger reduced form model
(output per hectare, millions of 2003 dollars) *(continued)*

Country/region	Actual, 2003	Present	Model-predicted[a] Future Without CF	With CF	Model-predicted change as percent of actual base Without CF	With CF
Colombia	186	337	−15	29	−100.0	−100.0
Cuba	285	−210	−547	−504	−100.0	−100.0
Democratic Republic of the Congo	422	−9	−422	−378	−97.8	−87.5
Ecuador	176	300	75	119	−100.0	−100.0
Egypt	3,516	−393	−833	−789	−12.5	−11.3
Ethiopia	253	−243	−632	−588	−100.0	−100.0
France	1,176	300	240	283	−5.1	−1.4
Germany	881	221	272	316	5.8	10.8
Ghana	434	−459	−932	−889	−100.0	−99.0
Greece	2,400	207	43	87	−6.8	−5.0
India	777				−36.8	−31.2
Northeast	777	−78	−273	−230	−25.2	−19.6
Northwest	777	−442	−782	−738	−43.7	−38.1
Southeast	777	−440	−801	−757	−46.4	−40.8
Southwest	777	−382	−696	−652	−40.4	−34.8
Indonesia	1,051	273	−15	29	−27.4	−23.3
Iran	883	−87	−407	−364	−36.3	−31.3
Iraq	370	−266	−728	−685	−100.0	−100.0
Italy	1,648	280	171	214	−6.6	−4.0
Ivory Coast	518	−269	−695	−652	−82.2	−73.8
Japan	9,032	530	515	559	−0.2	0.3
Kazakhstan	110	−64	78	122	129.6	169.3
Kenya	446	−346	−696	−653	−78.6	−68.8
Madagascar	447	115	−204	−160	−71.3	−61.6
Malawi	267	30	−329	−285	−100.0	−100.0
Malaysia	1,368	344	42	85	−22.1	−18.9
Mali	350	−898	−1,564	−1,520	−100.0	−100.0
Mexico	136	−47	−405	−361	−100.0	−100.0
Morocco	801	−14	−291	−247	−34.5	−29.1
Mozambique	253	−142	−532	−489	−100.0	−100.0
Myanmar	386	234	−21	22	−66.1	−54.8
Nepal	728	220	251	294	4.3	10.2
Netherlands	4,568	267	299	343	0.7	1.7
New Zealand	254	600	634	678	13.5	30.7
Niger	243	−822	−1,367	−1,324	−100.0	−100.0
Nigeria	460	−431	−873	−830	−96.1	−86.6

(table continues next page)

Table F.1   Impact of climate change by 2070–99 on agricultural output: Mendelsohn-Schlesinger reduced form model

(output per hectare, millions of 2003 dollars) *(continued)*

Country/region	Actual, 2003	Present	Model-predicted[a] Future Without CF	Model-predicted[a] Future With CF	Model-predicted change as percent of actual base Without CF	Model-predicted change as percent of actual base With CF
North Korea	2,222	214	393	437	8.1	10.0
Other Central Asia	605	−51	−89	−46	−6.3	0.9
Other Equatorial Africa	478	−82	−477	−434	−82.7	−73.6
Other Horn of Africa	20,118	−736	−1,160	−1,116	−2.1	−1.9
Other South America	118	−79	−446	−403	−100.0	−100.0
Other Southern Africa	44	−171	−550	−507	−100.0	−100.0
Other West Africa	419	−50	−452	−409	−96.0	−85.6
Pakistan	856	−337	−673	−629	−39.3	−34.2
Peru	171	173	−75	−32	−100.0	−100.0
Philippines	1,054	142	−145	−101	−27.1	−23.0
Poland	239	168	240	283	29.9	48.2
Portugal	713	241	51	95	−26.6	−20.5
Romania	490	198	179	222	−3.9	5.0
Russia	87				223.4	255.0
Caspian Black Sea	87	112	157	200	51.6	102.0
Far Eastern	87	−1,767	−621	−578	0.0	0.0
North European	87	−149	215	258	421.0	471.3
North Urals Siberia	87	−1,167	−233	−190	0.0	0.0
Northeast Siberia	87	−2,359	−1,011	−968	0.0	0.0
South Urals Siberia	87	−363	113	157	550.5	600.8
Southeast Siberia	87	−967	−194	−150	0.0	0.0
Saudi Arabia	2,654	−591	−1,109	−1,066	−19.5	−17.9
Scandinavia	397	−134	202	245	84.6	95.6
Senegal	441	−703	−1,219	−1,175	−100.0	−100.0
South Africa	407	30	−238	−194	−65.6	−54.9
South Korea	8,707	482	468	512	−0.2	0.3
Southeast Europe	949	288	217	261	−7.5	−2.9
Spain	716	213	36	80	−24.6	−18.6
Sri Lanka	1,808	−235	−544	−501	−17.1	−14.7
Sudan	417	−679	−1,194	−1,150	−100.0	−100.0
Syria	912	−7	−312	−268	−33.4	−28.6
Tanzania	430	−38	−380	−336	−79.5	−69.3
Thailand	738	−209	−549	−505	−46.0	−40.1
Turkey	935	182	78	122	−11.2	−6.5
Uganda	280	0	−334	−290	−100.0	−100.0
Ukraine	207	160	183	226	11.1	32.1
United Kingdom	760	372	439	482	8.8	14.5

(table continues next page)

Table F.1 Impact of climate change by 2070–99 on agricultural output: Mendelsohn-Schlesinger reduced form model
(output per hectare, millions of 2003 dollars) *(continued)*

Country/region	Actual, 2003	Model-predicted[a] Present	Future Without CF	Future With CF	Model-predicted change as percent of actual base Without CF	Model-predicted change as percent of actual base With CF
United States	260				−14.8	−2.9
Alaska	62	−943	−218	−174	0.0	0.0
Lakes, Northeast	411	265	302	346	9.1	19.7
Pacific Northwest	320	191	269	313	24.5	38.1
Rockies, Plains	133	47	146	190	74.6	107.3
Southeast	383	346	86	129	−67.9	−56.6
South Pacific Coast	1,135	116	51	95	−5.7	−1.9
Southwest Plains	127	80	−159	−116	−100.0	−100.0
Uzbekistan	721	61	−97	−53	−21.8	−15.8
Venezuela	114	−9	−441	−398	−100.0	−100.0
Vietnam	969	53	−285	−241	−34.9	−30.4
Yemen	973	−480	−869	−826	−40.0	−35.5
Zambia	189	2	−399	−356	−100.0	−100.0
Zimbabwe	901	−79	−455	−412	−41.8	−36.9
Total					−18.6	−13.0

CF = carbon fertilization

a. Converted from 1990 to 2003 prices by US farm deflator (0.745).

Note: Total weighting by output (see table 5.8).

five subzones in Australia and one in the United States (Southwest Plains: Arizona, New Mexico, Texas, and parts of Utah, Colorado, Kansas, and Oklahoma).[4] The results also screen out "ice to ice" cases, where the base output function is highly negative because of low temperature and the future output function is also negative because temperature remains too low despite the warming. Otherwise these areas (e.g., Alaska) would show spurious large gains in agricultural output.

When the percentage changes in agricultural impacts for each country, region, or subzone are applied to the corresponding 2003 benchmark levels of agricultural output (see appendix table E.1), the aggregate result is that global agricultural output would fall by $217 billion in the case without carbon fertilization and by $152 billion in the case with carbon fertilization. These reductions amount to a reduction in global output by

4. Note, however, that the MS reduced form function does not take irrigation into account.

18.6 and 13 percent, respectively. On this basis, using the reduced form MS model, global warming would reduce underlying world agricultural capacity by about one-fifth to one-eighth from levels otherwise attainable by the 2080s. It should be noted, however, that the only MS reduced form estimates used in the main "preferred" estimates of this study are those for the United States, where they are given a weight of one-half alongside equally weighted results from the Rosenzweig-Iglesias crop models. For all other country estimates in the crop model framework, the Rosenzweig-Iglesias calculations are used, because they are specifically developed by scientists using agronomic data for the countries and regions in question.

Cross-Section (Ricardian) Results

A corresponding set of estimates can be obtained applying the cross-section (CS) model (equation 5.2 in chapter 5). As discussed in chapter 5, the Ricardian estimates of table F.2 (excluding carbon fertilization) provide the source for the "default" Ricardian estimates in the main text for countries and regions lacking specific estimates. In one sense this set of estimates has a more straightforward application than the reduced form (RF) estimates just discussed but in another it requires a more complicated implementation. The more straightforward application pertains to the majority of observations in which the base level of the agricultural productivity measure (rental equivalent opportunity cost of land) is positive. In the CS function, only 25 out of 116 cases are negative. So instead of necessarily resorting to the "model change relative to actual base" method used for the RF model, where about half the cases show negative base output, it is appealing simply to obtain the percentage change in land rental equivalent value by calculating the change in the model estimate against the model estimate of the base level. For translation into corresponding output changes, this proportionate change in land value (or land rental value) must then be multiplied by the ratio of net revenue to output (see the discussion for the directly estimated regions in chapter 5). For this purpose, the following ratios are applied: Africa, 0.78; India and South Asia, 0.67; United States, 0.41; Europe, Japan, Australia, and New Zealand, 0.45; Latin America, 0.50; and Asia and the Middle East, 0.60. The ratios for Africa, India, and the United States are estimated in chapter 5. For the other regions, intermediate ratios are set on the basis of relative development level, with the land share presumed to be inversely related to the stage of development. With the percent change in output potential in hand, for purposes of global aggregation this percent change is then applied to each country's actual base level of agricultural production. This method is applied to cases "a" in table F.2.

The more complicated dimension pertains to the cases with negative base estimates, as well as to a subgroup with such low base estimates that the model-estimated changes translate into extremely large negative

Table F.2 Impact of climate change by 2070–99 on agriculture: Mendelsohn-Schlesinger cross-section Ricardian model

| Country/region | Model-predicted land rental equivalent (2003 dollars per hectare) | | | | Percent change in agricultural capacity | |
| | | Future | | | | |
	Base	Without CF	With CF	Basis	Without CF	With CF
Afghanistan	20	17	25	a	−9.5	14.5
Algeria	11	−9	−1	b	−29.9	−17.9
Angola	16	3	11	a	−65.6	−26.4
Argentina	21	18	26	a	−7.4	11.7
Australia				a	−55.1	−39.6
Southeast	23	17	25	a	−11.6	4.1
Southwest	22	15	23	a	−15.3	1.3
Central East	14	0	8	a	−45.5	−20.0
Central West	9	−8	1	a	−80.9	−42.1
North	−1	−19	−11	a	−100.0	−100.0
Bangladesh	5	−11	−3	b	−14.3	−7.2
Belgium	22	26	34	b	2.2	6.7
Brazil					−59.5	−36.2
Amazon	0	−22	−14	b	−100.0	−100.0
Northeast	2	−16	−8	a	−100.0	−100.0
South	14	0	8	a	−49.6	−20.6
Burkina Faso	−9	−34	−25	b	−100.0	−100.0
Cambodia	−2	−19	−11	b	−53.5	−28.1
Cameroon	6	−9	−1	b	−24.4	−11.8
Canada					114.1	152.5
Arctic	−130	−59	−50	c	0.0	0.0
Central	−14	11	19	b	118.0	156.5
Northwest Territories	−71	−25	−16	c	0.0	0.0
Pacific Coast	−7	11	19	b	88.1	126.5
Southeast	−18	10	18	b	130.8	169.2
Central America	7	−8	0	b	−12.3	−5.6
Central Europe	18	25	33	b	7.3	15.9
Chile	19	23	31	a	9.1	30.0
China					3.6	13.9
Beijing Northeast	0	19	27	b	22.1	31.4
Central	17	22	30	a	16.3	44.9
Hong Kong Southeast	22	13	21	b	−3.8	−0.4
Northwest	11	22	30	b	17.2	29.8
South Central	22	15	23	a	−18.8	3.2
Tibetan Plateau	−22	4	12	b	39.9	52.3
Yellow Sea	25	21	29	b	−2.7	2.2
Colombia	5	−10	−2	a	−100.0	−67.4

(table continues next page)

Table F.2   Impact of climate change by 2070–99 on agriculture: Mendelsohn-Schlesinger cross-section Ricardian model *(continued)*

Country/region	Base	Model-predicted land rental equivalent (2003 dollars per hectare) Future Without CF	With CF	Basis	Percent change in agricultural capacity Without CF	With CF
Cuba	4	−9	−1	b	−56.3	−21.7
Democratic Republic of the Congo	9	−8	0	a	−100.0	−78.9
Ecuador	13	2	10	a	−43.5	−12.1
Egypt	13	−4	4	b	−5.9	−3.1
Ethiopia	10	−5	3	a	−100.0	−53.5
France	23	26	34	b	2.3	10.6
Germany	19	25	34	a	13.8	32.5
Ghana	−4	−24	−16	b	−54.7	−32.5
Greece	25	23	31	b	−1.2	2.9
India					−21.3	−8.8
Northeast	6	−4	4	b	−16.2	−3.7
Northwest	3	−12	−4	b	−23.5	−11.0
Southeast	−2	−19	−11	b	−25.9	−13.5
Southwest	0	−15	−7	b	−23.3	−10.8
Indonesia	0	−13	−5	b	−15.3	−6.1
Iran	21	10	18	a	−30.9	−7.5
Iraq	16	−2	6	a	−67.8	−36.6
Italy	23	23	31	b	0.1	6.0
Ivory Coast	0	−18	−10	b	−41.7	−22.7
Japan	22	24	32	b	0.4	1.4
Kazakhstan	11	24	32	a	65.6	109.1
Kenya	6	−9	−1	b	−40.3	−18.2
Madagascar	14	2	11	a	−63.7	−17.6
Malawi	16	2	10	a	−66.1	−27.0
Malaysia	2	−11	−3	b	−11.6	−4.7
Mali	−10	−38	−30	b	−96.5	−68.8
Mexico	17	5	13	a	−35.9	−12.0
Morocco	23	14	22	a	−30.1	−2.3
Mozambique	10	−5	3	a	−100.0	−54.1
Myanmar	11	−1	7	a	−67.5	−22.9
Nepal	13	13	21	b	−0.9	12.3
Netherlands	22	26	34	b	1.2	3.2
New Zealand	22	24	32	a	4.5	21.3
Niger	−5	−29	−21	b	−100.0	−77.3
Nigeria	−2	−22	−14	b	−50.5	−29.3

(table continues next page)

**Table F.2   Impact of climate change by 2070–99 on agriculture:
Mendelsohn-Schlesinger cross-section Ricardian model**
(continued)

Country/region	Base	Model-predicted land rental equivalent (2003 dollars per hectare) Future Without CF	With CF	Basis	Percent change in agricultural capacity Without CF	With CF
North Korea	11	23	31	b	6.3	10.6
Other Central Asia	15	19	27	a	13.3	45.0
Other Equatorial Africa	6	−11	−3	b	−40.9	−20.6
Other Horn of Africa	−3	−21	−13	b	−1.1	−0.6
Other South America	10	−4	4	a	−70.7	−31.5
Other Southern Africa	18	4	12	a	−59.8	−24.7
Other West Africa	1	−16	−7	b	−48.8	−25.3
Pakistan	10	−3	5	b	−17.9	−6.5
Peru	13	3	11	a	−39.1	−7.1
Philippines	2	−11	−2	b	−14.3	−5.1
Poland	19	25	34	a	16.7	36.7
Portugal	25	22	30	a	−6.6	7.6
Romania	20	26	34	a	11.2	28.9
Russia					152.2	204.8
Caspian Black Sea	18	25	33	a	18.5	39.2
Far Eastern	−88	−28	−20	c	0.0	0.0
North European	−2	19	28	b	293.1	405.9
North Urals Siberia	−57	−7	1	c, d	0.0	0.0
Northeast Siberia	−118	−48	−40	c	0.0	0.0
South Urals Siberia	−12	15	23	b	383.4	495.9
Southeast Siberia	−46	−5	3	c, d	0.0	0.0
Saudi Arabia	5	−16	−8	b	−9.8	−6.1
Scandinavia	−3	15	23	b	55.4	79.7
Senegal	−8	−28	−20	b	−56.8	−34.5
South Africa	23	14	22	a	−29.4	−1.7
South Korea	24	26	34	b	0.2	1.3
Southeast Europe	23	25	34	a	5.0	20.9
Spain	25	22	31	a	−4.5	10.2
Sri Lanka	−3	−17	−9	b	−9.5	−4.2
Sudan	−3	−25	−17	b	−62.8	−39.5
Syria	23	14	22	a	−25.2	−4.1
Tanzania	14	1	9	a	−74.4	−29.3
Thailand	0	−16	−8	b	−25.3	−12.2
Turkey	23	24	32	a	1.6	17.3
Uganda	14	1	9	a	−74.0	−29.1
Ukraine	19	26	34	a	15.3	34.3

(table continues next page)

Table F.2   Impact of climate change by 2070–99 on agriculture:
Mendelsohn-Schlesinger cross-section Ricardian model
(continued)

Country/region	Base	Model-predicted land rental equivalent (2003 dollars per hectare) Future Without CF	With CF	Basis	Percent change in agricultural capacity Without CF	With CF
United Kingdom	20	25	33	a	10.5	28.5
United States					4.7	21.0
Alaska	−44	−6	2	c, d	0.0	0.0
Lakes, Northeast	18	25	33	a	14.5	32.6
Pacific Northwest	17	24	33	a	16.6	36.1
Rockies, Plains	15	24	32	a	27.0	49.8
Southeast	24	16	24	a	−13.7	0.4
South Pacific Coast	22	23	31	b	0.1	8.6
Southwest Plains	23	17	25	a	−11.1	3.7
Uzbekistan	24	22	30	a	−5.5	14.6
Venezuela	2	−15	−7	a	−100.0	−100.0
Vietnam	7	−6	2	b	−17.2	−7.1
Yemen	9	−8	0	b	−20.2	−10.2
Zambia	16	1	10	a	−71.2	−31.8
Zimbabwe	17	3	11	b	−19.0	−8.0
Total					−6.8	8.0

CF = carbon fertilization

a. Percent change in predicted land rental equivalent multiplied by ratio of net revenue to output; see text.
b. Negative or low predicted base land rental equivalent; see text.
c. Ice to ice; see text.
d. Ice to thaw; see text.

Note: Total weighting by output (see table 5.8).

changes and hence into negative future output levels. In the CS function it is not possible to directly apply the method used for the RF function because the predicted variable is no longer output per hectare but land rental equivalent per hectare. For meaningful comparison to the actual output base the model-change estimate must somehow be translated to a comparable absolute output change before being compared with actual output.

The CS model (like the RF model) was originally estimated for the United States, so it is natural to consider the relationship of predicted rental equivalent per hectare to the actual base for the United States as a benchmark. When the CS model is applied to the 1961–90 base climate data, the farm area–weighted average of the estimated land rental equivalent for the non-Alaska subzones turns out to be 8.4 percent of the corresponding weighted average of actual 2003 output per hectare. On this basis, for those country cases in which it is necessary to apply the model-predicted change in land rental equivalent against the base output (rather than applying outright the percent change in land rental equivalent), the corresponding absolute change in output per hectare is simply imputed at 12 times the change in the land rental equivalent. The change in output per hectare is then compared with the base level of output per hectare to obtain the percent change in output potential.[5] The criterion chosen for application of this alternative calculation, or case "b", is that the country in question has a predicted base land rental equivalent per hectare that is either negative or less than 2 percent of 2003 output per hectare (i.e., one-fourth of the US level). This subset turns out to include 25 cases with negative base predicted land rental equivalent plus another 31 cases in which the estimated base is positive but falls below the 2 percent of actual output per hectare threshold.

The result is that somewhat fewer than half of the estimates for the CS function apply the percent change in the predicted land rental equivalent as translated into percent change in output potential multiplying by the ratio of net revenue to output (cases "a" in table F.2). Half apply the alternative method that first translates the model change into output change and then compares this absolute change with the actual base (cases "b" in the table). The remaining cases are "ice to ice," which as described earlier in the RF results are again set to zero change from global warming.

As expected, the Ricardian CS function results show lower agricultural damage from global warming than the crop model–derived RF results (the same comparative outcome found in Mendelsohn and Schlesinger 1999 and Mendelsohn et al. 2000). In the aggregate, world agricultural potential falls by 6.8 percent without carbon fertilization. In the case with carbon fertilization, world productive capacity *rises* by 8 percent.

The CS model damages are only about one-third as large as the RF model results, for the case without carbon fertilization. Mendelsohn et al. (2000, 557) suggest that the cross-section damages are smaller because this approach "carefully includes adaptation since it captures how people have adapted to where they live." This interpretation is somewhat at odds with Richard Adams' statement that the underlying process-based models developed in Adams et al. (1999)—the basis for the MS reduced form model—already incorporate adaptation. Moreover, considering that Adams et al. suggest that adaptation could offset only about half of the damages from moderate warming and a lesser amount for larger temperature changes (as noted earlier), the shrinkage of the global damage estimates from the RF to

5. In these cases, there is no need for an additional step of multiplying by the ratio of net revenue to output.

the CS estimates here would also seem to overstate the mitigation from additional adaptation in the CS model. The cutback is considerably more than half, yet cutback even by half from adaptation would imply that the RF model had incorporated no adaptation at all and in addition that the approximately 5°C of warming for land areas by the 2080s is "moderate," which it is not.

The results for the case with carbon fertilization differ considerably more between the RF and CS models. It should be kept in mind that carbon fertilization cannot be estimated by statistical regression across regions, unlike the rest of the CS function, because all farms face the same present-day atmospheric concentration of carbon. Instead, authors must arbitrarily impose the carbon fertilization parameter. As discussed in chapter 3, the parameter chosen by Mendelsohn and Schlesinger is somewhat higher for the CS Ricardian model than for the RF models. Based on the results of tables F.1 and F.2, implicitly the global weighted effect of carbon fertilization by the 2080s is to raise yields by 7 percent in the RF model but by 16 percent in the CS model.[6] In light of the central estimate of the present study of 15 percent yield increase from atmospheric carbon concentration of 735 ppm by the 2080s, on the basis of the recent free air concentration enrichment (FACE) studies as discussed earlier, the results for the carbon fertilization case in the MS estimates appear reasonable. As noted in chapter 3, however, in their corresponding global estimates (Mendelsohn et al. 2000), the authors substantially increased the carbon fertilization parameter and thus appear to have overstated the carbon fertilization effect.[7]

---

6. The multiple of implied future-period productivity with carbon fertilization to that without is: $(1 - 0.127)/(1 - 0.184) = 1.070$ for the RF model (table F.1) and $(1 + 0.083)/(1 - 0.066) = 1.160$ for the Ricardian CS model (table F.2).

7. Note further that the percentage increases discussed here are after the proportionate change from the CS function for land rental equivalent has been shrunk down to the corresponding percent increase in output by applying the ratio of net revenue to output, ranging from 0.41 for the United States to 0.78 for Africa. See chapter 3 for further discussion.

Appendix G
Ricardian Models for India, Africa, and Latin America

Mendelsohn, Dinar, and Sanghi (2001) provide a Ricardian climate impact model for agriculture in India. Their statistical regression estimates across 271 districts, with 10 annual cross-sections for India, are shown in table G.1. In addition to the climate variables, the model includes the following control variables: population density, literacy, latitude, high yield, bulls per hectare, tractors per hectare, number of hectares in district, and six soil types.

For Africa, the World Bank recently carried out a survey of 9,597 farms in Burkina Faso, Egypt, Ethiopia, Ghana, Niger, Senegal, South Africa, Zambia, Cameroon, Kenya, and Zimbabwe. Of the farms surveyed, 7,238 had dryland crops, 1,221 had irrigated crops, and 5,062 had livestock (as well as crops, in most cases). Of the irrigated-crop observations, 58 percent were in Egypt. A summary statistical analysis of these data provides Ricardian climate functions meant to be representative for Africa (Kurukulasuriya et al. 2006). The climate regression coefficients from this analysis, for dryland and irrigated agriculture are shown in table G.2. Although the analysis also included a model for livestock, it was specified in terms of net revenue "per farm" rather than per hectare, a form that is too ambiguous for meaningful application in the climate impact simulations of the present study because of variation in farm size.

As noted earlier in the present study, the Africa models include a variant for irrigated agriculture based only on observations excluding farms in Egypt. Although the authors do not report the full set of parameters for that model, they do report the parameters for the marginal impact of temperature and precipitation for the model including Egypt (called A) and

Table G.1   Ricardian model for India

Month	Temperature (°C)	Precipitation (mm per month)
January	−32.0 (0.8)	18.5 (7.3)
January squared	11.4 (3.6)	−0.227 (3.1)
April	−102 (3.6)	−9.81 (5.4)
April squared	−8.81 (1.8)	0.079 (3.6)
July	−299 (6.4)	−1.16 (6.3)
July squared	−6.04 (1.2)	0.002 (5.6)
October	353 (6.0)	3.85 (4.7)
October squared	12.9 (1.1)	0.005 (0.9)

Notes: *t*-statistics in parentheses. Dependent variable: natural logarithm of net revenue per hectare; value per hectare. The mean has been subtracted from each climate variable. Coefficients are multiplied by 1,000. The period covered is 1977–86. Average net revenue: 1,424.7 rupees of 1980 per hectare (Dinar et al. 1998, 98).

the model excluding Egypt (called B). These are as follows: The marginal impact of temperature is $68 per hectare for +1°C for model A, but −$74 per hectare for model B. The marginal impact of precipitation is $6.9 per hectare for 1 mm per month additional precipitation in model A but $34.2 in model B.

For Latin America, a recent series of studies sponsored by the World Bank provides Ricardian models for major countries.[1] Table G.3 reports the equation estimates from the four studies in this series used directly in the computations of the present study. Each of the equations includes parameters for other variables, such as soil types. As discussed earlier in the present study, however, with the linear formulation of these models, all

---

1. The series of studies are Cap and Lozanoff (2006); Avila, Irias, and de Lima (2006); González, Velasco, and Cares (2006); Rocha et al. (2006); Jativa and Seo (2006); and Pacheco, Caraballo, and Seo (2006).

Table G.2   Ricardian models for Africa

	Dryland	Irrigated
Temperature (°C)		
Winter	−68	181
	(1.1)	(1.1)
Winter squared	2.5	−3.2
	(1.6)	(0.6)
Spring	−28	−180
	(0.3)	(0.8)
Spring squared	−1.0	0.8
	(0.5)	(0.2)
Summer	125	1,277
	(1.8)	(4.1)
Summer squared	−1.4	−20.2
	(1.0)	(3.7)
Fall	−58	−1,517
	(0.8)	(3.3)
Fall squared	0.4	28.7
	(0.2)	(3.4)
Precipitation (mm per month)		
Winter	−4.6	11.8
	(3.4)	(1.5)
Winter squared	0.03	−0.05
	(4.0)	(1.0)
Spring	4.7	−12.2
	(3.8)	(1.6)
Spring squared	−0.01	−0.10
	(2.6)	(2.2)
Summer	3.6	27.9
	(4.7)	(4.9)
Summer squared	−0.01	−0.10
	(3.9)	(4.5)
Fall	−2.1	25.5
	(3.0)	(4.3)
Fall squared	0.01	0.08
	(5.5)	(4.7)

Notes: Robust t-statistic in parentheses. Dependent variable is net farm revenue per hectare in 2005 US dollars. Additional control variables include water flow, elevation, household size, household electricity, and 22 soil types. Average net revenue: dryland, $319 per hectare; irrigated, $1,261 per hectare. Seasons for the Southern Hemisphere are defined as: winter (May–July), spring (August–October), summer (November–January), and fall (February–April). The months are the same but the seasons reversed for the Northern Hemisphere.

that is needed to investigate the impact of climate change is to apply the base period and future period climate variables to their respective parameters, take the difference between the two results, and compare this change to the base period average land price.

Table G.3 Ricardian functions for Argentina, Brazil, Chile, and Ecuador

Variable	Season	Argentina	Brazil	Chile	Season	Ecuador[a]
T_1	Summer	−1,192	−3,569	−329.8	Dry	−1,744
T_1^2	Summer	33.75	76.04	−10.81	Dry	39.96
T_2	Winter	2,145	1,251	−4,272	Rainy	2,811
T_2^2	Winter	−122	−36.26	231.2	Rainy	−76.9
T_3	Fall			6,989		
T_3^2	Fall			−380.5		
T_4	Spring			−7,334		
T_4^2	Spring			453.6		
P_1	Summer	−253	9.398	−1,073	Dry	−32.72
P_1^2	Summer	1.19	−0.024	17.10	Dry	0.095
P_2	Winter	−36.6	5.142	−717.2	Rainy	−39.27
P_2^2	Winter	0.18	0.033	2.484	Rainy	0.1352
P_3	Fall			1,029.70		
P_3^2	Fall			−10.97		
P_4	Spring			−87.16		
P_4^2	Spring			7.895		
Average land price (US dollars)		3,452	2,134	7,300		2,280

Variables: P = precipitation (mm/month)
 T = temperature (°C)

Seasons: summer (December–February), winter (June–August), fall (March–May), spring (September–November), dry (May–September), and rainy (October–April).

a. Weighted average for small and large farms (72 and 28 percent, respectively, based on number of observations).

Sources: Argentina: Cap and Lozanoff (2006); Brazil: Avila, Irias, and de Lima (2006); Chile: González, Velasco, and Cares (2006); Ecuador: Jativa and Seo (2006).

Appendix H
Monthly Climate Data, 1961–90 and 2070–99

Table H.1 Average temperature, January–June (°C)

Country	January T0	January T1	February T0	February T1	March T0	March T1	April T0	April T1	May T0	May T1	June T0	June T1
Afghanistan	0.42	6.12	2.34	7.74	7.74	13.07	13.62	18.79	18.40	23.83	23.32	29.22
Algeria	12.31	16.59	14.93	19.60	18.07	23.06	22.04	27.23	26.53	32.14	30.83	36.33
Angola	22.63	26.24	22.70	26.25	22.77	26.24	22.34	26.03	20.76	24.89	18.43	22.86
Argentina	21.16	24.80	20.27	24.13	17.92	21.48	14.47	17.82	11.15	14.33	8.17	11.02
Australia												
Central East	28.11	32.33	27.55	31.65	25.74	29.63	22.43	26.63	18.41	22.19	15.05	18.94
Central West	30.53	34.69	29.68	33.74	27.78	31.82	23.80	28.08	19.13	22.93	15.87	19.58
North	29.46	33.10	28.89	32.42	28.26	31.79	26.70	30.48	24.15	27.68	21.34	24.95
Southeast	23.65	27.46	23.52	27.08	21.04	24.43	17.04	20.62	13.07	16.29	10.15	13.35
Southwest	25.30	28.84	24.85	28.17	22.61	25.83	18.85	22.24	14.83	18.05	12.11	15.22
Bangladesh	17.63	22.19	19.94	25.10	24.29	29.45	26.98	31.47	27.61	30.92	27.67	30.18
Belgium	2.24	6.41	2.84	6.99	5.42	9.12	8.21	11.47	12.45	15.47	15.34	19.23
Brazil												
Amazon	25.92	29.59	25.95	29.38	25.99	29.39	26.14	29.81	25.74	29.99	25.20	30.11
Northeast	25.84	29.38	25.79	29.18	25.74	29.15	25.59	29.37	25.12	29.05	24.44	28.44
South	24.59	28.03	24.84	28.16	24.16	27.54	22.36	25.99	20.27	24.30	18.51	22.64
Burkina Faso	24.96	29.62	27.76	32.42	30.47	35.03	31.91	36.39	31.41	35.93	29.32	33.41
Cambodia	24.54	28.46	26.11	29.79	27.39	31.20	28.62	32.08	28.19	31.69	27.51	30.67
Cameroon	23.86	27.67	25.43	29.06	26.35	29.86	26.51	29.86	25.63	28.94	24.47	27.86
Canada												
Arctic	-31.54	-20.59	-32.26	-22.81	-29.97	-21.60	-21.43	-14.80	-9.19	-3.61	1.15	6.68
Central	-20.46	-13.39	-16.64	-9.73	-9.85	-3.35	0.56	7.48	8.41	13.52	13.89	18.48
Northwest Territories	-28.29	-19.52	-26.37	-18.76	-21.56	-14.72	-11.27	-5.11	-1.21	5.10	6.77	12.44
Pacific Coast	-12.48	-7.78	-9.25	-4.49	-5.06	-0.35	1.27	6.14	6.52	10.87	10.55	14.54
Southeast	-18.49	-9.18	-16.96	-9.03	-10.67	-4.37	-2.24	4.28	5.44	11.28	11.32	16.53

Central America	22.75	25.90	23.36	26.61	24.54	27.98	25.40	29.07	25.56	29.34	24.92	28.93
Central Europe	-2.85	2.42	-0.88	4.61	2.92	7.78	7.51	11.39	12.19	15.32	15.32	19.60
Chile	13.39	16.29	12.93	15.95	11.60	14.56	9.27	12.23	6.95	9.96	4.94	7.82
China												
Beijing Northeast	-17.88	-11.25	-14.51	-7.56	-5.55	1.23	4.93	11.91	12.58	19.45	17.83	24.04
Central	-2.28	3.53	-0.24	5.39	4.74	10.16	10.21	15.71	14.66	19.86	17.89	22.62
Hong Kong Southeast	8.93	13.85	9.89	14.61	13.65	17.91	18.55	22.51	22.68	26.16	25.29	28.82
Northwest	-11.77	-5.92	-8.26	-2.53	0.09	6.05	8.65	14.89	14.89	21.12	19.04	25.09
South Central	9.10	13.74	10.47	15.14	14.22	18.64	18.26	22.38	21.57	24.97	23.14	26.54
Tibetan Plateau	-12.90	-7.03	-10.70	-4.93	-6.23	-0.74	-1.24	4.29	3.05	9.07	7.13	12.86
Yellow Sea	1.34	6.77	2.95	8.24	8.12	13.40	14.55	19.78	19.95	24.84	24.15	28.72
Colombia	24.49	27.85	24.88	27.96	25.05	28.20	24.67	27.89	24.26	27.72	23.81	27.52
Cuba	22.40	25.23	22.62	25.41	23.80	26.62	24.80	27.72	26.08	28.99	27.01	30.04
Democratic Republic of the Congo	24.04	27.52	24.42	27.90	24.65	28.17	24.55	28.01	24.27	28.25	23.23	27.71
Ecuador	22.58	25.66	22.73	25.72	22.81	25.83	22.73	25.78	22.35	25.51	21.63	24.97
Egypt	12.89	16.96	14.62	18.80	17.84	22.04	22.49	26.55	26.35	30.48	28.92	33.36
Ethiopia	21.52	25.18	22.62	26.29	23.93	27.65	24.42	28.29	24.45	28.31	24.21	28.40
France	3.13	7.06	4.20	8.12	6.39	9.88	9.07	12.52	12.73	16.48	16.13	20.77
Germany	-0.67	4.22	0.35	5.30	3.59	8.09	7.38	11.02	12.00	15.00	15.23	19.05
Ghana	26.81	31.20	28.92	33.12	29.38	33.14	29.03	32.61	28.07	31.70	26.59	29.98
Greece	4.82	8.33	5.96	9.71	8.39	12.09	12.20	15.72	16.67	20.48	20.66	25.18
India												
Northeast	11.94	16.79	14.24	19.27	19.03	24.01	23.51	28.35	26.05	30.34	26.69	29.89
Northwest	13.95	18.61	16.41	20.96	21.71	26.09	27.01	31.73	30.24	34.61	30.81	34.48
Southeast	22.23	26.15	24.59	28.90	27.82	32.08	30.65	34.53	32.05	35.17	29.90	32.52
Southwest	22.50	26.03	24.43	28.25	27.56	31.43	30.04	33.62	30.64	33.64	28.19	30.81

(table continues next page)

Table H.1 Average temperature, January–June (°C) *(continued)*

Country	January T0	January T1	February T0	February T1	March T0	March T1	April T0	April T1	May T0	May T1	June T0	June T1
Indonesia	25.54	28.30	25.63	28.41	25.85	28.65	26.08	28.89	26.09	28.95	25.64	28.45
Iran	4.78	9.28	6.80	11.31	11.67	16.20	17.19	22.00	22.43	27.85	26.87	32.88
Iraq	8.16	12.43	10.39	14.91	14.46	19.14	19.99	24.92	25.74	31.17	30.00	35.77
Italy	4.16	8.12	5.10	9.23	7.22	11.02	10.25	13.93	14.39	18.25	18.12	22.44
Ivory Coast	25.82	30.15	27.60	31.71	28.12	31.70	27.91	31.40	27.08	30.60	25.76	29.03
Japan	-0.85	3.27	-0.51	3.94	2.91	7.00	9.01	13.23	13.86	18.06	17.68	21.85
Kazakhstan	-12.51	-6.10	-11.99	-5.07	-4.15	-2.79	8.03	14.48	15.62	22.10	20.76	27.23
Kenya	24.78	27.49	25.52	28.35	25.90	28.93	25.24	28.39	24.27	27.85	23.27	27.49
Madagascar	24.52	27.76	24.56	27.76	24.26	27.37	23.35	26.41	21.50	24.69	19.68	22.87
Malawi	23.24	26.56	23.17	26.45	23.04	26.40	22.14	25.60	20.21	24.08	18.30	22.60
Malaysia	24.80	27.69	24.96	27.93	25.40	28.41	25.78	28.82	25.95	28.99	25.70	28.55
Mali	21.27	25.99	24.15	28.98	27.33	32.32	30.44	35.52	32.97	38.24	33.24	38.13
Mexico	14.99	18.58	16.34	19.99	18.58	22.52	21.42	25.80	23.53	27.82	25.00	29.21
Morocco	9.83	13.59	11.38	15.53	13.36	17.44	15.30	19.95	18.82	23.90	22.48	27.40
Mozambique	25.75	29.10	25.62	28.86	25.22	28.48	23.90	27.27	21.80	25.60	19.73	23.81
Myanmar	17.74	21.79	19.45	23.83	22.43	26.85	25.01	28.73	25.44	28.46	24.89	27.67
Nepal	4.15	8.93	5.75	10.70	10.17	15.24	14.53	19.58	17.17	21.78	19.18	22.92
Netherlands	1.96	6.19	2.41	6.61	4.91	8.70	7.70	10.92	12.02	14.93	14.87	18.49
New Zealand	15.10	17.70	15.18	17.86	13.83	16.43	10.95	13.44	7.89	10.41	5.60	8.17
Niger	19.03	23.41	21.91	26.36	25.98	30.68	30.17	34.80	32.53	37.34	32.63	37.18
Nigeria	24.52	28.85	26.92	31.08	29.07	32.92	29.82	33.55	28.86	32.48	27.27	30.85
North Korea	-12.08	-5.97	-9.14	-2.76	-1.93	4.24	6.43	12.70	12.68	18.44	17.08	22.19
Other Central Asia	-6.67	-1.37	-5.13	0.27	1.39	7.05	8.97	14.49	13.88	20.12	18.40	24.99
Other Equatorial Africa	24.99	28.35	25.74	29.09	26.08	29.44	26.00	29.26	25.57	28.92	24.24	27.69
Other Horn of Africa	24.00	27.58	24.90	28.54	26.31	30.07	27.51	31.45	28.41	32.32	29.29	33.52

Other South America	25.06	28.95	24.71	28.51	23.87	27.61	22.02	25.90	19.86	24.05	17.98	22.45
Other Southern Africa	25.11	29.19	24.35	28.32	23.34	27.27	20.81	25.13	17.30	21.92	14.39	19.02
Other West Africa	24.79	28.62	26.39	30.11	27.47	30.91	27.90	31.31	27.45	30.91	26.16	29.60
Pakistan	8.61	13.70	10.72	15.57	15.94	20.65	21.55	26.48	25.80	30.80	28.86	33.82
Peru	20.16	23.53	20.22	23.44	20.11	23.43	19.85	23.33	19.30	23.22	18.44	22.68
Philippines	24.17	26.79	24.40	27.05	25.25	27.85	26.32	29.12	26.75	29.67	26.23	28.93
Poland	-2.98	3.27	-1.47	5.07	2.56	8.46	7.39	11.94	12.91	15.86	15.92	19.73
Portugal	8.43	11.70	9.39	12.67	11.04	14.16	12.87	16.44	15.93	20.37	19.57	24.26
Romania	-3.49	1.79	-1.27	4.39	3.40	8.33	9.33	13.25	14.43	17.83	17.59	22.49
Russia												
Caspian Black Sea	-7.31	-0.96	-6.51	0.13	-0.77	5.02	9.06	13.94	15.97	20.22	19.82	25.13
Far Eastern	-28.49	-17.50	-27.67	-18.10	-23.13	-15.41	-14.13	-7.50	-2.27	3.61	6.65	14.40
North European	-13.46	-4.22	-11.82	-3.15	-5.58	1.98	2.06	9.05	9.42	16.21	14.36	19.13
North Urals Siberia	-25.68	-15.69	-24.10	-14.48	-16.37	-7.20	-9.32	-2.51	-0.91	6.50	8.15	16.21
Northeast Siberia	-40.34	-30.39	-36.80	-27.03	-26.44	-17.43	-14.18	-7.17	-1.94	3.88	8.55	15.93
South Urals Siberia	-19.29	-11.58	-17.97	-10.16	-9.24	-1.46	1.15	8.59	9.12	17.36	15.60	21.95
Southeast Siberia	-28.86	-20.91	-25.31	-17.05	-15.05	-7.47	-3.51	3.01	5.43	12.63	12.51	19.14
Saudi Arabia	15.44	19.68	17.12	21.32	20.54	24.75	24.40	29.07	28.79	33.82	31.42	36.67
Scandinavia	-7.56	-1.71	-6.95	-0.94	-3.27	2.30	1.53	6.82	7.54	12.40	12.33	16.09
Senegal	24.14	28.16	26.37	30.33	28.40	32.12	30.00	33.64	31.06	34.74	30.11	33.99
South Africa	23.30	27.22	22.74	26.56	21.22	24.95	17.86	21.87	14.37	18.66	11.30	15.54
South Korea	-3.02	1.48	-1.08	3.78	4.01	8.56	10.54	15.06	15.73	20.22	19.98	24.44
Southeastern Europe	0.54	4.60	2.21	6.50	5.65	9.77	10.25	13.99	14.98	18.78	18.45	23.31
Spain	5.97	9.55	7.08	10.73	8.89	12.36	10.92	15.05	14.47	19.85	18.55	24.55
Sri Lanka	25.20	27.96	25.99	28.85	27.22	30.04	28.01	30.77	28.17	30.98	27.67	30.62
Sudan	21.84	26.00	23.48	27.59	26.42	30.39	28.70	32.79	30.02	34.45	29.85	34.33
Syria	5.92	9.55	7.70	11.70	11.25	15.45	16.21	20.59	21.28	26.07	25.78	30.90
Tanzania	22.95	26.09	23.12	26.17	23.13	26.33	22.62	26.02	21.67	25.55	20.36	24.69

(table continues next page)

Table H.1 Average temperature, January–June (°C) (continued)

Country	January T0	January T1	February T0	February T1	March T0	March T1	April T0	April T1	May T0	May T1	June T0	June T1
Thailand	23.14	26.98	25.19	28.92	27.27	31.06	28.80	32.12	28.27	31.34	27.46	30.32
Turkey	0.09	3.79	1.57	5.71	5.30	9.31	10.48	14.52	14.95	19.60	18.98	24.35
Uganda	22.82	25.85	23.31	26.45	23.39	26.81	22.80	26.11	22.30	25.90	21.77	26.03
Ukraine	-5.21	1.30	-3.80	3.16	1.06	6.97	9.02	13.59	15.09	18.43	18.46	22.96
United Kingdom	3.18	6.51	3.21	6.48	4.87	7.88	6.93	9.72	9.96	12.61	12.88	15.79
United States												
Alaska	-19.13	-10.59	-18.32	-11.33	-14.19	-7.15	-7.14	-1.36	2.14	7.87	8.24	13.24
Lakes and Northeast	-6.96	-0.58	-4.99	1.83	1.20	7.28	8.09	14.25	14.27	19.52	19.25	24.67
Pacific Northwest	-2.00	2.22	0.64	4.64	3.04	6.63	6.21	9.80	10.35	14.06	14.56	19.58
Rockies and Plains	-7.69	-2.07	-4.72	1.15	-0.08	5.34	6.29	11.71	12.09	17.20	17.27	23.04
Southeast	5.52	9.79	7.52	12.17	12.21	16.50	16.79	21.41	20.93	25.80	24.73	29.75
South Pacific Coast	3.08	7.37	5.36	9.18	7.01	10.50	10.00	13.78	14.47	18.72	18.93	23.86
Southwest Plains	3.61	8.16	6.17	10.64	9.99	14.33	14.76	19.87	19.23	24.86	23.72	29.54
Uzbekistan	-3.29	1.87	-1.87	3.43	5.10	10.61	13.92	19.30	20.35	26.53	25.28	31.76
Venezuela	25.14	28.70	25.68	28.85	26.27	29.54	26.22	29.64	25.72	29.37	24.94	28.80
Vietnam	19.60	23.52	20.83	24.61	22.42	26.11	25.42	28.87	26.77	30.07	26.96	30.16
Yemen	18.96	23.01	19.86	23.87	21.48	25.47	24.14	28.51	26.47	30.71	28.33	32.77
Zambia	22.90	26.44	22.91	26.41	22.87	26.41	21.89	25.67	19.61	23.79	17.40	21.97
Zimbabwe	23.97	27.60	23.55	27.07	22.93	26.43	21.13	24.91	18.38	22.65	15.75	20.31

T0 = temperature for 1961–90
T1 = temperature for 2070–99

Table H.2 Average temperature, July–December (°C)

Country	July T0	July T1	August T0	August T1	September T0	September T1	October T0	October T1	November T0	November T1	December T0	December T1
Afghanistan	25.22	31.15	23.75	29.70	19.15	25.34	13.20	19.13	7.27	12.66	2.74	8.27
Algeria	32.53	38.03	32.01	37.55	28.88	34.26	23.45	28.82	17.48	22.60	13.03	17.49
Angola	18.00	22.38	19.89	24.21	22.15	26.41	23.11	27.57	22.78	26.78	22.61	26.55
Argentina	7.95	10.73	9.52	12.39	11.99	15.04	15.10	18.23	17.94	21.09	20.19	23.67
Australia												
Central East	14.23	17.88	16.14	20.02	19.54	23.60	23.36	27.79	26.01	30.57	27.68	31.94
Central West	14.88	18.45	17.02	21.10	20.79	25.19	24.88	29.48	27.75	32.40	29.79	34.04
North	20.75	24.28	22.72	26.27	25.57	29.26	28.50	32.30	30.03	34.02	30.16	33.98
Southeast	9.23	12.19	10.65	13.96	13.33	17.02	16.71	20.95	19.61	23.78	22.17	26.10
Southwest	11.19	14.12	12.32	15.64	14.99	18.58	18.20	21.98	21.21	25.00	23.68	27.34
Bangladesh	27.35	29.65	27.37	29.92	27.35	30.37	26.04	29.61	22.56	25.93	18.74	22.85
Belgium	17.20	22.05	17.21	22.75	14.50	19.39	10.78	14.77	5.96	10.02	3.32	6.98
Brazil												
Amazon	25.21	30.35	26.05	31.31	26.60	31.60	26.86	31.70	26.57	31.06	26.23	30.27
Northeast	24.23	28.26	25.03	29.02	26.20	30.20	26.50	30.63	26.35	30.68	26.12	30.11
South	18.47	22.47	19.89	24.17	21.24	25.71	22.65	26.82	23.46	27.43	24.03	27.55
Burkina Faso	27.20	30.67	26.52	29.84	27.11	30.60	28.66	32.72	27.37	31.99	25.19	30.00
Cambodia	27.11	30.17	27.02	29.99	26.73	29.71	26.34	29.30	25.58	28.50	24.54	28.32
Cameroon	23.54	26.92	23.41	26.98	23.82	27.45	24.35	28.04	24.24	27.85	23.62	27.41
Canada												
Arctic	5.85	10.19	3.91	7.56	-2.80	2.50	-12.79	-3.53	-23.47	-11.16	-28.52	-16.18
Central	16.83	22.26	15.42	21.03	9.16	14.35	2.74	7.64	-8.33	-2.80	-17.36	-10.57
Northwest Territories	10.95	15.53	9.12	13.34	2.94	7.39	-5.34	0.13	-17.57	-9.55	-24.72	-15.27
Pacific Coast	12.96	17.63	12.27	17.24	7.81	12.15	2.51	6.78	-6.55	-1.87	-11.13	-6.12
Southeast	14.96	20.50	13.76	19.39	8.67	14.12	2.63	7.56	-4.99	0.87	-14.65	-6.89

(table continues next page)

Table H.2 Average temperature, July–December (°C) *(continued)*

Country	July T0	July T1	August T0	August T1	September T0	September T1	October T0	October T1	November T0	November T1	December T0	December T1
Central America	24.76	28.72	24.72	28.32	24.51	27.92	24.09	27.51	23.32	26.72	22.85	26.09
Central Europe	17.08	22.65	16.74	23.37	13.50	19.38	8.69	13.27	2.96	7.49	-1.16	3.25
Chile	4.63	7.47	5.42	8.36	6.90	9.77	8.82	11.63	10.81	13.54	12.52	15.39
China												
Beijing Northeast	20.71	25.93	19.12	24.38	12.74	17.99	4.43	9.14	-6.50	-0.47	-15.09	-8.07
Central	20.16	24.27	19.63	23.74	15.31	19.66	10.32	14.57	4.20	8.91	-0.74	5.36
Hong Kong Southeast	27.69	30.86	27.26	30.64	24.79	28.49	20.47	23.93	15.44	18.72	10.76	15.54
Northwest	21.14	27.13	19.97	26.38	14.38	20.42	6.67	11.86	-2.42	3.74	-9.64	-3.30
South Central	24.17	27.33	23.76	26.97	21.96	25.50	18.58	22.00	14.24	17.31	10.46	14.70
Tibetan Plateau	9.32	14.58	8.74	13.76	5.49	10.47	-0.89	4.45	-7.63	-1.43	-11.50	-5.59
Yellow Sea	26.90	30.66	26.38	30.39	21.65	25.91	16.06	19.84	9.50	13.31	3.47	9.08
Colombia	23.68	27.51	23.93	27.83	24.13	27.83	24.21	27.81	24.32	27.83	24.28	27.80
Cuba	27.52	30.50	27.53	30.47	27.13	30.12	26.22	29.28	24.69	27.81	23.18	26.14
Democratic Republic of the Congo	22.75	27.31	23.41	27.90	23.99	28.31	24.17	28.63	24.04	27.84	23.91	27.59
Ecuador	21.18	24.57	21.47	24.84	21.79	25.12	22.02	25.33	22.13	25.40	22.35	25.57
Egypt	29.21	34.76	29.20	35.03	27.41	32.55	24.12	28.98	18.60	23.28	14.32	18.71
Ethiopia	23.28	27.34	23.04	26.93	23.38	27.31	22.92	26.88	21.95	25.58	21.28	24.85
France	18.62	24.42	18.26	24.64	15.81	21.33	11.77	16.00	6.71	10.79	3.89	7.45
Germany	16.94	21.76	16.71	22.34	13.63	18.77	9.21	13.41	4.03	8.49	0.69	4.99
Ghana	25.57	28.79	25.31	28.57	25.77	29.03	26.76	30.33	27.19	31.29	26.39	30.71
Greece	23.13	28.32	22.94	28.24	19.81	24.58	14.85	18.90	10.41	13.98	6.51	10.04
India												
Northeast	25.14	27.68	24.62	27.38	23.97	27.32	21.44	25.37	16.92	20.77	12.96	17.33
Northwest	28.46	31.39	27.24	30.00	26.85	30.05	24.75	28.67	19.79	23.93	15.33	19.75

Southeast	27.51	29.93	27.01	29.39	27.24	30.03	26.34	29.51	23.88	27.09	21.94	25.42
Southwest	26.26	28.77	25.72	28.16	26.14	28.74	26.28	29.07	24.36	27.42	22.64	25.91
Indonesia	25.32	28.13	25.44	28.30	25.71	28.54	26.01	28.90	26.02	28.88	25.79	28.60
Iran	28.88	35.22	27.56	33.81	23.80	30.07	18.15	23.93	12.07	17.32	6.93	11.68
Iraq	32.57	38.79	32.13	38.28	28.71	34.99	22.87	28.46	15.45	20.76	9.87	14.29
Italy	20.90	26.21	20.76	26.58	17.88	22.94	13.55	17.77	8.80	12.75	5.26	9.02
Ivory Coast	24.77	27.91	24.65	27.85	25.18	28.32	25.82	29.21	26.18	30.03	25.35	29.54
Japan	21.68	25.67	23.13	27.21	19.14	23.30	13.13	17.19	7.43	11.49	2.12	6.21
Kazakhstan	23.20	30.08	20.69	27.54	14.82	20.60	5.97	11.14	-2.08	3.93	-8.82	-2.38
Kenya	22.70	27.06	22.98	26.96	23.79	27.54	24.64	28.41	24.42	27.92	24.44	27.56
Madagascar	19.21	22.44	19.59	22.84	20.77	24.02	22.31	25.78	23.47	26.90	24.19	27.52
Malawi	17.99	22.45	19.36	23.55	21.78	25.74	24.00	28.62	24.47	29.21	23.75	27.36
Malaysia	25.44	28.26	25.41	28.33	25.39	28.29	25.30	28.22	25.07	27.92	24.96	27.81
Mali	31.70	36.16	30.56	34.70	30.51	34.72	29.46	34.25	25.57	30.63	21.65	26.50
Mexico	24.95	28.98	24.75	28.79	23.63	27.85	21.21	25.55	17.96	22.04	15.60	19.38
Morocco	26.28	30.90	26.06	30.44	23.01	27.84	18.42	23.14	13.89	18.48	10.32	14.28
Mozambique	19.37	23.58	20.77	24.81	22.91	26.91	24.79	29.35	25.64	30.28	25.72	29.29
Myanmar	24.67	27.36	24.59	27.33	24.60	27.59	23.73	26.92	21.15	24.24	18.34	22.14
Nepal	19.13	22.17	18.71	21.83	17.50	21.19	13.79	18.10	9.17	13.19	5.56	9.98
Netherlands	16.68	20.97	16.79	21.66	14.12	18.65	10.51	14.37	5.89	9.96	3.24	7.02
New Zealand	4.92	7.49	6.04	8.44	7.89	10.27	9.87	12.16	11.75	14.07	13.64	16.09
Niger	31.05	35.02	30.18	33.79	30.18	34.13	28.33	32.88	23.59	28.13	20.01	24.66
Nigeria	25.82	29.04	25.33	28.38	25.91	29.19	26.71	30.38	25.86	29.91	24.61	28.87
North Korea	20.71	25.20	20.69	25.25	14.84	19.57	7.98	12.22	-0.61	4.13	-8.81	-2.86
Other Central Asia	21.12	27.73	19.81	26.59	14.87	21.23	7.99	13.38	1.52	7.24	-3.76	2.04
Other Equatorial Africa	23.29	26.82	23.48	27.24	24.21	27.90	24.67	28.36	24.65	28.04	24.49	27.90
Other Horn of Africa	29.02	33.03	28.84	32.66	28.55	32.32	26.72	30.53	25.07	28.67	24.07	27.50
Other South America	18.10	22.49	19.82	24.47	21.76	26.52	23.52	27.97	24.41	28.63	24.94	28.96

(table continues next page)

Table H.2 Average temperature, July–December (°C) (continued)

Country	July T0	July T1	August T0	August T1	September T0	September T1	October T0	October T1	November T0	November T1	December T0	December T1
Other Southern Africa	14.24	18.75	16.57	21.12	20.28	24.88	22.91	27.83	24.13	28.66	24.81	29.10
Other West Africa	25.00	28.23	24.69	27.80	25.18	28.24	25.74	28.96	25.73	29.22	24.46	28.19
Pakistan	28.57	32.94	27.49	31.79	25.15	29.90	20.77	25.94	15.19	20.16	10.30	15.32
Peru	18.10	22.48	18.73	23.11	19.35	23.40	19.78	23.63	20.12	23.94	20.14	23.87
Philippines	25.87	28.59	25.83	28.59	25.79	28.54	25.58	28.40	25.24	27.97	24.67	27.37
Poland	17.47	22.07	17.10	22.58	13.36	18.45	8.72	13.23	3.33	8.43	-0.68	4.59
Portugal	22.49	27.17	22.46	26.94	20.39	24.73	16.32	20.20	11.56	15.24	8.73	11.98
Romania	19.22	25.97	18.85	26.37	15.20	21.46	9.77	14.70	4.16	8.57	-0.78	3.65
Russia												
Caspian Black Sea	22.00	28.42	20.81	27.22	15.45	21.02	7.87	13.09	1.55	7.02	-3.69	2.04
Far Eastern	10.06	14.98	8.31	13.06	2.49	7.99	-9.14	-1.28	-21.87	-11.09	-27.54	-15.47
North European	16.98	21.54	14.77	19.64	9.36	14.07	2.46	7.87	-4.17	2.66	-9.77	-1.60
North Urals Siberia	13.46	18.59	10.51	15.83	4.50	10.21	-5.94	1.61	-16.62	-6.03	-22.04	-11.16
Northeast Siberia	13.43	17.89	9.50	14.68	1.60	7.56	-12.98	-4.28	-30.95	-18.69	-37.15	-25.11
South Urals Siberia	18.21	24.07	15.17	21.55	9.38	14.87	0.29	6.05	-9.14	-1.56	-16.29	-8.26
Southeast Siberia	15.81	21.23	13.48	19.54	6.65	12.36	-3.93	1.97	-17.65	-8.91	-26.55	-17.86
Saudi Arabia	31.89	36.94	31.91	36.41	30.07	35.00	25.78	30.87	20.79	25.75	16.75	21.29
Scandinavia	14.20	17.87	13.06	17.04	8.89	13.00	4.20	8.42	-1.43	3.58	-5.42	0.20
Senegal	28.40	31.95	27.61	30.86	27.75	31.03	28.60	32.18	26.99	30.97	24.14	28.15
South Africa	11.20	15.31	13.11	17.39	16.16	20.63	18.47	23.18	20.60	24.97	22.30	26.37
South Korea	23.51	27.53	24.18	28.23	19.24	23.44	13.20	17.17	6.20	10.01	-0.15	4.08
Southeastern Europe	20.76	27.03	20.55	27.07	17.11	22.65	11.98	16.48	6.78	10.60	2.48	6.27
Spain	22.02	28.21	21.82	27.89	19.11	24.48	14.32	18.82	9.34	13.46	6.42	9.89
Sri Lanka	27.33	30.29	27.14	30.03	27.07	29.99	26.58	29.42	25.88	28.61	25.32	28.06

Sudan	28.59	32.97	28.19	31.99	28.36	32.27	27.74	32.03	24.84	28.98	22.40	26.65
Syria	28.61	34.26	28.36	34.10	25.09	30.76	19.47	24.36	12.61	17.15	7.50	11.39
Tanzania	20.08	24.50	20.95	25.17	22.23	26.09	23.38	27.57	23.44	27.39	23.11	26.58
Thailand	27.08	29.89	26.82	29.55	26.68	29.50	26.17	29.03	24.61	27.38	22.87	26.61
Turkey	22.23	28.48	22.06	28.44	18.53	24.11	13.01	17.72	7.34	11.35	2.51	6.25
Uganda	21.32	25.85	21.56	25.65	21.96	25.87	22.36	26.35	22.30	25.84	22.35	25.78
Ukraine	19.98	26.07	19.32	26.06	14.75	20.61	8.57	13.73	2.69	7.82	-1.97	3.35
United Kingdom	14.63	18.09	14.51	18.53	12.48	16.28	9.65	12.97	5.78	9.13	4.04	7.20
United States												
Alaska	10.91	14.60	9.33	13.44	4.31	8.60	-4.99	0.70	-14.16	-5.88	-18.11	-8.64
Lakes and Northeast	21.81	28.10	20.64	27.15	16.33	22.74	10.15	15.47	3.28	8.33	-3.92	1.23
Pacific Northwest	18.18	24.26	17.84	23.78	13.54	18.71	8.12	12.75	2.08	6.36	-1.66	2.52
Rockies and Plains	20.91	27.31	19.74	26.31	14.14	20.46	8.12	13.68	0.11	5.03	-6.03	-0.93
Southeast	26.50	31.16	26.02	31.21	23.09	28.65	17.34	22.56	12.19	16.81	7.48	11.46
South Pacific Coast	22.63	27.75	21.82	26.98	18.19	23.05	13.22	18.03	7.29	11.87	3.39	7.61
Southwest Plains	26.16	31.52	25.18	30.68	21.50	27.32	15.98	21.75	9.53	14.50	4.78	9.22
	27.70	34.37	25.25	31.95	19.49	25.57	11.47	16.66	5.13	10.40	-0.21	5.20
Uzbekistan	24.76	28.88	25.02	29.25	25.37	29.41	25.54	29.48	25.52	29.26	25.11	28.83
Venezuela	26.96	30.06	26.69	29.70	25.97	29.09	24.56	27.60	22.49	25.32	20.39	24.16
Vietnam	27.64	31.44	27.42	30.80	26.70	30.34	23.66	27.55	20.96	24.70	19.61	23.50
Yemen	17.12	21.90	19.47	24.17	22.81	27.51	24.60	29.96	24.15	28.96	23.10	27.09
Zambia	15.61	20.26	17.88	22.38	21.40	26.14	23.75	29.46	24.22	29.59	23.84	27.82

T0 = temperature for 1961–90
T1 = temperature for 2070–99

Table H.3 Average precipitation, January–June (millimeters per day)

Country	January P0	January P1	February P0	February P1	March P0	March P1	April P0	April P1	May P0	May P1	June P0	June P1
Afghanistan	1.39	1.61	1.73	1.80	2.07	2.08	1.58	1.50	0.75	0.43	0.18	0.09
Algeria	0.28	0.25	0.30	0.28	0.30	0.29	0.26	0.23	0.22	0.27	0.11	0.19
Angola	5.03	5.01	5.11	4.99	5.54	5.41	3.67	3.67	0.53	0.39	0.02	0.00
Argentina	2.36	2.36	2.37	2.42	2.33	2.33	1.65	1.68	1.25	1.30	1.02	1.15
Australia												
Central East	3.31	3.31	3.07	3.08	2.25	2.26	1.25	1.25	1.18	1.18	0.75	0.75
Central West	1.93	1.93	2.10	2.10	1.35	1.35	0.57	0.57	0.59	0.59	0.50	0.50
North	7.14	7.14	7.79	7.78	5.69	5.70	1.78	1.79	0.65	0.65	0.30	0.30
Southeast	2.01	2.02	1.60	1.60	1.67	1.67	1.63	1.63	1.78	1.78	1.45	1.45
Southwest	0.61	0.61	0.71	0.71	0.59	0.59	0.75	0.75	1.06	1.06	1.19	1.18
Bangladesh	0.27	0.08	0.66	0.60	1.56	1.29	4.56	4.57	7.98	9.54	15.39	17.85
Belgium	2.20	3.16	1.89	2.58	2.19	2.60	1.82	1.85	2.13	1.76	2.47	1.96
Brazil												
Amazon	8.36	8.49	9.17	9.66	9.34	9.83	7.97	7.98	6.01	5.75	3.90	3.60
Northeast	5.82	6.05	6.83	7.08	6.95	7.16	5.66	5.65	2.69	2.43	1.51	1.48
South	6.78	7.13	5.86	6.19	4.83	5.15	3.25	3.34	2.48	2.52	1.84	1.98
Burkina Faso	0.01	0.11	0.05	0.11	0.34	0.47	1.01	0.89	2.12	1.99	3.41	3.46
Cambodia	0.53	0.42	0.67	0.43	1.29	0.94	2.61	2.61	6.41	6.34	9.23	8.52
Cameroon	0.51	1.08	1.03	1.15	2.89	2.81	4.37	4.17	5.57	5.86	5.70	6.05
Canada												
Arctic	0.18	0.43	0.19	0.39	0.20	0.39	0.26	0.46	0.33	0.56	0.51	0.84
Central	0.65	0.87	0.55	0.78	0.65	0.85	0.80	1.25	1.32	1.69	2.20	2.50
Northwest Territories	0.45	0.81	0.43	0.71	0.43	0.66	0.48	0.79	0.64	1.07	1.18	1.59
Pacific Coast	2.52	3.14	2.16	2.79	1.75	2.21	1.39	1.77	1.73	1.91	2.36	2.42
Southeast	1.72	2.18	1.50	1.91	1.63	2.03	1.68	2.07	1.98	2.41	2.74	3.17

Central America	2.90	2.98	1.99	1.93	1.59	1.48	2.66	2.74	6.88	6.36	10.39	9.39
Central Europe	2.02	2.45	2.06	2.45	2.06	2.35	2.58	2.65	3.14	2.96	3.80	3.56
Chile	1.11	0.96	1.14	1.06	1.04	0.86	1.33	1.23	2.30	2.18	2.41	2.44
China												
Beijing Northeast	0.09	0.21	0.14	0.27	0.27	0.33	0.75	0.98	1.23	1.63	2.43	2.86
Central	0.27	0.43	0.41	0.81	0.90	1.63	1.88	2.57	2.76	3.80	3.56	4.06
Hong Kong Southeast	1.81	1.87	3.11	3.36	4.39	4.75	6.76	7.24	8.15	7.90	8.78	10.12
Northwest	0.08	0.26	0.09	0.25	0.19	0.36	0.32	0.76	0.45	0.78	0.64	0.65
South Central	0.82	0.89	1.16	1.36	1.51	1.75	3.44	3.67	5.39	6.01	7.17	7.93
Tibetan Plateau	0.22	0.38	0.32	0.46	0.49	0.52	0.67	0.80	0.97	1.32	2.38	3.32
Yellow Sea	0.87	1.01	1.53	1.96	2.16	2.76	3.25	3.91	3.61	3.71	4.72	5.25
Colombia	3.76	4.21	4.28	4.65	5.41	5.23	8.62	8.68	9.83	10.22	9.86	10.35
Cuba	1.33	1.63	1.45	1.44	1.56	1.44	2.39	2.58	5.55	5.73	6.22	5.67
Democratic Republic of the Congo	4.10	4.79	4.35	4.51	5.36	5.48	5.38	5.76	3.59	3.51	2.12	2.18
Ecuador	6.04	6.32	7.26	7.60	7.76	8.02	8.11	8.12	6.41	7.20	5.73	6.78
Egypt	0.20	0.20	0.16	0.15	0.14	0.09	0.12	0.14	0.10	0.09	0.07	0.05
Ethiopia	0.35	0.65	0.61	0.88	1.20	1.28	2.69	2.64	2.88	2.35	2.28	1.38
France	2.39	2.90	2.35	2.70	2.19	2.37	2.21	1.89	2.64	1.88	2.24	1.52
Germany	1.71	2.38	1.53	2.14	1.64	2.04	1.82	2.00	2.21	2.06	2.70	2.44
Ghana	0.27	0.54	1.00	1.11	2.40	2.53	3.48	3.46	4.82	4.77	6.14	6.44
Greece	2.54	2.21	2.45	1.98	1.98	1.58	1.53	1.16	1.36	1.00	0.96	0.71
India												
Northeast	0.51	0.45	0.69	0.70	0.85	0.70	1.61	1.62	2.59	3.47	6.52	8.27
Northwest	0.30	0.37	0.38	0.40	0.43	0.40	0.32	0.26	0.47	0.55	1.96	2.41
Southeast	0.30	0.10	0.42	0.32	0.48	0.44	0.91	1.05	1.58	2.48	4.88	5.70
Southwest	0.08	-0.17	0.11	0.06	0.21	0.21	0.70	0.79	1.68	2.78	6.67	7.91

(table continues next page)

Table H.3 Average precipitation, January–June (millimeters per day) *(continued)*

Country	January		February		March		April		May		June	
	P0	P1	P0	P1	P0	P1	P0	P1	P0	P1	P0	P1
Indonesia	9.11	9.53	8.83	9.49	9.18	9.43	9.11	9.62	8.05	8.53	6.39	6.65
Iran	1.15	1.27	1.15	1.13	1.18	1.17	1.03	0.93	0.59	0.40	0.17	0.04
Iraq	1.10	1.05	1.10	0.98	1.07	0.94	1.03	0.95	0.45	0.38	0.05	0.00
Italy	2.50	2.46	2.55	2.42	2.36	2.16	2.45	2.13	2.24	1.81	2.08	1.82
Ivory Coast	0.38	0.68	1.36	1.49	2.65	2.97	4.05	4.32	5.44	5.29	7.39	8.08
Japan	2.42	2.24	2.60	2.48	3.07	2.89	4.05	4.03	4.47	4.54	6.82	7.23
Kazakhstan	0.54	0.76	0.50	0.69	0.58	0.78	0.78	1.01	0.82	0.86	0.85	0.73
Kenya	1.03	1.82	1.10	1.51	2.06	2.30	4.82	5.05	3.25	2.79	1.37	1.17
Madagascar	9.15	8.98	9.25	9.36	6.06	5.98	3.24	2.85	1.94	1.72	1.75	1.57
Malawi	7.60	7.68	7.42	7.56	6.81	7.10	3.54	3.48	0.88	0.93	0.29	0.22
Malaysia	8.11	7.59	6.47	6.25	6.60	5.12	7.43	7.91	7.84	8.42	6.53	6.70
Mali	0.00	0.06	0.01	0.03	0.05	0.08	0.21	0.18	0.52	0.29	1.26	1.13
Mexico	0.80	0.44	0.59	0.21	0.47	0.15	0.63	0.37	1.36	1.21	3.57	3.50
Morocco	1.24	1.06	1.54	1.38	1.20	1.01	1.30	1.11	0.75	0.72	0.28	0.27
Mozambique	6.44	6.86	6.69	6.85	5.37	5.87	2.84	2.73	1.08	1.07	0.68	0.53
Myanmar	0.30	0.21	0.45	0.42	0.75	0.75	2.22	2.52	6.37	7.54	12.81	13.87
Nepal	0.67	0.70	0.93	0.79	1.13	0.73	1.64	1.22	2.89	3.65	6.55	8.58
Netherlands	2.16	3.05	1.68	2.37	1.98	2.40	1.66	1.81	1.90	1.78	2.30	1.99
New Zealand	4.33	4.61	3.77	4.12	4.63	4.82	4.68	4.73	5.05	5.37	5.21	5.61
Niger	0.00	0.05	0.01	0.04	0.02	0.07	0.06	-0.01	0.23	0.15	0.62	0.75
Nigeria	0.13	0.28	0.35	0.41	1.04	1.20	2.31	2.33	3.70	4.18	5.21	5.35
North Korea	0.47	0.51	0.66	0.62	0.99	0.94	2.08	2.25	2.66	2.97	4.35	4.81
Other Central Asia	0.98	1.17	1.13	1.23	1.57	1.64	1.67	1.81	1.35	1.05	0.64	0.40
Other Equatorial Africa	3.08	3.64	3.78	3.95	5.37	5.45	5.89	5.92	5.74	5.72	3.16	3.23
Other Horn of Africa	0.19	0.49	0.33	0.52	0.62	0.67	1.69	1.80	1.33	0.93	0.43	-0.05

Other South America	5.10	5.38	4.99	5.46	4.12	4.57	3.18	3.55	2.18	2.35	1.45	1.62
Other Southern Africa	2.56	2.23	2.58	2.33	1.84	1.84	0.92	0.72	0.14	0.05	0.05	0.00
Other West Africa	0.25	0.43	0.73	0.81	1.29	1.61	2.61	3.00	5.10	5.01	8.62	9.04
Pakistan	0.67	0.83	0.94	0.98	1.12	1.08	0.80	0.73	0.54	0.49	0.54	0.64
Peru	5.64	5.73	6.14	6.63	5.83	6.02	4.87	4.94	3.65	3.97	2.84	3.15
Philippines	4.32	4.31	3.22	3.15	2.63	2.38	2.97	2.39	5.77	5.85	8.46	8.86
Poland	1.10	1.57	1.01	1.46	1.04	1.47	1.31	1.62	1.98	2.11	2.56	2.74
Portugal	3.42	3.39	3.72	3.57	2.32	1.97	2.29	1.62	1.70	1.12	1.18	0.88
Romania	1.22	1.38	1.26	1.36	1.17	1.27	1.70	1.62	2.38	2.04	3.01	2.51
Russia												
Caspian Black Sea	1.15	1.27	1.00	1.17	0.93	1.18	1.19	1.38	1.50	1.49	1.87	1.57
Far Eastern	0.84	1.29	0.69	1.07	0.53	0.90	0.61	1.00	0.77	1.26	1.18	1.78
North European	1.21	1.81	1.01	1.60	0.97	1.48	1.17	1.61	1.40	1.92	2.04	2.33
North Urals Siberia	0.90	1.32	0.73	1.21	0.73	1.21	0.88	1.23	1.11	1.51	1.64	2.06
Northeast Siberia	0.34	0.58	0.31	0.57	0.35	0.65	0.48	0.77	0.75	1.27	1.37	1.99
South Urals Siberia	0.77	1.30	0.62	1.11	0.60	0.97	0.96	1.38	1.43	2.00	2.00	2.23
Southeast Siberia	0.36	0.65	0.31	0.60	0.39	0.65	0.85	1.19	1.37	1.97	2.25	2.97
Saudi Arabia	0.21	0.31	0.22	0.26	0.40	0.42	0.58	0.56	0.32	0.25	0.08	0.03
Scandinavia	1.81	2.48	1.44	2.04	1.45	1.96	1.29	1.67	1.45	1.73	1.94	2.04
Senegal	0.01	0.00	0.01	0.01	0.01	0.03	0.03	0.04	0.45	0.16	2.38	1.79
South Africa	2.20	2.25	2.31	2.23	1.95	2.02	1.36	1.19	0.62	0.52	0.53	0.37
South Korea	1.05	0.96	1.40	1.35	1.97	1.92	3.46	3.62	3.37	3.47	5.90	6.51
Southeastern Europe	2.28	2.17	2.33	2.13	2.13	1.90	2.25	1.90	2.32	1.91	2.29	1.93
Spain	2.17	2.10	2.33	2.15	1.75	1.39	2.05	1.39	1.82	1.19	1.34	0.97
Sri Lanka	2.63	1.86	2.51	2.10	2.70	2.60	5.19	5.35	4.55	3.75	2.99	3.09
Sudan	0.05	0.13	0.09	0.17	0.29	0.25	0.67	0.62	1.28	1.34	1.90	1.68
Syria	1.80	1.50	1.69	1.27	1.51	1.21	1.19	1.02	0.55	0.43	0.09	0.04
Tanzania	4.78	5.26	4.94	5.18	5.75	5.89	5.68	5.62	2.07	2.01	0.49	0.52

(table continues next page)

Table H.3 Average precipitation, January–June (millimeters per day) *(continued)*

Country	January PO	January P1	February PO	February P1	March PO	March P1	April PO	April P1	May PO	May P1	June PO	June P1
Thailand	0.52	0.39	0.64	0.51	1.15	1.04	2.79	3.23	6.47	7.90	7.26	7.25
Turkey	2.31	1.95	2.16	1.71	1.93	1.59	2.02	1.74	1.75	1.35	1.12	0.89
Uganda	1.31	1.99	1.99	1.95	3.28	3.14	5.06	5.63	4.38	3.92	2.75	2.67
Ukraine	1.31	1.46	1.24	1.40	1.06	1.34	1.36	1.53	1.66	1.62	2.32	1.92
United Kingdom	3.87	4.88	2.93	3.70	3.11	3.60	2.27	2.53	2.36	2.22	2.44	2.23
United States												
Alaska	0.75	1.27	0.77	1.25	0.73	1.21	0.63	1.05	0.74	1.21	1.42	1.85
Lakes and Northeast	1.59	1.73	1.61	1.94	2.23	2.63	2.65	3.09	3.02	3.39	3.26	3.22
Pacific Northwest	3.22	4.09	2.62	3.31	2.31	2.68	1.68	1.55	1.49	1.25	1.34	0.97
Rockies and Plains	0.59	0.82	0.58	0.84	0.93	1.24	1.35	1.75	1.97	2.02	2.12	2.07
Southeast	3.20	2.93	3.61	3.57	3.92	4.03	3.39	3.71	3.82	3.78	3.78	3.81
South Pacific Coast	2.22	2.94	2.15	2.68	1.87	2.04	1.09	0.91	0.60	0.38	0.43	0.35
Southwest Plains	0.74	0.67	0.91	0.89	0.99	0.84	1.10	0.90	1.73	1.43	1.67	1.64
Uzbekistan	0.68	0.71	0.70	0.66	1.05	1.04	1.07	1.04	0.61	0.35	0.18	0.05
Venezuela	1.73	2.11	1.68	2.27	1.96	2.25	4.45	4.46	7.35	6.94	9.85	9.57
Vietnam	1.05	0.96	0.87	0.69	1.20	1.01	2.50	2.46	5.50	5.88	7.76	7.69
Yemen	0.22	0.30	0.29	0.27	0.46	0.45	0.81	0.72	0.61	0.52	0.36	0.30
Zambia	7.10	7.25	6.93	6.97	4.99	5.00	1.76	1.39	0.20	0.10	0.02	0.00
Zimbabwe	4.90	5.09	4.84	5.07	2.49	3.00	1.09	0.82	0.28	0.19	0.13	0.05

P0 = precipitation for 1961–90
P1 = precipitation for 2070–99

Table H.4 Average precipitation, July–December (millimeters per day)

Country	July P0	July P1	August P0	August P1	September P0	September P1	October P0	October P1	November P0	November P1	December P0	December P1
Afghanistan	0.34	0.36	0.33	0.39	0.15	0.16	0.32	0.28	0.51	0.54	0.99	1.08
Algeria	0.07	0.05	0.12	0.27	0.17	0.19	0.23	0.18	0.31	0.27	0.30	0.31
Angola	0.02	−0.01	0.12	0.09	0.73	0.54	2.36	1.97	4.82	4.58	5.05	4.83
Argentina	0.94	0.95	0.85	0.83	1.07	1.02	1.62	1.66	1.95	2.08	2.14	2.18
Australia												
Central East	0.84	0.84	0.67	0.67	0.60	0.59	1.06	1.05	1.64	1.64	2.51	2.52
Central West	0.36	0.36	0.25	0.25	0.21	0.21	0.35	0.34	0.59	0.59	0.96	0.96
North	0.24	0.24	0.13	0.13	0.25	0.25	0.68	0.68	1.98	1.98	3.92	3.92
Southeast	1.58	1.58	1.64	1.64	1.50	1.49	1.73	1.72	1.62	1.61	1.67	1.67
Southwest	1.10	1.09	0.92	0.92	0.79	0.78	0.68	0.68	0.58	0.57	0.52	0.52
Bangladesh	16.93	18.79	13.19	14.07	10.09	11.32	5.08	5.53	1.03	0.71	0.32	0.15
Belgium	2.33	1.65	2.12	1.44	2.14	1.60	2.35	2.34	2.65	3.25	2.49	3.03
Brazil												
Amazon	2.88	2.65	2.55	2.33	3.34	2.91	4.74	4.06	6.10	5.64	7.29	7.14
Northeast	1.16	1.12	0.72	0.90	1.01	0.85	2.29	1.92	3.59	2.77	4.79	4.85
South	1.64	1.67	1.72	1.57	2.71	2.62	4.41	4.56	5.50	5.92	6.76	7.20
Burkina Faso	5.48	5.57	6.79	6.91	4.74	5.81	1.28	1.65	0.11	0.36	0.04	0.12
Cambodia	9.19	9.16	9.97	9.61	10.61	10.66	7.94	8.91	3.94	3.63	1.27	1.28
Cameroon	6.28	6.07	7.27	7.04	8.68	8.43	7.02	6.94	2.36	3.04	0.62	1.38
Canada												
Arctic	0.89	1.29	1.04	1.44	0.76	1.16	0.59	0.99	0.36	0.81	0.22	0.54
Central	2.29	2.34	1.94	1.88	1.64	1.66	0.97	1.12	0.81	1.00	0.72	0.98
Northwest Territories	1.58	1.90	1.49	1.82	1.10	1.58	0.89	1.44	0.72	1.26	0.50	0.93
Pacific Coast	2.36	2.16	2.06	1.93	2.11	2.29	2.35	3.02	2.60	3.46	2.58	3.32
Southeast	3.03	3.13	2.98	2.98	3.02	3.05	2.45	2.60	2.34	2.72	1.99	2.42

(table continues next page)

Table H.4 Average precipitation, July–December (millimeters per day) (*continued*)

Country	July P0	July P1	August P0	August P1	September P0	September P1	October P0	October P1	November P0	November P1	December P0	December P1
Central America	9.53	8.75	9.10	8.51	10.70	9.53	9.92	9.84	6.49	6.71	4.15	4.08
Central Europe	3.41	2.74	3.46	2.75	2.57	1.88	2.11	2.05	2.61	2.94	2.26	2.57
Chile	2.46	2.42	2.02	1.97	1.40	1.27	1.06	0.96	0.94	0.82	1.07	1.00
China												
Beijing Northeast	4.36	4.98	3.67	4.37	1.68	1.90	0.73	0.72	0.31	0.30	0.14	0.25
Central	4.26	4.50	3.75	3.95	3.52	3.95	1.92	2.24	0.82	0.77	0.29	0.48
Hong Kong Southeast	4.96	5.33	5.63	6.44	4.15	4.94	2.68	2.91	1.90	1.68	1.28	1.30
Northwest	0.90	0.62	0.79	0.64	0.43	0.33	0.26	0.25	0.17	0.19	0.10	0.24
South Central	6.48	6.90	6.66	7.35	4.55	5.43	3.28	3.76	1.81	1.65	0.80	0.69
Tibetan Plateau	3.04	4.40	2.81	3.75	1.69	2.12	0.58	0.72	0.22	0.27	0.20	0.25
Yellow Sea	5.54	5.96	4.33	4.89	3.10	3.82	1.95	2.19	1.40	1.07	0.75	0.91
Colombia	8.49	9.04	7.96	8.15	7.88	7.45	8.76	8.84	7.36	7.72	4.76	4.79
Cuba	4.31	3.86	5.07	4.57	6.09	5.31	5.05	5.22	2.58	3.05	1.25	1.47
Democratic Republic of the Congo	2.08	2.17	2.96	2.63	4.24	3.86	5.52	4.79	6.01	6.25	4.88	5.24
Ecuador	4.25	5.44	3.51	4.09	4.05	3.69	4.55	5.08	4.28	5.26	4.26	4.56
Egypt	0.09	0.09	0.09	0.17	0.05	0.10	0.09	0.08	0.10	0.11	0.17	0.16
Ethiopia	3.97	3.52	4.10	3.78	2.85	2.36	2.14	2.43	1.05	1.72	0.34	0.61
France	1.80	1.26	2.12	1.53	2.31	1.86	2.54	2.29	2.71	2.74	2.52	2.68
Germany	2.42	2.00	2.42	1.71	1.96	1.49	1.67	1.79	2.01	2.55	1.95	2.50
Ghana	4.89	4.67	4.48	3.65	5.68	5.20	3.75	4.23	1.25	1.86	0.54	0.82
Greece	0.70	0.52	0.64	0.49	0.99	0.76	2.12	1.69	2.89	2.45	3.22	3.04
India												
Northeast	10.47	12.81	9.66	11.38	6.44	7.92	2.02	2.66	0.44	0.44	0.33	0.30
Northwest	5.70	6.75	5.71	7.06	2.83	3.95	0.36	0.75	0.33	0.49	0.21	0.24

Southeast	7.56	8.03	7.48	8.16	6.04	7.10	3.87	4.77	2.15	2.21	0.92	0.70
Southwest	9.45	9.52	7.36	7.75	5.69	6.85	2.85	4.02	1.28	1.61	0.41	0.24
Indonesia	5.54	5.73	5.50	5.50	6.20	6.31	7.07	6.66	8.53	8.81	9.34	9.94
Iran	0.14	0.12	0.12	0.18	0.10	0.19	0.32	0.39	0.53	0.66	0.94	0.96
Iraq	0.02	0.02	0.02	0.06	0.02	0.25	0.33	0.48	0.73	0.84	0.99	0.96
Italy	1.65	1.33	2.16	1.80	2.42	1.97	3.01	2.80	3.44	3.13	2.91	2.89
Ivory Coast	5.35	5.07	5.66	4.70	6.91	6.01	4.44	4.92	2.10	2.77	0.83	1.12
Japan	6.69	7.42	6.05	6.72	6.55	6.88	4.24	4.08	3.38	2.86	2.45	2.12
Kazakhstan	0.89	0.71	0.67	0.58	0.54	0.43	0.76	0.72	0.76	0.85	0.63	0.85
Kenya	1.16	1.09	1.12	1.07	1.15	1.02	2.13	1.94	3.45	4.09	1.61	2.41
Madagascar	1.86	1.62	1.63	1.47	1.09	0.75	1.98	1.42	3.92	3.74	7.63	7.48
Malawi	0.26	0.18	0.09	0.00	0.10	-0.05	0.54	-0.39	2.61	2.16	7.00	7.62
Malaysia	6.18	6.65	6.98	7.46	8.28	8.87	9.36	9.77	11.03	11.66	10.57	10.29
Mali	2.46	2.23	3.20	3.38	1.90	2.31	0.50	0.56	0.04	0.10	0.00	0.10
Mexico	4.38	3.83	4.34	3.91	4.71	4.30	2.38	2.56	1.00	0.96	0.89	0.63
Morocco	0.09	0.08	0.14	0.14	0.37	0.35	0.80	0.72	1.43	1.23	1.36	1.22
Mozambique	0.59	0.47	0.39	0.27	0.37	0.16	0.95	0.12	2.53	2.11	5.89	6.54
Myanmar	12.92	13.67	12.82	13.54	8.96	10.07	5.60	6.29	2.00	1.82	0.45	0.23
Nepal	11.18	15.98	9.37	12.03	6.60	8.04	1.94	2.36	0.33	0.26	0.48	0.45
Netherlands	2.36	1.84	2.17	1.55	2.26	1.84	2.33	2.51	2.66	3.42	2.46	3.15
New Zealand	5.13	5.53	5.12	5.50	5.21	5.46	4.96	4.99	4.62	4.76	4.73	4.82
Niger	1.60	2.21	2.17	3.24	0.78	1.39	0.08	0.19	0.00	0.01	0.00	0.03
Nigeria	6.83	6.94	7.32	7.43	6.52	6.54	3.04	3.52	0.47	1.00	0.15	0.33
North Korea	8.06	9.43	7.90	9.34	3.95	4.43	1.70	1.50	1.13	0.87	0.48	0.45
Other Central Asia	0.33	0.27	0.20	0.22	0.20	0.14	0.77	0.71	0.91	1.00	1.00	1.21
Other Equatorial Africa	2.51	2.46	3.21	2.63	5.64	5.25	8.26	8.07	6.67	7.18	3.41	4.05
Other Horn of Africa	0.84	0.78	0.94	1.02	0.63	0.52	0.93	1.33	0.80	1.39	0.27	0.68
Other South America	1.02	1.09	1.06	0.95	1.77	1.59	3.05	3.10	3.94	4.03	4.61	4.48

(table continues next page)

Table H.4 Average precipitation, July–December (millimeters per day) *(continued)*

Country	July		August		September		October		November		December	
	P0	P1	P0	P1	P0	P1	P0	P1	P0	P1	P0	P1
Other Southern Africa	0.01	-0.03	0.02	-0.05	0.13	0.04	0.49	0.29	1.22	1.14	1.56	1.34
Other West Africa	11.27	11.24	13.02	12.60	11.65	10.98	6.65	6.97	2.30	2.78	0.66	0.91
Pakistan	1.93	2.37	1.78	2.30	0.69	0.97	0.24	0.31	0.23	0.31	0.48	0.53
Peru	2.46	2.74	2.24	2.39	3.09	3.04	4.21	4.60	4.51	4.77	5.11	5.08
Philippines	9.46	9.92	9.49	10.16	9.03	9.15	8.98	9.70	8.19	8.53	5.69	5.79
Poland	2.55	2.30	2.31	1.80	1.73	1.39	1.42	1.52	1.58	2.05	1.37	1.77
Portugal	0.33	0.23	0.32	0.20	1.25	1.01	2.61	2.05	3.38	2.94	3.42	3.24
Romania	2.50	1.73	2.03	1.50	1.54	1.04	1.19	0.88	1.44	1.37	1.40	1.53
Russia												
Caspian Black Sea	1.73	1.23	1.41	1.11	1.33	1.06	1.13	1.13	1.44	1.52	1.42	1.68
Far Eastern	1.76	2.29	1.75	2.12	1.33	1.91	1.16	1.67	1.09	1.54	0.84	1.37
North European	2.36	2.54	2.21	2.24	2.02	2.08	1.84	2.19	1.69	2.30	1.47	2.00
North Urals Siberia	1.89	2.08	2.05	2.35	1.84	2.03	1.47	1.95	1.24	1.90	1.04	1.50
Northeast Siberia	1.58	1.87	1.49	1.79	1.06	1.34	0.77	1.21	0.55	1.01	0.44	0.76
South Urals Siberia	2.32	2.35	2.14	2.03	1.58	1.51	1.41	1.53	1.23	1.63	0.92	1.45
Southeast Siberia	3.11	3.53	2.90	3.26	1.92	2.23	1.00	1.27	0.69	1.07	0.52	0.82
Saudi Arabia	0.15	0.32	0.13	0.68	0.04	0.46	0.08	0.26	0.24	0.29	0.21	0.23
Scandinavia	2.44	2.51	2.50	2.57	2.64	2.91	2.46	3.10	2.38	3.10	2.05	2.71
Senegal	5.15	4.48	7.24	6.96	5.97	5.82	1.99	2.03	0.11	0.17	0.00	0.07
South Africa	0.43	0.28	0.58	0.40	0.74	0.52	1.35	1.06	1.80	1.79	1.83	1.78
South Korea	9.47	10.76	8.12	9.15	5.15	5.77	2.04	1.92	1.79	1.31	0.87	0.72
Southeastern Europe	1.71	1.29	1.69	1.32	1.95	1.49	2.30	1.84	3.12	2.78	2.87	2.87
Spain	0.64	0.43	0.76	0.56	1.40	1.23	2.07	1.62	2.51	2.10	2.25	2.05
Sri Lanka	2.84	4.26	3.09	4.48	4.51	5.56	8.54	9.67	9.45	10.22	7.02	6.63
Sudan	2.87	2.87	3.34	3.53	2.15	2.49	1.15	1.48	0.29	0.62	0.08	0.17

Syria	0.02	0.00	0.02	0.03	0.05	0.11	0.66	0.61	1.11	0.96	1.74	1.58
Tanzania	0.30	0.32	0.32	0.37	0.60	0.47	1.14	0.46	3.41	3.33	5.14	5.53
Thailand	7.18	8.05	8.54	8.81	8.82	9.54	5.46	6.23	2.66	2.47	1.02	0.91
Turkey	0.50	0.28	0.44	0.25	0.63	0.53	1.42	1.22	1.93	1.66	2.56	2.37
Uganda	2.86	3.19	3.63	3.57	3.82	3.13	3.99	3.16	3.95	4.66	1.88	2.57
Ukraine	2.31	1.69	1.74	1.35	1.45	1.09	1.09	1.00	1.45	1.49	1.56	1.77
United Kingdom	2.40	2.05	2.97	2.58	3.49	3.30	3.78	4.08	3.97	4.71	3.93	4.58
United States												
Alaska	1.83	2.47	1.96	2.48	1.69	2.29	1.21	1.92	1.00	1.73	0.94	1.66
Lakes and Northeast	3.11	2.90	3.09	3.04	3.06	2.80	2.35	2.32	2.40	2.47	2.06	2.10
Pacific Northwest	0.66	0.42	0.87	0.71	1.18	0.96	1.75	1.61	3.23	3.49	3.44	4.06
Rockies and Plains	1.62	1.27	1.44	1.26	1.35	1.20	0.94	0.94	0.69	0.79	0.62	0.72
Southeast	3.94	3.77	3.54	3.31	3.54	3.32	2.71	2.58	3.27	3.15	3.51	3.37
South Pacific Coast	0.37	0.35	0.49	0.53	0.57	0.65	0.88	0.85	1.98	2.05	2.03	2.55
Southwest Plains	1.73	1.56	1.98	1.74	2.11	1.74	1.44	1.42	0.99	0.84	0.84	0.72
Uzbekistan	0.12	0.07	0.05	0.07	0.09	0.07	0.41	0.34	0.57	0.56	0.72	0.78
Venezuela	9.23	8.62	8.44	8.33	6.69	6.30	5.49	5.42	4.40	4.61	2.64	2.85
Vietnam	8.05	7.96	8.63	8.78	8.66	9.07	7.10	7.99	5.03	4.83	2.12	2.00
Yemen	0.85	1.14	0.78	1.32	0.32	0.82	0.21	0.86	0.30	0.54	0.26	0.40
Zambia	0.01	−0.04	0.01	−0.07	0.15	−0.01	1.03	0.08	3.71	3.50	7.13	7.11
Zimbabwe	0.07	0.02	0.09	0.00	0.25	0.08	0.86	−0.04	2.51	2.26	4.71	5.25

P0 = precipitation for 1961–90
P1 = precipitation for 2070–99

Appendix I
Dispersion of Climate Projections Across General Circulation Models

It is often argued that climate general circulation models (GCMs) give such widely divergent projections at detailed geographical levels that they do not provide the basis for examining future climate change effects at such levels. This appendix examines the degree of dispersion across the six GCMs used in this study for projected temperature and precipitation by 2070–99. The average levels for this period are shown in 4.2 in chapter 4.

This appendix considers the coefficient of variation of these projections across the six climate models listed in table 4.1. This measure, which is the ratio of the standard deviation (square root of the sum of square residuals from mean) to the mean, is the most natural gauge of dispersion to consider. Even so it is inherently problematic for climate measures. It depends on the level of the mean, and of course as the mean approaches zero it approaches infinity even if the variation around the mean is small. As usually measured (in Celsius or Fahrenheit), temperature in particular is not a "ratio scale" number with absolute zero but a relative number with arbitrary zero. In contrast, temperature measured in kelvin (K) is in a ratio scale. Because it will show a much larger mean value (e.g., 287 K rather than 14°C), the coefficient of variation will be much smaller when calculated using kelvin than when using Celsius.[1]

---

1. Moreover, because Celsius is not a ratio scale number it is meaningless to say that post-warming temperatures will be x percent higher than today's levels. Some of the Ricardian

Similarly, the coefficient of variation will be quite different if it is calculated for alternative future levels of temperature and precipitation against future means from what would be calculated using instead the change in temperature or change in precipitation from present-day levels. The change variables will have much smaller means than the level variables, potentially generating an extreme measure of coefficient of variation.

With these caveats in mind, it is useful to consider the coefficient of variation for the projected future *levels* of temperature and precipitation across the six GCM projections for 2070–99. These are reported in table I.1. For future temperatures, the coefficient of variation shows a relatively low median of 0.10. That is, for the typical case, the standard deviation across the six models is only 10 percent of the mean value, even though the measure used is Celsius. For precipitation, the median coefficient of variation is 0.33. This extent of dispersion is considerably higher. However, as noted in the discussion of the estimates using the various Ricardian models (chapter 5), the coefficients in these empirically estimated models tend to show lesser agricultural impact from future changes in precipitation than from future changes in temperature. Significant variability in the precipitation projections is unlikely to be particularly problematic for the impact projections, given the relatively low dispersion in the temperature projections.

As expected, the measured dispersion can be large where the level of the mean is close to zero (e.g., in Alaska the coefficient of variation for future temperature is 6.68; it is negative for Arctic Canada because the future mean temperature is below zero). Aside from such cases, the only surprisingly high coefficient of variation for temperature is in the case of Northeastern India, where it reaches 3.64. Otherwise, it seems fair to say that the variability of the climate model projections of future temperature is perhaps surprisingly modest, in light of the seeming reputation of such models for sharp variability.

The same can largely be said about the results for precipitation. The cases with high coefficients of variation (e.g., above 1) tend to be regions with low present and future precipitation (e.g., Algeria at 0.23 mm per day, Egypt at 0.12 mm per day, Niger at 0.68 mm per day, and Yemen at 0.64 mm per day; future levels in all cases). Once again, however, there are intriguing exceptions. The coefficient of variation for future precipitation is relatively high for Argentina, Brazil's Northeast, India's Northwest, Mexico, and the US South Pacific Coast, even though none of these regions has a level of future precipitation below 1 mm per day. True variability across the models appears to be present in such cases. Nonetheless,

---

impact studies have slipped into the misnomer of identifying "elasticities" of impact with respect to temperature—a concept that instead would require a meaningful percentage change in temperature and hence the use of kelvin.

Table I.1   Coefficient of variation for future climate projections of six models

Country	Temperature	Precipitation
Afghanistan	0.19	0.47
Algeria	0.09	2.90
Angola	0.09	0.45
Argentina	0.07	0.65
Australia	0.05	0.34
Bangladesh	0.09	0.13
Belgium	0.20	0.27
Brazil		
Amazon	0.12	0.32
Northeast	0.09	0.77
South	0.07	0.27
Burkina Faso	0.03	0.41
Cambodia	0.05	0.21
Cameroon	0.04	0.23
Canada		
Arctic	−0.93	0.38
Central	0.20	0.33
Northwest Territories	1.79	0.41
Pacific Coast	0.63	0.25
Southeast	1.76	0.16
Central America	0.08	0.22
Central Europe	0.32	0.17
Chile	0.10	0.98
China		
Beijing Northeast	0.75	0.34
Central	0.24	0.31
Hong Kong Southeast	0.07	0.25
Northwest	0.37	0.89
South Central	0.09	0.34
Tibetan Plateau	2.00	0.67
Yellow Sea	0.13	0.24
Colombia	0.07	0.36
Cuba	0.04	0.38
Democratic Republic of the Congo	0.07	0.27
Ecuador	0.05	0.46
Egypt	0.10	1.44
Ethiopia	0.05	0.70
France	0.21	0.22
Germany	0.28	0.28
Ghana	0.03	0.23
Greece	0.14	0.24

(table continues next page)

Table I.1　Coefficient of variation for future climate projections of six models *(continued)*

Country	Temperature	Precipitation
India		
Northeast	3.64	0.37
Northwest	0.07	0.60
Southeast	0.04	0.30
Southwest	0.03	0.34
Indonesia	0.04	0.22
Iran	0.12	0.67
Iraq	0.11	0.63
Italy	0.20	0.24
Ivory Coast	0.03	0.24
Japan	0.22	0.18
Kazakhstan	0.32	0.47
Kenya	0.07	0.44
Madagascar	0.04	0.23
Malawi	0.08	0.27
Malaysia	0.04	0.14
Mali	0.04	1.57
Mexico	0.11	0.60
Morocco	0.14	0.40
Mozambique	0.07	0.35
Myanmar	0.08	0.26
Nepal	0.26	0.42
Netherlands	0.22	0.28
New Zealand	0.11	0.12
Niger	0.03	1.41
Nigeria	0.03	0.35
North Korea	0.39	0.23
Other Central Asia	0.29	0.70
Other Equatorial Africa	0.05	0.31
Other Horn of Africa	0.04	0.73
Other South America	0.11	0.49
Other South Africa	0.08	0.55
Other West Africa	0.03	0.15
Pakistan	0.13	0.69
Peru	0.09	0.35
Philippines	0.03	0.23
Poland	0.36	0.22
Portugal	0.13	0.26
Romania	0.28	0.24
Russia		
Caspian Black Sea	0.32	0.31
Far Eastern	−0.06	0.29
North European	0.63	0.29

(table continues next page)

Table I.1   Coefficient of variation for future climate projections of six models *(continued)*

Country	Temperature	Precipitation
Russia *(continued)*		
North Urals Siberia	3.48	0.31
Northeast Siberia	−1.60	0.28
South Urals Siberia	0.98	0.33
Southeast Siberia	0.23	0.27
Saudi Arabia	0.07	1.79
Scandinavia	0.67	0.24
Senegal	0.05	0.20
South Africa	0.06	0.46
South Korea	0.21	0.20
Southeast Europe	0.20	0.26
Spain	0.16	0.41
Sri Lanka	0.03	0.26
Sudan	0.04	1.18
Syria	0.13	0.43
Tanzania	0.07	0.33
Thailand	0.04	0.27
Turkey	0.18	0.31
Uganda	0.06	0.37
Ukraine	0.35	0.28
United Kingdom	0.18	0.23
United States		
Alaska	6.68	0.41
Lakes and Northeast	0.27	0.20
Pacific Northwest	0.18	0.55
Rockies, Plains	0.24	0.45
Southeast	0.15	0.27
South Pacific Coast	0.14	0.87
Southwest Plains	0.16	0.46
Uzbekistan	0.18	1.15
Venezuela	0.08	0.37
Vietnam	0.05	0.21
Yemen	0.05	1.57
Zambia	0.07	0.23
Zimbabwe	0.07	0.41

Note: For future levels, see table 4.2; for climate models, see table 4.1.

the surprising pattern is that such cases seem to be the exception rather than the rule. So whether the models are correct or not, they seem to adhere more closely to each other, even for precipitation, than might be expected given much of the discussion about GCM projections.

References

ABS (Australian Bureau of Statistics). 2005. *Value of Agricultural Commodities Produced, Australia 2004–05*. Canberra. Available at www.abs.gov.au (accessed April 12, 2007).

Adams, R. M., C. Rosenzweig, R. Peart, J. Ritchie, B. McCarl, J. Glyer, B. Curry, J. Jones, K. Boote, and L. Allen. 1990. Global Climate Change and U.S. Agriculture. *Nature* (May): 219–24.

Adams, Richard M., Bruce A. McCarl, Kathleen Segerson, Cynthia Rosenzweig, Kelly J. Bryant, Bruce L. Dixon, Richard Conner, Robert E. Evenson, and Dennis Ojima. 1999. Economic Effects of Climate Change on US Agriculture. In *The Impact of Climate Change on the United States Economy*, ed. Robert Mendelsohn and James E. Neumann. Cambridge, UK: Cambridge University Press.

Avila, Antonio Flavio Dias, Luiz José Maria Irias, and Magda Aparecida de Lima. 2006. Global Warming Effects on the Brazilian Agriculture: Economic Impact Assessment on Land Values. World Bank, Washington. Photocopy (December).

BEA (Bureau of Economic Analysis). 2006. *National Income and Product Accounts*. Washington: US Department of Commerce. Available at www.bea.gov (accessed June 29, 2006).

Boer, G., G. Flato, and D. Ramsden. 2000. A Transient Climate Change Simulation with Greenhouse Gas and Aerosol Forcing: Projected Climate to the Twenty-First Century. *Climate Dynamics* 16, no. 6 (June): 427–50.

Cap, Eugenio, and Jorge Lozanoff. 2006. El Impacto del Cambio Climatico sobre la Agricultura Argentina: Un Estudio Económico. World Bank, Washington. Photocopy (December).

CEA (Council of Economic Advisers). 1994. *Economic Report of the President*. Washington.

Cline, William R. 1992. *The Economics of Global Warming*. Washington: Peterson Institute for International Economics.

Cline, William R. 1996. The Impact of Global Warming on Agriculture: Comment. *American Economic Review* 86, no. 5 (December): 1309–11.

Cline, William R. 2004. Climate Change. In *Global Crises, Global Solutions*, ed. Bjørn Lomborg. Cambridge, UK: Cambridge University Press.

Darwin, Roy, Marinos Tsigas, Jan Lewandrowski, and Anton Raneses. 1995. *World Agriculture and Climate Change*. Agricultural Economic Report no. 703 (June). Washington: US Department of Agriculture, Economic Research Service.

Darwin, R. F. 1999. A FARMer's View of the Ricardian Approach to Measuring Agricultural Effects of Climate Change. *Climatic Change* 41: 371–411.

Darwin, R. F., and D. Kennedy. 2000. Economic Effects of CO_2 Fertilization of Crops: Transforming Changes in Yield into Changes in Supply. *Environmental Modeling and Assessment* 5, no. 3:157–68.

Deininger, Klaus. 1999. *Making Negotiated Land Reform Work: Initial Experiences from Brazil, Colombia, and South Africa.* World Bank Policy Research Working Paper no. 2040 (January). Washington: World Bank.

Dinar, Ariel, Robert Mendelsohn, Robert Evenson, Jyoti Parikh, Apurva Sanghi, Kavi Kumar, James McKinsey, and Stephen Lonergan. 1998. *Measuring the Impact of Climate Change on Indian Agriculture.* World Bank Technical Paper no. 402 (March). Washington: World Bank.

Emori, S., T. Nozawa, A. Abe-Ouchi, A. Numaguti, M. Kimoto, and T. Nakajima. 1999. Coupled Ocean-Atmosphere Model Experiments of Future Climate Change with an Explicit Representation of Sulfate Aerosol Scattering. *Journal of the Meteorological Society of Japan* 77: 1299–307.

EPA (Environmental Protection Agency). 1989. *The Potential Effects of Global Climate Change on the United States,* eds. Joel B. Smith and Dennis Tirpak. Washington.

ERS (Economic Research Service). 2006a. *China Agricultural and Economic Data.* Washington: US Department of Agriculture. Available at www.ers.usda.gov/data/china (accessed June 29, 2006).

ERS (Economic Research Service). 2006b. *Data Sets: International Food Consumption Patterns.* Washington: US Department of Agriculture.

FAO (Food and Agriculture Organization). 2005. *Compendium of Food and Agriculture Indicators 2005.* Rome. Available at www.fao.org (accessed June 29, 2006).

FAO (Food and Agriculture Organization). 2006a. *World Census of Agriculture: Results by Country.* Rome. Available at www.fao.org (accessed June 29, 2006).

FAO (Food and Agriculture Organization). 2006b. *FAO Country Profiles and Mapping Information System.* Rome. Available at www.fao.org.

Federal Register. 2006. US Government. *Federal Register* 71, no. 158 (August 16).

Fischer, Günther, Harrij vanVelthuizen, Mahendra Shah, and Freedy Nachteergaele. 2002. *Global Agro-Ecological Assessment for Agriculture in the 21st Century: Methodology and Results.* Laxenburg, Austria: International Institute for Applied Systems Analysis.

Flato, G. M., and G. J. Boer. 2001. Warming Asymmetry in Climate Change Experiments. *Geophysical Research Letters* 28: 195–98.

González U., Jorge, Roberto Velasco H., and José Cares G. 2006. Cambio Climático en Sistemas Agrícolas de Chile: I: Evaluación Preliminar del Efecto de Variables de Clima Sobre el Valor Económico Estimado del Suelo. World Bank, Washington. Photocopy (December).

Gordon, H. B., and S. P. O'Farrell. 1997. Transient Climate Change in the CSIRO Coupled Model with Dynamic Sea Ice. *Monthly Weather Review* 125: 875–907.

Gordon, C., C. Cooper, C. A. Senior, H. T. Banks, J. M. Gregory, T. C. Johns, J. F. B. Mitchell, and R. A. Wood. 2000. The Simulation of SST, Sea Ice Extents and Ocean Heat Transports in a Version of the Hadley Centre Coupled Model without Flux Adjustments. *Climate Dynamics* 16: 147–68.

Hitz, Sam, and Joel Smith. 2004. Estimating Global Impacts from Climate Change. In *The Benefits of Climate Change Policies: Analytical and Framework Issues.* Paris: Organisation for Economic Cooperation and Development.

IBGE (Instituto Brasileiro de Geografia e Estatística). 2006. *Censo Agropecuário de 1995–1996.* Rio de Janeiro. Available at www.ibge.gov.br (accessed June 29, 2006).

IEA (International Energy Agency). 2006. *Energy Technology Perspectives: Scenarios and Strategies to 2050.* Paris.

IPCC (Intergovernmental Panel on Climate Change). 1996. *Climate Change 1995: Impacts, Adaptations and Mitigation of Climate Change: Scientific-Technical Analyses,* ed. Robert T. Watson, Marufu C. Zinyuwera, and Richard H. Moss. IPCC Second Assessment Report: Climate Change 1995. Cambridge, UK: Cambridge University Press.

IPCC (Intergovernmental Panel on Climate Change). 1999. Guidelines on the Use of Scenario Data for Climate Impact and Adaptation Assessment, Version 1. Intergovernmental Panel on Climate Change, Task Group on Scenarios for Climate Impact Assessment (December). Available at http://ipcc-ddc.cru.uea.ac.uk.

IPCC (Intergovernmental Panel on Climate Change). 2001a. *Climate Change 2001: The Scientific Basis*, ed. J. T. Houghton et al. IPCC Third Assessment Report: Climate Change 2001. Cambridge, UK: Cambridge University Press.

IPCC (Intergovernmental Panel on Climate Change). 2001b. *Climate Change 2001: Impacts, Adaptation, and Vulnerability*, ed. James J. McCarthy et al. IPCC Third Assessment Report: Climate Change 2001.Cambridge, UK: Cambridge University Press.

IPCC (Intergovernmental Panel on Climate Change). 2007a. Summary for Policymakers. *Climate Change 2007: The Physical Science Basis*. Working Group I Contribution to IPCC Fourth Assessment Report: Climate Change 2007. Geneva.

IPCC (Intergovernmental Panel on Climate Change). 2007b. Summary for Policymakers. *Climate Change 2007: Climate Change Impacts, Adaptation, and Vulnerability*. Working Group II Contribution to IPCC Fourth Assessment Report: Climate Change 2007. Geneva (April 6).

IMF (International Monetary Fund). 2006. *International Financial Statistics*. Washington.

Jativa, Pablo, and S. Niggol Seo. 2006. A Cross-Sectional Examination of Climate Change Impacts on Agriculture in Ecuador. World Bank, Washington. Photocopy (December).

Jorgenson, Dale W., Richard J. Goettle, Brian H. Hurd, and Joel B. Smith. 2004. *U.S. Market Consequences of Global Climate Change*. Arlington, VA: Pew Center on Global Climate Change (April).

Knutson, T. R., T. L. Delworth, K. W. Dixon, and R. J. Stouffer. 1999. Model Assessment of Regional Surface Temperature Trends (1949–1997). *Journal of Geophysical Research* 104: 30981–96.

Kurukulasuriya, Pradeep, and Shane Rosenthal. 2003. *Climate Change and Agriculture*. World Bank Environment Department Paper no. 91 (June). Washington: World Bank.

Kurukulasuriya, Pradeep, Robert Mendelsohn, Rashid Hassan, James Benhin, Temesgen Deressa, Mbaye Diop, Helmy Mohamed Eid, K. Yerfi Fosu, Glwadys Gbetibouo, Suman Jain, Ali Mahamadou, Renneth Mano, Jane Kabubo-Mariara, Samia El-Marsafawy, Ernest Molua, Samiha Ouda, Mathieu Ouedraogo, Isidor Sène, David Maddison, S. Niggol Seo, and Ariel Dinar. 2006. Will African Agriculture Survive Climate Change? *World Bank Economic Review*, no. 21 (October).

Kurukulasuriya, Pradeep, and Robert Mendelsohn. 2006. A Ricardian Analysis of the Impact of Climate Change on African Cropland. CEEPA Discussion Paper no. 8 (July). Pretoria, South Africa: Centre for Environmental Economics and Policy in Africa.

Li, Yi-Fan. 1996. *Global Population Distribution Database*. Downsview, Ontario: Environment Canada (August 12). Available at http://grid.cr.usgs.gov.

Long, Stephen P., Elizabeth A. Ainsworth, Andrew D. B. Leakey, and Patrick B. Morgan. 2005. Global Food Insecurity: Treatment of Major Food Crops with Elevated Carbon Dioxide or Ozone under Large-scale Fully Open-Air Conditions Suggests Recent Models May Have Overestimated Future Yields. *Philosophical Transactions of the Royal Society B* 360: 2011–20.

Long, Stephen P., Elizabeth A. Ainsworth, Andrew D. B. Leakey, Josef Nösberger, and Donald R. Ort. 2006. Food for Thought: Lower-than-Expected Crop Yield Stimulation with Rising CO_2 Concentrations. *Science* 312 (June 30): 1918–21.

Mendelsohn, Robert, William D. Nordhaus, and Daigee Shaw. 1994. The Impact of Global Warming on Agriculture: A Ricardian Analysis. *American Economic Review* 84, no. 4 (September): 753–71.

Mendelsohn, Robert, and James E. Neumann, eds. 1999. *The Impact of Climate Change on the United States Economy*. Cambridge, UK: Cambridge University Press.

Mendelsohn, Robert, and William D. Nordhaus. 1999. The Impact of Global Warming on Agriculture: A Ricardian Analysis: Reply. *American Economic Review* 89, no. 4 (September): 1053–55.

Mendelsohn, Robert, and Michael E. Schlesinger. 1999. Climate Response Functions. *Ambio* 28, no. 4 (June): 362–66.

Mendelsohn, Robert, Wendy Morrison, Michael E. Schlesinger, and Natalia G. Andronova. 2000. Country-Specific Market Impacts of Climate Change. *Climatic Change* 45: 553–69.

Mendelsohn, Robert, Ariel Dinar, and Apurva Sanghi. 2001. The Effect of Development on the Climate Sensitivity of Agriculture. *Environment and Development Economics* 6: 85–101.

Mendelsohn, Robert, and Ariel Dinar. 2003. Climate, Water, and Agriculture. *Land Economics* 79, no. 3 (August): 328–41.

Mendelsohn, Robert, and Michelle Reinsborough. 2007. A Ricardian Analysis of US and Canadian Farmland. Yale University, New Haven, CT. Photocopy.

Nakićenović, N., and R. Swart, eds. 2000. *IPCC Special Report on Emissions Scenarios*. Cambridge, UK: Cambridge University Press.

NAST (National Assessment Synthesis Team). 2001. *Climate Change Impacts on the United States: The Potential Consequences of Climate Variability and Change.* Report to the US Global Change Research Program. Cambridge, UK: Cambridge University Press.

NOAA (National Oceanic and Atmospheric Administration). 2007. Comparative Climatic Data: Data Tables. Washington: US Department of Commerce. Available at http://ols.nndc.noaa.gov (accessed March 29, 2007).

Nordhaus, William D., and Joseph Boyer. 2000. *Warming the World: Economic Models of Global Warming.* Cambridge, MA: MIT Press.

OECD (Organisation for Economic Cooperation and Development). 2004. *The Benefits of Climate Change Policies: Analytical and Framework Issues.* Paris.

OECD (Organisation for Economic Cooperation and Development). 2005. *OECD in Figures, 2005 Edition.* Paris. Available at http://ocde.p4.siteinternet.com (accessed June 29, 2006).

Pacheco, Rafael, Luisa Caraballo, and S. Niggol Seo. 2006. Global Warming and Agriculture in Venezuela: An Economic Valuation. World Bank, Washington. Photocopy (December).

Parry, M., C. Rosenzweig, A. Iglesias, G. Fischer, and M. Livermore. 1999. Climate Change and World Food Security: A New Assessment. *Global Environmental Change* 9: S51–S67.

Parry, M., C. Rosenzweig, A. Iglesias, M. Livermore, and G. Fischer. 2004. Effects of Climate Change on Global Food Production under SRES Emissions and Socio-Economic Scenarios. *Global Environmental Change* 11, no. 3: 1–3.

Parry, Martin, Cynthia Rosenzweig, and Matthew Livermore. 2005. Climate Change, Global Food Supply and Risk of Hunger. *Philosophical Transactions of the Royal Society B* 360: 2125–38 (October 24).

Quiggin, John, and John K. Horowitz. 1999. The Impact of Global Warming on Agriculture: A Ricardian Analysis: Comment. *American Economic Review* 89, no. 4 (September): 1044–45.

Reilly, J., N. Hohmann, and S. Kane. 1994. Climate Change and Agricultural Trade: Who Benefits, Who Loses? *Global Environmental Change* 4, no. 1: 24–36.

Reilly, John M., and 22 coauthors. 1996. Agriculture in a Changing Climate: Impacts and Adaptation. In *Climate Change 1995: Impacts, Adaptations and Mitigation of Climate Change,* ed. Robert T. Watson, Marufu C. Zinyuwera, and Richard H. Moss. Cambridge, UK: Cambridge University Press.

Reilly, John M., and 19 coauthors. 2001. *Agriculture: The Potential Consequences of Climate Variability and Change for the United States.* US National Assessment of the Potential Consequences of Climate Variability and Change, US Global Change Research Program. New York: Cambridge University Press.

Reinsborough, Michelle J. 2003. A Ricardian Model of Climate Change in Canada. *Canadian Journal of Economics* 36, no. 1 (February): 21–40.

Rocha, Jorge Granados, Irma Baquero Haeberlin, Margarita Ramírez Gómez, and Fabiola Gómez. 2006. Efectos del Cambio Climático Global en la Agricultura Colombiana. World Bank, Washington. Photocopy (December).

Roeckner, E., K. Arpe, L. Bengtsson, M. Christoph, M. Claussen, L. Dümenil, M. Esch, M. Giorgetta, U. Schlese, and U. Schulzweida. 1996. *The Atmospheric General Circulation Model ECHAM-4: Model Description and Simulation of Present-Day Climate.* Max-Planck Institute for Meteorology Report no. 218. Hamburg, Germany: Max-Planck Institute for Meteorology.

Rosenberg, Norman J., and Pierre R. Crosson. 1991. *Processes for Identifying Regional Influences of and Responses to Increasing Atmospheric CO_2 and Climate Change: The MINK Project—An Overview.* DOE/RL/01830T-H5 (August). Washington: US Department of Energy.

Rosenzweig, C., M. L. Parry, G. Fischer, and K. Frohberg. 1993. *Climate Change and World Food Supply.* Research Report no. 3. Oxford: University of Oxford, Environmental Change Unit. Available at www.ciesin.org (accessed August 9, 2006).

Rosenzweig, Cynthia, and Ana Iglesias, eds. 1994. *Implications of Climate Change for International Agriculture: Crop Modeling Study.* EPA 230-B-94-003. Washington: US Environmental Protection Agency.

Rosenzweig, C., and M. L. Parry. 1994. Potential Impacts of Climate Change on World Food Supply. *Nature* 367: 133–38.

Rosenzweig, C., M. Parry, and G. Fischer. 1995. World Food Supply. In *As Climate Changes: International Impacts and Implications,* ed. K. M. Strzepek and J. B. Smith. Cambridge, UK: Cambridge University Press.

Rosenzweig, Cynthia, and Ana Iglesias. 2006. *Potential Impacts of Climate Change on World Food Supply: Data Sets from a Major Crop Modeling Study.* New York: Goddard Institute for Space Studies, Columbia University. Available at http://sedac.ciesin.columbia.edu (accessed August 9, 2006).

Sanghi, Apurva, Robert Mendelsohn, and Ariel Dinar. 1998. The Climate Sensitivity of Indian Agriculture. In *Measuring the Impact of Climate Change on Indian Agriculture,* by Dinar et al. World Bank Technical Paper no. 402 (March). Washington: World Bank.

Statistics Canada. 2007. *Agriculture 2001 Census: Data Tables.* Ottawa. Available at www.statcan.ca.

Stern Review. 2006. *Stern Review Report on the Economics of Climate Change,* by Nicholas Stern. Prepublication edition available at www.hm-treasury.gov.uk. Published edition available as *The Economics of Climate Change: The Stern Review.* Cambridge, UK: Cambridge University Press, 2007.

Tol, Richard S. J. 2002. Estimates of Damage Costs of Climate Change. *Environmental and Resource Economics* 21: 47–73.

Tubiello, F. N., C. Rosenzweig, R. A. Goldberg, S. Jagtap, and J. W. Jones. 2002. Effects of Climate Change on US Crop Production: Simulation Results Using Two Different GCM Scenarios. Part I: Wheat, Potato, Maize, and Citrus. *Climate Research* 20 (April): 259–70.

Tubiello, Francesco N., Jeffrey S. Amthor, Kenneth J. Boote, Marcello Donatelli, William Easterling, Gunther Fischer, Roger M. Gifford, Mark Howden, John Reilly, and Cynthia Rosenzweig. 2007. Crop Response to Elevated CO_2 and World Food Supply. (A Comment on "Food for Thought" by Long et al., 2006, *Science* 312: 1918–21.) *European Journal of Agronomy* 26: 215–23.

United Nations. 2006. *World Population Prospects: The 2004 Revision Population Database.* New York: United Nations, Department of Economic and Social Affairs.

USDA (US Department of Agriculture). 2004. *2002 Census of Agriculture: Summary and State Data,* volume 1. Geographic Area Series, Part 51 (June). Washington.

USDA (US Department of Agriculture). 2005. *Cotton and Wool Outlook* (December 12). Washington.

USDA (US Department of Agriculture, Foreign Agricultural Service). 2006. *World Agricultural Production*. WAP 09-06 (September). Washington.

Washington, W. M., J. W. Weatherly, G. A. Meehl, A. J. Semtner Jr., T. W. Bettge, A. P. Craig, W. G. Strand Jr., J. Arblaster, V. B. Wayland, R. James, and Y. Zhang. 2000. Parallel Climate Model (PCM): Control and Transient Solutions. *Climate Dynamics* 16, no. 10-11 (October): 755–74.

World Bank. 1978. *World Development Report 1978*. Washington.

World Bank. 1984. *World Development Report 1984*. Washington.

World Bank. 2005. *World Development Indicators 2005*. Washington.

World Bank. 2006. *World Development Indicators 2006*. Washington.

Worldwatch Institute. 1998. *United States Leads World Meat Stampede*. Washington (July 1).

Zhang, X-H., J. M. Oberhuber, A. Bacher, and E. Roeckner. 1998. Interpretation of Interbasin Exchange in an Isopycnal Ocean. *Climate Dynamics* 14: 725–40.

Glossary

benchmark 2 × CO$_2$ warming. Eventual equilibrium warming from a doubling of atmospheric concentration of carbon dioxide above preindustrial levels (280 parts per million by volume, or ppm, prior to the Industrial Revolution). The present concentration of CO$_2$ is about 380 ppm. Equilibrium climate simulations commonly assume a radiative forcing equivalent to a doubling of preindustrial CO$_2$ concentration.

C3 and C4 crops. Crops are generally divided into two groups—C3 and C4—depending on the number of carbon atoms in the first stable compound into which carbon dioxide is incorporated during photosynthesis (process by which plants use sunlight to make carbohydrates from CO$_2$ and water, with oxygen as a waste product). Plants belonging to the C3 group include rice, wheat, soybeans, barley, oats, potatoes, fine grains, legumes, and most trees. Those in the C4 group include maize, millet, sorghum, and sugarcane. Because of differences in the photosynthesis process between the two groups, C3 crops benefit substantially more than C4 crops from "carbon fertilization" associated with higher atmospheric concentrations of CO$_2$.

carbon dioxide equivalent. Measure that expresses the amount of other greenhouse gases in terms of the amount of carbon dioxide that would have the same global warming potential.

carbon fertilization. Enhancement of the growth of plants as a result of increased atmospheric carbon dioxide concentration, resulting from the fact that CO$_2$ is an input into the process of photosynthesis.

crop process models. Agronomic models that predict yields and other aspects of crop production as a function of temperature, precipitation, availability of irrigation, soil type, crop management, and other variables.

equilibrium climate simulation. Mode of running a global climate model in which greenhouse gas concentrations are suddenly changed (typically double the preindustrial values) and the model allowed to come into equilibrium with the new forcing (*see also* benchmark 2 × CO_2 warming *and* ocean thermal lag).

evapotranspiration. Combined loss of moisture from soil through evaporation and from plants through stomatal transpiration.

free air concentration enrichment (FACE). Method whereby carbon dioxide levels can be elevated in a specified area of forest or other biomass. Unlike controlled environments such as growth chambers and greenhouses, this experiment enables scientists to study the response of plant growth to increased levels of CO_2 under natural conditions.

general circulation models (GCMs). Computer models of the earth's climate system that simulate the physical processes whereby the atmosphere and oceans affect global climate. They have been developed over two decades and require extensive computations to run. They can be run to estimate current climates and the sensitivity of climate to different conditions such as different levels of greenhouse gases.

greenhouse gas emissions. Release of gases from the burning of fossil fuels for residential, commercial, and industrial purposes and to power transport vehicles (automobiles, trucks, airplanes, trains, and ships) and from other emissions-producing processes and activities. Globally these emissions are measured in gigatons (1 billion metric tons).

greenhouse effect. Warming of the earth attributable to the opacity of water vapor, carbon dioxide, and other greenhouse gases to outbound long-wave infrared radiation from the earth, relative to their transparency to inbound short-wave solar radiation. The result of this differential is that about half of the sun's radiation is permitted to enter through the atmosphere, but about 80 to 90 percent of the returning radiation from the earth is trapped. Natural greenhouse gases keep the earth's average surface temperature about 33°C warmer than it otherwise would be (at about +15°C rather than −18°C). In its 2007 report, the Intergovernmental Panel on Climate Change judged that anthropogenic (manmade) emissions of greenhouse gases have been the main reason for the observed rise in average global surface temperatures by about 0.8°C from 1850–99 to 2001–05.

Kyoto Protocol. Agreement made under the United Nations Framework Convention on Climate Change. Industrial and transition-economy, but not developing, countries that ratify this protocol commit to reducing their emissions of carbon dioxide and five other greenhouse gases by at least 5 percent below 1990 levels in the commitment period 2008–2012 or engage in emissions trading if they maintain or increase emissions of these gases (*see* greenhouse gas emissions). The protocol was negotiated in Kyoto, Japan in December 1997 and came into force on February 16, 2005 following ratification by Russia in November 2004. As of October 2006, a total of 166 countries and other governmental entities have ratified the agreement (representing over 61.6 percent of emissions). Notable exceptions include the United States and Australia. Although India and China have ratified the protocol, as developing countries they are not required to reduce carbon emissions despite their large populations and (especially in the case of China) current emissions.

MMSA. Mendelsohn, Morrison, Schlesinger, and Andronova (2000).

MS. Mendelsohn and Schlesinger (1999).

ocean thermal lag. Length of time (some three decades for benchmark $2 \times CO_2$ warming) between increase in atmospheric concentration of greenhouse gases and the resulting eventual equilibrium warming, attributable to ocean thermal dynamics. During this period surface warming is slowed as the deep ocean is warmed to maintain an equilibrium differential from ocean surface temperatures.

permanent crop land. Land under crops that last many seasons and are not replanted after each harvest. Permanent crops include tea, coffee, rubber, flowering shrubs, fruit and nut trees, and vines.

Ricardian models. Family of Ricardian or cross-section (CS) models relating agricultural capacity to temperature and precipitation, usually in a nonlinear fashion, on the basis of statistical estimates from farm survey or county-level data across varying climatic zones. The classical economist David Ricardo developed the theory that the value of land depends on the difference between its fertility and that of the least fertile land just brought into cultivation at the margin. The seminal Ricardian agricultural impact model (Mendelsohn, Nordhaus, and Shaw 1994) argued that statistical regressions relating land values to climate differences could capture the impact of climate on agricultural productivity and thus be used to calculate prospective effects of global warming.

SRES scenarios. A suite of emissions scenarios developed by the Intergovernmental Panel on Climate Change (IPCC) in its Special Report on Emissions Scenarios (SRES) for the Third Assessment Report and also used in the Fourth Assessment Report. The six families of scenarios are A1FI, A1B, A1T, A2, B1, and B2. The central scenario set used in the present study is SRES A2, in which carbon dioxide emissions rise from about 7.3 GtC (gigatons of carbon) in 1990 to about 29 GtC by 2100.

transient climate simulation. Mode of running a global climate model in which a period of time is simulated with continuously varying concentrations of greenhouse gases so that the climate of the model represents prospective changes already realized by the time of each future date in question, rather than the higher long-run equilibrium warming eventually resulting from atmospheric concentrations at each such date. The difference stems from ocean thermal lag.

Sources: The present study; Cline (1992); IPCC Data Distribution Center, www.ipcc-data.org; US Department of Agriculture, www.usda.gov; Environmental Protection Agency, www.epa.gov; United Nations Environment Program, www.unep.org; Pew Center on Global Climate Change, www.pewclimate.org; and United Nations Framework Convention on Climate Change, http://unfccc. int. All Web sites accessed on June 8, 2007.

Index

need for, and climate change, 26–27, 28f, 30
   in US, 26–27, 28f
   water availability for, 9, 16, 26, 29, 84–85
irrigation compensation, 84
iso-production curves, for MS model, 44f, 44–45

Jorgensen et al. (2004) study, 18

kelvin, 163, 164n
Kurukulasuriya et al. (2006) study, 48, 53, 63, 84–85
Kurukulasuriya and Mendelsohn (2006) study, 85
Kyoto Protocol, 97

land area. See also agricultural land; farm area
   by country, region, and subzone, 115–18, 119t–21t
   ratio of farm land to, 115–16
   weighting by, 41–42, 42t
land class coverage, percent changes in, 12
land classification, 5–6
   by growing season length, 11–12
   by utilization type, 15–16, 16n
land rental equivalent, in Ricardian estimates, 25–26, 129–35, 130t–33t
land rental value, output potential and, 46–47, 47t
land surface air temperature, 41, 41n, 95
land value models, 5, 57, 57t
land zone model, 11, 13–14
   in Fischer (2002) study, 15–17
   versus Rosenzweig model, 13
Latin America. See also specific country
   agricultural production in, 58
   Ricardian models for, 56–58, 57t, 83, 138–39, 140t
   vulnerability of, 80, 96
   World Bank study on, 48, 48n, 56–58, 57t, 65, 85
latitude
   agroecological zone model by, 16
   crop yields by, 19
   grid land area calculations by, 6
   land zone model approach to, 12
   regional differences due to, 9, 18, 49, 49n, 73, 74f–75f, 95–96
Long et al. (2005) study, 24
Long et al. (2006) study, 25n

maize
   carbon fertilization effect on, 20
   ethanol produced from, 89
   production of, 90t, 90–91
   Rosenzweig model on, 62
   temperature thresholds for, 10
   yield impacts, 9–10, 91, 92t
mapping methodology, 115–16
meat consumption per capita, 93t, 93–94, 94n
Mendelsohn, Dinar, and Sanghi (1998) study, 17
Mendelsohn, Dinar, and Sanghi (2001) study, 48, 48n, 49, 49n, 50t, 65, 83–84
Mendelsohn and Dinar (2003) study, 32n
Mendelsohn, Morrison, Schlesinger, and Andronova (2000) study (MMSA), 20, 81–83
   carbon fertilization effect in, 25–26, 26n, 82
   grid specification in, 82n
   versus MS model, 46
   positive effects found in, 2
   turning point identified in, 41
Mendelsohn, Nordhaus, and Shaw (1994) model, 4–5, 45, 63n
   irrigation in, 29
   quadratic functional form in, 20
Mendelsohn and Nordhaus (1999) study
   irrigation in, 29–31
   mathematical error in, 30n, 30–31
Mendelsohn and Reinsborough (2007) study, 58–59
Mendelsohn, Robert, 3, 63n
Mendelsohn and Schlesinger (1999) study (MS model), 5
   adaptation in, 45
   agricultural response functions in, 43–46
   carbon fertilization effect in, 25, 124, 125t–28t, 129–35, 130t–33t
   country-specific results for, 6, 63–80, 123–35
   crop models in, 65
   dispersion across climate models, 59, 60t, 61
   versus MMSA model, 46
   reduced form, 43–46, 123–29, 125t–28t
   for US, 46–47, 47t, 63, 133–34
MINK study, 8
model-source studies, estimates in, comparison to, 80–86
monthly climate data, 142t–61t

Other Publications from the Peterson Institute

WORKING PAPERS

* = out of print

POLICY ANALYSES IN INTERNATIONAL ECONOMICS Series

72 **Roots of Competitiveness: China's Evolving Agriculture Interests** Daniel H. Rosen, Scott Rozelle, and Jikun Huang
July 2004 ISBN 0-88132-376-4
73 **Prospects for a US-Taiwan FTA** Nicholas R. Lardy and Daniel H. Rosen
December 2004 ISBN 0-88132-367-5
74 **Anchoring Reform with a US-Egypt Free Trade Agreement** Ahmed Galal and Robert Z. Lawrence
April 2005 ISBN 0-88132-368-3
75 **Curbing the Boom-Bust Cycle: Stabilizing Capital Flows to Emerging Markets** John Williamson
July 2005 ISBN 0-88132-330-6
76 **The Shape of a Swiss-US Free Trade Agreement** Gary Clyde Hufbauer and Richard E. Baldwin
February 2006 ISBN 978-0-88132-385-6
77 **A Strategy for IMF Reform** Edwin M. Truman
February 2006 ISBN 978-0-88132-398-6
78 **US-China Trade Disputes: Rising Tide, Rising Stakes** Gary Clyde Hufbauer, Yee Wong, and Ketki Sheth
August 2006 ISBN 978-0-88132-394-8
79 **Trade Relations Between Colombia and the United States** Jeffrey J. Schott, editor
August 2006 ISBN 978-0-88132-389-4
80 **Sustaining Reform with a US-Pakistan Free Trade Agreement** Gary C. Hufbauer and Shahid Javed Burki
November 2006 ISBN 978-0-88132-395-5
81 **A US–Middle East Trade Agreement: A Circle of Opportunity?** Robert Z. Lawrence
November 2006 ISBN 978-0-88132-396-2
82 **Reference Rates and the International Monetary System** John Williamson
January 2007 ISBN 978-0-88132-401-3
83 **Toward a US-Indonesia Free Trade Agreement** Gary Clyde Hufbauer and Sjamsu Rahardja
June 2007 ISBN 978-0-88132-402-0

BOOKS

IMF Conditionality* John Williamson, editor
1983 ISBN 0-88132-006-4
Trade Policy in the 1980s* William R. Cline, ed.
1983 ISBN 0-88132-031-5
Subsidies in International Trade* Gary Clyde Hufbauer and Joanna Shelton Erb
1984 ISBN 0-88132-004-8

International Debt: Systemic Risk and Policy Response* William R. Cline
1984 ISBN 0-88132-015-3
Trade Protection in the United States: 31 Case Studies* Gary Clyde Hufbauer, Diane E. Berliner, and Kimberly Ann Elliott
1986 ISBN 0-88132-040-4
Toward Renewed Economic Growth in Latin America* Bela Balassa, Gerardo M. Bueno, Pedro-Pablo Kuczynski, and Mario Henrique Simonsen
1986 ISBN 0-88132-045-5
Capital Flight and Third World Debt* Donald R. Lessard and John Williamson, editors
1987 ISBN 0-88132-053-6
The Canada-United States Free Trade Agreement: The Global Impact* Jeffrey J. Schott and Murray G. Smith, editors
1988 ISBN 0-88132-073-0
World Agricultural Trade: Building a Consensus* William M. Miner and Dale E. Hathaway, editors
1988 ISBN 0-88132-071-3
Japan in the World Economy* Bela Balassa and Marcus Noland
1988 ISBN 0-88132-041-2
America in the World Economy: A Strategy for the 1990s* C. Fred Bergsten
1988 ISBN 0-88132-089-7
Managing the Dollar: From the Plaza to the Louvre* Yoichi Funabashi
1988, 2d. ed. 1989 ISBN 0-88132-097-8
United States External Adjustment and the World Economy* William R. Cline
May 1989 ISBN 0-88132-048-X
Free Trade Areas and U.S. Trade Policy* Jeffrey J. Schott, editor
May 1989 ISBN 0-88132-094-3
Dollar Politics: Exchange Rate Policymaking in the United States* I. M. Destler and C. Randall Henning
September 1989 ISBN 0-88132-079-X
Latin American Adjustment: How Much Has Happened?* John Williamson, editor
April 1990 ISBN 0-88132-125-7
The Future of World Trade in Textiles and Apparel* William R. Cline
1987, 2d ed. June 1999 ISBN 0-88132-110-9
Completing the Uruguay Round: A Results-Oriented Approach to the GATT Trade Negotiations* Jeffrey J. Schott, editor
September 1990 ISBN 0-88132-130-3
**Economic Sanctions Reconsidered (2 volumes)
Economic Sanctions Reconsidered: Supplemental Case Histories** Gary Clyde Hufbauer, Jeffrey J. Schott, and Kimberly Ann Elliott
1985, 2d ed. Dec. 1990 ISBN cloth 0-88132-115-X
ISBN paper 0-88132-105-2

Economic Sanctions Reconsidered: History and
Current Policy   Gary Clyde Hufbauer,
Jeffrey J. Schott, and Kimberly Ann Elliott
December 1990   ISBN cloth 0-88132-140-0
                         ISBN paper 0-88132-136-2
**Pacific Basin Developing Countries: Prospects for
Economic Sanctions Reconsidered: History
and Current Policy**   Gary Clyde Hufbauer,
Jeffrey J. Schott, and Kimberly Ann Elliott
December 1990   ISBN cloth 0-88132-140-0
                         ISBN paper 0-88132-136-2
**Pacific Basin Developing Countries: Prospects
for the Future***   Marcus Noland
January 1991   ISBN cloth 0-88132-141-9
                         ISBN paper 0-88132-081-1
Currency Convertibility in Eastern Europe*
John Williamson, editor
October 1991   ISBN 0-88132-128-1
**International Adjustment and Financing: The
Lessons of 1985-1991***   C. Fred Bergsten, editor
January 1992   ISBN 0-88132-112-5
**North American Free Trade: Issues and
Recommendations***
Gary Clyde Hufbauer and Jeffrey J. Schott
April 1992   ISBN 0-88132-120-6
Narrowing the U.S. Current Account Deficit*
Alan J. Lenz/*June 1992*   ISBN 0-88132-103-6
The Economics of Global Warming
William R. Cline/*June 1992*   ISBN 0-88132-132-X
**US Taxation of International Income: Blueprint
for Reform***   Gary Clyde Hufbauer,
assisted by Joanna M. van Rooij
October 1992   ISBN 0-88132-134-6
**Who's Bashing Whom? Trade Conflict
in High-Technology Industries**
Laura D'Andrea Tyson
November 1992   ISBN 0-88132-106-0
Korea in the World Economy*
Il SaKong
January 1993   ISBN 0-88132-183-4
**Pacific Dynamism and the International
Economic System***
C. Fred Bergsten and Marcus Noland, editors
May 1993   ISBN 0-88132-196-6
Economic Consequences of Soviet Disintegration*
John Williamson, editor
May 1993   ISBN 0-88132-190-7
**Reconcilable Differences? United States-Japan
Economic Conflict***
C. Fred Bergsten and Marcus Noland
June 1993   ISBN 0-88132-129-X
Does Foreign Exchange Intervention Work?
Kathryn M. Dominguez and Jeffrey A. Frankel
September 1993   ISBN 0-88132-104-4
Sizing Up U.S. Export Disincentives*
J. David Richardson
September 1993   ISBN 0-88132-107-9

NAFTA: An Assessment
Gary Clyde Hufbauer and Jeffrey J. Schott/*rev. ed.*
October 1993   ISBN 0-88132-199-0
Adjusting to Volatile Energy Prices
Philip K. Verleger, Jr.
November 1993   ISBN 0-88132-069-2
The Political Economy of Policy Reform
John Williamson, editor
January 1994   ISBN 0-88132-195-8
**Measuring the Costs of Protection
in the United States**
Gary Clyde Hufbauer and Kimberly Ann Elliott
January 1994   ISBN 0-88132-108-7
**The Dynamics of Korean Economic
Development***   Cho Soon
March 1994   ISBN 0-88132-162-1
Reviving the European Union*
C. Randall Henning, Eduard Hochreiter, and
Gary Clyde Hufbauer, editors
April 1994   ISBN 0-88132-208-3
China in the World Economy
Nicholas R. Lardy
April 1994   ISBN 0-88132-200-8
**Greening the GATT: Trade, Environment,
and the Future**   Daniel C. Esty
July 1994   ISBN 0-88132-205-9
Western Hemisphere Economic Integration*
Gary Clyde Hufbauer and Jeffrey J. Schott
July 1994   ISBN 0-88132-159-1
**Currencies and Politics in the United States,
Germany, and Japan**   C. Randall Henning
September 1994   ISBN 0-88132-127-3
Estimating Equilibrium Exchange Rates
John Williamson, editor
September 1994   ISBN 0-88132-076-5
**Managing the World Economy: Fifty Years after
Bretton Woods**   Peter B. Kenen, editor
September 1994   ISBN 0-88132-212-1
Reciprocity and Retaliation in U.S. Trade Policy
Thomas O. Bayard and Kimberly Ann Elliott
September 1994   ISBN 0-88132-084-6
The Uruguay Round: An Assessment*
Jeffrey J. Schott, assisted by Johanna W. Buurman
November 1994   ISBN 0-88132-206-7
Measuring the Costs of Protection in Japan*
Yoko Sazanami, Shujiro Urata, and Hiroki Kawai
January 1995   ISBN 0-88132-211-3
Foreign Direct Investment in the United States,
3d ed., Edward M. Graham and Paul R. Krugman
January 1995   ISBN 0-88132-204-0
**The Political Economy of Korea-United States
Cooperation***
C. Fred Bergsten and Il SaKong, editors
February 1995   ISBN 0-88132-213-X
International Debt Reexamined*
William R. Cline
February 1995   ISBN 0-88132-083-8

WORKS IN PROGRESS

DISTRIBUTORS OUTSIDE THE UNITED STATES

Australia, New Zealand,
and Papua New Guinea
D. A. Information Services
648 Whitehorse Road
Mitcham, Victoria 3132, Australia
Tel: 61-3-9210-7777
Fax: 61-3-9210-7788
Email: service@dadirect.com.au
www.dadirect.com.au

India, Bangladesh, Nepal, and Sri Lanka
Viva Books Private Limited
Mr. Vinod Vasishtha
4737/23 Ansari Road
Daryaganj, New Delhi 110002
India
Tel: 91-11-4224-2200
Fax: 91-11-4224-2240
Email: viva@vivagroupindia.net
www.vivagroupindia.com

Mexico, Central America, South America,
and Puerto Rico
US PubRep, Inc.
311 Dean Drive
Rockville, MD 20851
Tel: 301-838-9276
Fax: 301-838-9278
Email: c.falk@ieee.org

Asia *(Brunei, Burma, Cambodia, China,*
Hong Kong, Indonesia, Korea, Laos, Malaysia,
Philippines, Singapore, Taiwan, Thailand,
and Vietnam)
East-West Export Books (EWEB)
University of Hawaii Press
2840 Kolowalu Street
Honolulu, Hawaii 96822-1888
Tel: 808-956-8830
Fax: 808-988-6052
Email: eweb@hawaii.edu

Canada
Renouf Bookstore
5369 Canotek Road, Unit 1
Ottawa, Ontario KlJ 9J3, Canada
Tel: 613-745-2665
Fax: 613-745-7660
www.renoufbooks.com

Japan
United Publishers Services Ltd.
1-32-5, Higashi-shinagawa
Shinagawa-ku, Tokyo 140-0002
Japan
Tel: 81-3-5479-7251
Fax: 81-3-5479-7307
Email: purchasing@ups.co.jp
For trade accounts only. Individuals will find
Institute books in leading Tokyo bookstores.

Middle East
MERIC
2 Bahgat Ali Street, El Masry Towers
Tower D, Apt. 24
Zamalek, Cairo
Egypt
Tel. 20-2-7633824
Fax: 20-2-7369355
Email: mahmoud_fouda@mericonline.com
www.mericonline.com

United Kingdom, Europe
(including Russia and Turkey), **Africa,**
and Israel
The Eurospan Group
c/o Turpin Distribution
Pegasus Drive
Stratton Business Park
Biggleswade, Bedfordshire
SG18 8TQ
United Kingdom
Tel: 44 (0) 1767-604972
Fax: 44 (0) 1767-601640
Email: eurospan@turpin-distribution.com
www.eurospangroup.com/bookstore

Visit our Web site at:
www.petersoninstitute.org
E-mail orders to:
petersonmail@presswarehouse.com